"When I spoke to Frances Keenan on the phone about *Elvis, You're Unforgettable*, I found her to be warm, friendly, and a genuine fan of Elvis...she carries over these qualities into this book and throws in some great Elvis candid photos. I recommend it."

—Roger Bailey
Roger Reviews
Elvis International Forum

"This book is a wonderful read for anyone who is, has been, or might be an Elvis lover."

—Jane Dystel, President
Jane Dystel Literary Management

"After 20 years—a fan speaks (as only a fan can do). The true story of an Elvis fan who had a fantasy to meet and talk to Elvis. You will learn a lot about him as he helps her through her teen years...It will make you laugh, lift your spirits, and cry. You will not be able to put the book down...outstanding book. Highly recommended."

—Kathy Ferguson, President
Presleyites Fan Club

"Frances' descriptive narrative took me back to Papa and Granny Minton's front porch where our grandparents spun their yarns. She has inherited their gift of storytelling! Wonderful book! A real page-turner. I laughed and I cried while I relived it all."

—Sandra Polk Ross (Author's cousin)
Daughter-in-law of Col. Tom Parker

Every American, especially Elvis fans, should read this remarkable book written by my long time friend Frances Minton Keenan. It is superbly written and will make you laugh and cry as Frances reveals so much about her life and how her obsession with Elvis consoled her through tough times and embellished the good times. Her raw gutsiness will amaze you as it did the undisputed King of Rock and Roll himself. Frances has fulfilled her promise to Elvis to not write this book until after he was dead and to make him "live again". Elvis fans will love him even more as they learn of his great love for them and how he was humbled by their adoration. Elvis was an all American original and is truly "unforgettable".

—Cliff Denison, President
Love America, Inc.

"If you are an Elvis fan, you will love Frances Keenan's book. She has experienced what every fan would like...having a one-on-one with Elvis Presley. She did exactly what he told her to do...write a book after his death that brings him very much back to life!

If you are not an Elvis fan, you will still love this book. It is filled with special memories of growing up in the fifties. Frances writes with so many "little" descriptions that you can feel the Coca-Cola burn your throat and hear the rustle of your petticoats! She has managed to bring back the memories that most of us living in that time period had long ago buried.

Her life is not unlike many of us growing up and becoming grown-ups at a time when rules were more standard and life was sometimes hard and inconvenient.

As a president of an Elvis Fan Club, I am honored to have Frances as part of our organization and a fellow Floridian!"

—Sue Manuszak, President
Elvis Presley Continentals
Orlando, Florida

"Ms. Keenan has demonstrated great courage in transcribing the buoyant, but largely bittersweet events of her past. As a result, we are not only able to experience her pain, but also her triumphs; in particular, her lifelong dream of meeting and becoming acquainted with Elvis Presley.

In her early years, Presley was the author's anchor to innocence and sanity in a sinful, and often incomprehensible world. Meeting Mr. Presley as an adult, and becoming intimate with him, was more than the fulfillment of a young girls fantasy. It gave definition to a woman and mother in search of greater identity, who needed to be taken seriously, and was struggling to overcome the demons of her childhood.

Elvis, You're Unforgettable serves to remind us that all things are possible, if we can only find the strength to keep holding on and believing."

—Todd Rheingold, Author
Dispelling the Myths

In *Elvis You're Unforgettable: Memoirs From a Fan*, Frances Keenan writes from the heart and offers her readers a mother lode of Elvis memories—upclose, personal, and guaranteed to give goosebumps. She recreates Elvis' magic and brings the King back to life, just as he asked her to do. Readers will find Elvis' spirit alive and well in this wonderful memoir. Thank you, Frances. Thank you very much.

—Pauline Bartel, Author Reel Elvis!

I have known Frances for over twenty years and have been her pastor for the majority of those years. I was *before* the Elvis generation, but after reading *Elvis You're Unforgettable* I felt as if I knew him.

I was aware that Frances knew Elvis Presley, however, I was totally unprepared for her presentation of Elvis as confidant of a young girl, his picture absorbing her joys and her agonies, giving her comfort and "I understand" and assuring her that she is not alone. It was very touching.

Frances has an uncanny sense, not only of what Elvis meant to her, but to others as well. I feel that by tapping into the "Spiritual side" of Elvis, Frances opened another dimension of Elvis, persuading you to look inward, as well as enjoy the romance of the book. Frances, with her unconditional love for Elvis the biggest part of her life is able to transcend the physical realm and reach the Spirit.

As I read the book, it was as if Frances, in her straight-forward manner was sitting with me, talking to me. Good work, Frances! You have made Elvis Unforgettable! Looking forward to your next book!

—Rev. John Stanton
Friend and pastor of Frances Keenan

Elvis, You're Unforgettable takes the reader on a warm and loving trip back through the memories and into a special friendship that lasted for a lifetime. Learn about the Elvis that only his family and special friends knew.

Donna Presley Early
Elvis' First Cousin
Author—Elvis: Precious Memories

ELVIS, YOU'RE UNFORGETTABLE

by

Frances Keenan

Cover photograph by Moss Photo of New York
Cover design and Typesetting by Drawing Board Studios
Edited by Margie Weber
Printed in the United States of America

"An Evening Prayer" by C.M. Battersby and Charles H. Gabriel copyright © 1911; renewed 1939 by The Rodeheaver Co. (A div. of WORD MUSIC). All rights reserved. Used by permission. "An Evening Prayer" is one of 7,000 songs written by turn of the century composer Charles Gabriel.

Publisher's Cataloging in Publication
(Prepared by Quality Books, Inc.)

Keenan, Frances, 1943–
    Elvis, you're unforgettable: memoirs from a fan/Frances Keenan.
    p. cm
    Includes bibliographical references.
    ISBN 0-936417-53-6
    LCCN 96-079569

    1. Presley, Elvis 1935-1977.   2. Rock Musicians—United States—Biography.   3. Singers—United States—Biography.
    I. Title

ML420.P96K44 1997   782.42'166'092
                                            QB196-40679

Note to the reader: *Elvis, You're Unforgettable* is a true story based upon my memoirs. Conversations have been reconstructed to the best of my memory. Some names have been changed with respect to the individuals' privacy. All judgments, opinions, conclusions, and emotions are mine and with no malice intended. *Elvis, You're Unforgettable* is a love story from the heart of a fan.

In Memory of Mama Artie Mae
Sheffield Minton Leaman
1924-1991

How To Enjoy This Book

Elvis fans, you are about to embark upon a journey into another era called Elvis. Travel with me back in time to the year 1955, when it all began. Laugh and cry with me as I grow from a child to a grandmother. And through it all, experience Elvis as if you were there.

Put on one of his tapes or CDs. For the best effect, I suggest *Elvis Presley, A Valentine For You*. It contains my favorite song, *I Was The One*, which plays a significant role in this story. And if you want to experience the costumes, songs, audience participation— if you want to see it as it was when I was there, watch *Elvis, That's The Way It Is*. This movie was completed the day before I arrived in Vegas; subsequently, some of the people I write about are in the picture. Two other films you might want to view are *Follow That Dream* and *Jailhouse Rock*.

Now, kick off your shoes and get comfortable because I promise you, if you love Elvis, you won't be able to put this book down.

Elvisly Yours,
Frances Keenan

Love is a different laughter in the spirit.
It is a wild assault that hushes you to your awakening.
It is a new dawn upon the earth,
A day not yet achieved in your eyes or mine,
But already achieved in its own greater heart.

Kahlil Gibran
THE EARTH GODS

Table of Contents

Introduction

My name is Frances Keenan and I'm a natural born cracker—probably seventh to ninth generation Floridian. My religious upbringing came from the Assemblies of God and the Southern Baptists.

Even though *Elvis, You're Unforgettable* is targeted toward Elvis fans, it carries a witness of faith in God from a child who, over a lengthy period of time, had been the victim of sexual molestation. I've not chosen to dwell on the details of that childhood abuse, but I feel that I had to address the issue, since the secret I held within me affected every aspect of my life. The reader needs to know this to understand the spiritual battle going on inside me; a battle I fought, through five marriages and several attempted suicides—the one I had to conquer through my faith in the Lord.

Before I had Knowledge, there was faith—an innocent, blind faith, And that's why there are miracles in my story.

Close to the time that this book went to press, I read Donna Presley Early and Edie Hand's *Precious Memories.* I was deeply touched by their recollections of the sweet, compassionate, Christian side of their cousin, Elvis Presley, and received answers to questions I'd wondered about since 1971. Why did Elvis do the things he did for me? Who was I to deserve his special attention?

Now I know. I was a human being in pain, and Elvis saw into my suffering and wanted to make it better.

From start to finish, God has opened each and every door to success for this book; placing people, opportunity, and knowledge before me but, only at the precise moment of His perfect timing—confirming things I already knew in my spirit, after I had written it the way I remembered it.

Just as He laid the way for me to write *Elvis, You're Unforgettable*, so, also, did God give me the courage to do it.

Foreword

From October 1958 to April 1959, Elvis was assigned to drive my army jeep, Bumper number HQ 31. During the seven and one-half months that Elvis Presley served as my Reconnaissance Scout/Driver, a period in which I had almost daily contact with him, my primary interest was keeping Elvis and 38 other enlisted soldiers prepared for immediate combat, should the world situation require that type of action.

Since we had no American television, and had been in Germany almost two years, we knew very little about a soldier named Elvis. Of course, the romantic dreams of Frances Keenan (and many hundreds of thousands of teenage girls) would have been very alien to me (but not so for the soldiers with teenage daughters, I think).

For we who were considerably older than Elvis (he was 23, I was 35), it was easy to consider him as a mischievous younger brother, or the older or more experienced brother of soldiers his age. To the ladies of various clubs and groups, Elvis was a prize whether he was visiting groups or in their homes. To all of us, he soon was the talk of coffee calls.

To all, Elvis was rather shy. He loved to sing and, in fact, he loved to soldier. That does not mean that he did not miss his show-biz career, but since he had a job to do, he was going to do it and do it well.

I left Germany in April 1959. I communicated with the reconnaissance platoon members and (after a fashion) with Elvis until he was discharged in 1960. I stayed in the U.S. Army until 1963 (retired) and then became acquainted with the young ladies who, like Frances, had the UNIMAGINABLE DREAM of touching Elvis. I managed to get tickets to a couple of his performances and was startled at the enthralled look on most of the (all ages) female faces in the audience.

Back in Germany, we soldiers liked to tease Elvis...Soldier: "Elvis, you must stay awfully tired having young girls trying to take your clothes off." Elvis answered with a question: "Did you ever have hundreds of beautiful women trying to make love to you at the same time?"

A farm boy from Kentucky muttered: "Elvis, if you have that problem again, call us, we are ready............"

Frances Keenan has been putting in lots of hours getting this book together for Elvis fans. Congratulations on your work, Frances. In Germany, I have consoled young (and old) ladies who broke down and cried if they happened to get a glimpse of Elvis. The same is true if they just missed seeing him. Now and then, a few of the chasers were for me.....

Love and respects,
Ira Jones

Elvis, You're Unforgettable

Part 1 1955-1969

THIS IS THE PHOTOGRAPH FRANCES CONFIDED IN FROM AGE 12.
(ELVIS CIRCA 1956)

1

I Got Stung

1955

Some fool once said that only the weak need idols. Nobody said that when everybody cheered Lindbergh for crossin' the Atlantic.

———*Elvis Presley*

Outside, the weather was hot and humid. Not a hint of a breeze stirred the leaves on the old Brazilian pepper tree that sprawled across the front yard, shading our house from the blistering Florida sun. It was June 1955, and school was out for the summer. I stood looking through the ripped hole in the front screen door, listening to energetic shouts coming from neighborhood kids playing baseball in the street in front of our house.

"You're out!" screamed one boy.

"You're crazy. That was a foul ball!" yelled back another. I recognized the familiar voices of my two younger brothers, Sam and Tommy, who were getting more than their two-cents' worth into the shouting match.

Just the same old thing, I thought. As much as I loved my family and neighbors, they just didn't have whatever IT was I was searching for. Would things ever be different? I consoled myself with thoughts of school. I'd be entering junior high in the fall and Oak Grove promised dances, football games, and I hoped a little romance. I was mighty young to be concerning myself with romance, but I can't remember a time when I didn't think about it.

I backed away from the screen door, turned around, and walked over to the radio. The old Philco console stood proudly in the living room, just waiting to fill the house with hillbilly music. I think most people learn to appreciate, at least to a certain degree, the music they were raised on. I was raised on hillbilly and gospel. I liked the faster songs. The ones that didn't drag out with a twang so corny it made my hair curl.

I turned the radio on and sure enough, found one of those hair-curling twangies playing. Leaning backwards against the radio, I slowly slid down until I was sitting on the floor, then, glancing around the small room, I stopped for a moment to focus on the shabby condition of our old sofa with its busted springs. A smile tugged at the corners of my mouth as I remembered Aunt Ruby sliding off the couch and onto the floor. She'd been drunk, and not paying attention to the failing divan; she flopped down and ker-plunk! She hit the floor. I giggled at my memory; you had to respect those springs.

Our living room held four pieces of furniture. Besides the old sofa and the radio, we had a rocking chair, and a console television that stayed broken most of the time. Mama was literally that old cliche: "We might be poor but we're clean." And the tiles covering our floor were a testament to her immaculacy—always gleaming with a waxed shine. Mama liked 'em clean enough to eat off, and that's something I couldn't understand, since we never did.

Tilting my head back, I leisurely closed my eyes and drifted to that spacey-far-off-haven of daydreams where I often found myself, but was soon yanked back to reality by the irritating voice of the singer.

"Oh, hurry up and lay that egg," I lamented, and the song finally came to an end on my sour note of sentiment.

"And now," the deejay announced in a roll-off-the-tongue sounding voice, "I'm gonna play a song by a new singer who's really been stirrin' things up in his hometown of Memphis, Tennessee. Here's Elvis Presley, singing 'That's Alright Mama.'"

My ears perked up at the sound of the unusual name, then I heard a voice singing, the likes of which I'd never heard before.

> *Well, that's alright, little mama, that's alright for*
> *you, that's alright, mama, just any way you do.*

It's hard to describe all the feelings that lusty, shake-'em-up voice stirred in me, because there were so many. Elvis' articulation, his music and style, all blended into a distinctly different sound, and the man behind the lyrics touched my soul. He put a new twinkle in my eyes, made my romantic heart faint, and goosed up the rhythm in my feet. I felt fresh and alive and so tremendously excited, I jumped to my feet and buck-danced all over the living room.

And so began my love affair with Elvis Presley, who was, for now, a voice without a face. His magic embraced me and it felt like dream dust, that stuff Mama teased me about having for brains. I would often be reminded of this day when, later on, after he became famous, people trashed him for his vulgar movements. I wanted to tell them all that they were full of grits and gravy and didn't know what they were talking about. Elvis had turned this little girl inside out with nothing more than a communicating voice. That man had the "IT" I'd been looking for. What IT was, I wasn't completely sure, but I knew he had IT, and I wanted more of IT.

Even his name, Elvis Presley, was strange, exotic, different, and his tantalizing verbalization, which conveyed an essence of romance, identified with my spirit and seemed to be saying to me as I sat glued to the radio: *Frances Minton, we're one...you're mine and I'm yours. I'll always love you and never let you down. I'll be your friend and confidant and I won't betray you. I'll be your shoulder to cry on and I'll put a smile on your face when you're sad. I'll give you something to look forward to and I'll be there for you any time, any place. I'll give you what you want and, always, make your*

*life exciting...but most of all, I'll love you from a distance so you'll
never be hurt—I'll be someone to tell your troubles to.*

The last part (someone to tell your troubles to), was especially
meaningful to me. I had hurts inside me nobody knew about.
Things I didn't understand. And for some reason, Elvis Presley's
voice was like a balm to my wounds; soothing the pain, wrapping it
in bandages of song, and distancing the injury from the little girl in
me. The little girl who dreamed of impossible things and believed,
with all her heart, in answered prayers and wishes that came true if
only she believed hard enough.

I was excited over my discovery and couldn't wait to tell the
whole world about Elvis Presley. But when I did, nobody knew
who I was talking about. They all said, "What's an Elvis Presley?"
My cousin Ester Rose who'd been stung by the Elvis bug, too, was
the only person of the ones I asked who had heard of him. Ester
Rose told me she'd seen a picture of him in a songbook when she
was at the drugstore with her mama. She attempted to describe
Elvis to me, but her description failed to give me any kind of vision
beyond sideburns.

I tried to conjure up a face for the voice I'd fallen in love with,
but was in no way prepared for the one that looked back at me
from the country and western song book I purchased on the way
home from my cousin's house. The picture was a small, black and
white head shot, and the caption beneath it read, "Sun's Newest
Star." I remember standing in that drugstore, completely mesmerized by a face that screamed mystique. Elvis Presley didn't just
have IT—he had ALL OF IT!

Sun's newest star possessed a sultry sexiness; a sensual mouth
with a slow, flirty smile that harmonized perfectly with his mysterious, searching, shadowed, faraway, brooding, hypnotizing, yet
laughing eyes. Even before I knew their color those talking blues
spoke to me. They said, *You ain't seen nothin' like me, baby!*

In a time when crewcuts were the fashion, Elvis' long hair and
sideburns really made a statement for "Cool." He was the coolest
guy I'd ever seen, exuding a sexy blend—looking like a tough guy
who wasn't afraid to show his soft side. His extraordinary perfection set a new standard for good-looking: a take-my-breath-away

flawlessness, all his own. And the writer called him the Hillbilly Cat.

From then on, I endured all the unmoving, old-fashioned, flat-as-a-flitter songs played on the radio, in anticipation of the only voice that could move me.

The conventional world, the one Elvis took by storm and the one I lived in, was not ready for him. Eisenhower was in office, and in the South, segregation was considered the norm. Every school day began with The Lord's Prayer and the Pledge of Allegiance to the flag. Drive-in movies and drive-in restaurants were a way of life: special outings for families and hangouts for teenagers. Hamburgers were patted out and cooked to order, french fries were cut from fresh potatoes, and a Coca-Cola cost a nickel and made your eyes sting.

There were no interstate highways, nor color televisions, and only a few places advertised, "Come in! Cool air-conditioning!" My box office favorites were Marlon Brando, James Dean, and Marilyn Monroe. Perry Como was at the top of the hit parade.

In Tampa, where I lived, there was a place called the Super Test Amusement Park. For every fifteen to twenty cent gallon of gasoline purchased from the Super Test station, we received a ticket good for a ride at the park. Here, the family could make a fun night out. Daisy Mae and Ole Brother Charlie sang the come-on commercial. It seemed like any time you turned on the radio, there they were, singing, *Drive up your car, park it and say, fill it with Super Test today*. In addition to the promotional tickets, we also got our windows cleaned, air in our tires, and our water, battery, and oil were checked. The fifties served it up with a smile.

I was ten years old when we moved into the house on Elm Street, located a block from Lowry Park (now, the Lowry Park Zoo), and the Hillsborough River. Daddy had moved our family back and forth between Florida and Seattle, Washington, from the time I was born until I was in fifth grade. That's when Mama put her foot down and said, "No more!"

Our house was a small, three-bedroom, stuccoed concrete-block structure with a flat roof that held water when it rained, and, eventually yielding to the weight, leaked so bad it took all the pots and tubs we owned to catch the drips and downpours. My brothers adjusted their beds around the leaks, but it didn't stop the ceiling from caving in on Tommy one night while he was sleeping. He wasn't seriously injured, but when gallons of water and busted sheetrock came crashing on top of him, he nearly screamed the rest of the roof down. Tommy was so shook up he stuttered for a week afterwards.

Four grotesque gargoyles on each corner of the roof totaled sixteen reasons for nightmares. These creatures' demonic-looking faces frightened me, while Daddy called them kinfolks. I can still see him coming home drunk and sailing his hat up to land, perfectly, on top of a gargoyle's head. He'd be yelling at the top of his voice, "Ya...hooo, I'm home, you ugly brother!" When he sobered up, he'd have one of my brothers climb up on the roof and get his hat down.

My mother, Artie Mae, worked as a bookkeeper for Protane Bottled Gas Company. So, since I was older than my two brothers, that meant I got the responsibilities that go along with being the eldest. It was my job to look after Sam and Tommy when I got home from school, and I straightened up the house and started supper before Mama came home from work.

We saved our laundry for the weekends because Mama didn't want me using the washing machine when she wasn't close by. She was afraid I might get my hand caught in the wringer. Then, of course, there was the ironing, which Mama and I shared. Everything had to be starched and ironed, right down to the sheets and pillowcases.

Life in our neighborhood was safe, simple, and boring for a romantic, daydreaming young girl with stardust in her eyes and boys on her mind, and a deep dark secret to guard.

I loved our caring neighbors, who seemed like one big extended family. They looked after each other while their children played ball in the middle of tree-lined streets.

We held neighborhood parties at different houses almost every weekend, and the rest of the time somebody was always dropping in for coffee and conversation. Not everyone was lucky enough to own a television, and the ones who did found their living rooms filled with neighborhood kids who gathered to watch *Captain Mac's Adventure Trails* and *Davy Crockett*.

I remember when coonskin hats were the fad. One time a couple of brothers who lived on the street behind us decided when their mother wasn't at home to cut up her mink coat. They sold the pelts for a nickel apiece to the neighborhood kids so they could make coonskin hats. Now I didn't know many people who owned a mink coat, so this was a big deal. And even though a coonskin hat didn't interest me, a new collar for my sweater surely did. When those boys' mom got home and found the remains of her coat, we could hear her screaming clear over to our house.

ELVIS' DIVERSITY WAS a welcome invasion into my world and I yearned to see him in person. The probability of this happening was about as likely as walking on the moon. But, around my twelfth birthday, that is exactly what happened when Daddy was home.

Daddy was a merchant seaman who sailed around the world most of the time. His trips took him to far and distant places for months on end, sometimes for as long as a year. I liked it best when he was gone.

Daddy was an alcoholic and when he drank he got mean and crazy. Mama hated his drinking and this caused fights between them. Daddy would hit Mama, then Mama, not being a person to take his crap, would coldcock him with anything she could lay her hands on. Then he would lie, sprawled out on the floor wherever he had landed, until he'd slept the booze off.

On the day I went to see Elvis in person, Mama had taken Sam and Tommy with her to Grandaddy's farm in Keysville, which was about thirty-five miles from where we lived. This meant she would be gone all day. I stayed home to catch up on some house cleaning. Mama didn't usually leave me alone, but her friend Hazel, who lived in the house behind ours, had said she'd be home all day and would keep an eye out for me.

Daddy had been due in on the ship the day before but still hadn't made it home. We all knew what this could mean. If Mama didn't catch him right off the boat, chances were the nearest bar would get him first. Then, we wouldn't see him till we saw him, which was usually when he came dragging in with one or two of his drinking cronies, ready for a party. He'd think nothing of rousing our backsides out of bed in the middle of the night, shoving a cigar into Sam's mouth and ordering him to cut a few steps in his cowboy boots, and making me yodel and buck-dance. I hated performing for his skid-row companions, but usually complied to save peace.

Well, as fate would have it, Daddy got home not long after Mama had left. I heard a car pull up in the yard and went to the front door to see who it was. Daddy was just stepping out of a shiny, new, green and white Chevrolet, and as he walked around from the driver's side, I noticed him wobble and dread overtook me.

As a matter of ritual, Daddy removed his panama, tossed it up on top of a gargoyle's head, then noticing the absence of Mama's car, turned to me and asked where she was.

"She took Sam and Tommy with her to Grandma and Grandaddy's...but they'll be home tonight."

"Well, come on over here and give your old daddy a hug."

I hesitated for a moment, then stepped toward him and reached up to hug his neck. I was relieved to find, after I got a closer look at his eyes, that he wasn't quite as loaded as I had originally thought.

"Mama's been expectin' you since yesterday. When did your boat get in?"

He stretched his tall, thin body to its highest stature, locked his I-don't-want-none-of-your-shit eyes on me, and said, "Now, that ain't none of your business, is it, young lady?"

"No, sir."

"That's better. Well now, why don't you get in the house and change clothes, then you can tuck your little tail right in the front seat of this here new car and we'll take 'er for a spin."

"That's our car, Daddy?"

"Sure is. Ain't she a beauty? Just bought 'er yesterday."

It wasn't unusual for Daddy to come home with something extravagant. When he was on a drinking binge money seemed to burn a hole in his pocket. Mama used to say, "The roof might cave in on top of us but that wouldn't bother your daddy. Not as long as the Minton family drives a nice car, or is the first on the block to get a television set." Daddy could usually find the money for booze, too, or a new steel guitar for himself if he wanted one.

Mama was practical; a scrimper and a saver, and Daddy's foolish spending nearly sent her up a wall. Sometimes it was hard for me to figure out if we were rich or poor, depending upon whether Mama reached Daddy straight off the boat before he started drinking. It seemed like the only constant thing in our lives was Mama.

Daddy and I went inside the house, and while I was in my bedroom getting dressed, I heard Hazel as she came in through the back door. Then she and Daddy talked in the kitchen.

"She'll be all right, Hazel. I'm not drunk and she's my damn kid anyway."

"I know that. But I told Artie Mae I'd watch out for her."

"We're just gonna take a ride over to some friends of mine for a while. I bought a new Chevy and we're gonna try it out. Come on out and take a look at it." I heard the front screen door slam as they went outside to look at the car.

I knew better than to go off with Daddy when he was drinking. But he wasn't too soused, I rationalized, not being in the mood to fight with him. Besides, when he was only a little bit drunk, it was easy for me to manipulate him. Maybe I could talk him into buying me a record player, then I could listen to Elvis anytime I wanted.

The drive to his friend's house went smoother than I had expected and I started to relax. Daddy kept going on about how well the car ran and told me if I was good he might let me drive it. But I wasn't interested in getting behind the wheel of any automobile, much less our new one. I was too young for a license and just the thought of driving scared the pee out of me.

I didn't know these people we were going to visit, but once we arrived and I discovered their fourteen-year-old daughter liked Elvis, and owned a record player, I was in Elvis Heaven. I don't remember the girl's name, but we went into her bedroom to talk and spin platters.

We were chatting about something, kind of getting to know each other, when suddenly, she said, "I'm so mad at my parents. They won't let me go to the Armory to see Elvis today." I couldn't believe what my ears were hearing.

"What did you say? Did you say Elvis is in town, today? Where? What time?" I hadn't heard a thing about Elvis coming to Tampa.

She blew her bangs up and off her forehead with a raspberry-lip sigh and said, "In a couple hours from now."

I looked at the clock and it was half past noon. Carefully dropping the records I was holding onto the bed, I flew out of that room like a loony turned loose. Daddy was engaged in conversation when I sidled up next to him and gently nudged his shoulder in an effort to get his attention. He was a talker and didn't like being interrupted.

"What in blue blazes do you want? Can't you see I'm busy talkin' here?" I saw he was busy all right, lapping up the booze while he and his cronies thumped their guitars, so I pushed a little further.

"Daddy, can I talk to you for a minute?"

He stared at me for a second or two, then rising to his feet he said, "This better be good."

He excused himself from his circle of music playing buddies and followed me out onto the porch. "Now, what's so all fired urgent that it couldn't wait?"

"Daddy...you know my birthday is coming up in four days?" He was tenderhearted when it came to birthdays.

"Yeah, so get to the point."

"Well, I just found out Elvis is gonna be at the Armory today and I wanna see him so bad. Can I go, Daddy? Will you take me, please, for my birthday present? I won't ask for anything else, I promise."

"Who's this Elvis character you wanna see?"

I had forgotten Daddy was out to sea while Elvis was happening. "Oh, Daddy, he's just the best singer in the whole wide world."

"Then how come I ain't heard about him?"

Daddy was a guitar-playing man who loved music, singing, and the Grand Ole Opry, and he prided himself on knowing just about every singer you could name. "Well, that's because he's new," I explained, "and he's gonna be at the Armory in two hours."

He rubbed his chin, slowly shook his head, and said, "Well, I don't know about this. Your Mama will raise all kinds of hell if I let you go traipsin' off to some hillbilly show by yourself...and I ain't in the mood for this nonsense."

"You could just drop me off then do what you want to. I won't tell Mama if you'll just let me go," I promised.

"And how you gonna keep your big mouth shut? If she gets wind of this, she'll run me over the coals and I'll never hear the end of it." I was already getting excited. I knew, by the look on his face, I was wearing him down and the victory would soon be mine.

I reached up and hugged his neck, then backed away, pressing my hands together in a prayer position, and begged. "Daddy, please, please, please?"

"Damn," he laughed, "if you don't know how to wear me down. You just never give up, do you?" He finally made me a deal. "Tell you what, Daughter...you sing just one song for my friends in there...and cut a few steps for us, and I'll let you go see this Elvis person you wanna see so bad you're 'bout to shit your drawers."

"You promise, Daddy? Just one song?"

He nodded his head.

"You got a deal."

So, while Daddy played the steel guitar, I sang "More And More," a hillbilly song by Webb Pierce, and danced a huck-a-buck jig like I was auditioning for Arthur Godfrey.

After I'd performed for Elvis' performance, Daddy gave me some money and dropped me off in front of the Armory. He said he would pick me up at the same location when the show was over. "And remember to keep your trap shut about this or your mama will have my ass."

Getting in at the last minute presented no problem and the admission was only fifty cents because I wasn't twelve yet. The production drew a good-size crowd and my seat was near the back. The place was packed with mostly young people, whistling for the performance to start. Elvis wasn't billed as the headliner. Matter of fact, he was at the bottom of the list, but that didn't take away from the truth. He was the star. I felt embarrassed, even sorry, for the other performers who shared the billing with him. They didn't stand a chance. In fact, now I don't even recall who they were. Except Ernie Lee. I remember Ernie because he had a local television program.

The thing I held most dearly to my heart from this show was my excitement over Elvis. My emotions were very real to me: first-love's passions, and that part of the experience is something I'll never forget.

It was obvious who the crowd had paid their money to see when they started stomping and shouting, "We want Elvis!" When he finally took the stage wearing a sport coat and peg-legged pants, white loafers, a guitar strapped around his neck, and a mystery under his drooped eyelids, I mean to tell you that place got wild. I'd never seen anything like what was happening all over that audience. Girls screamed, and squealed, and hollered, and jumped, and pulled their hair out by the roots. When I raised up from my seat in an effort to see him better, I felt delirious and disappointed all at the same time; thrilled over Elvis but alas, frustrated because I wasn't close enough.

He just kind of stood there on stage for a minute, giving the crowd a slow, long, look. Then suddenly all hell broke loose. Elvis threw his whole body into a fast song and my eyes fixated on swinging and gyrating hips. Caught up in a storm of emotions, I couldn't even tell you what he sang. His rain of magic showered the building, hailing me to a world where I'd never been, and the unique style of Elvis was so earthshaking, my brain seemed to rattle while I ate the whole performance up.

He shook his legs, he dragged his toes, then he stretched out his arm, pointed his finger right at us and belched into the microphone. He broke all the rules, this handsome rebel with the faraway look in his blue, bedroom eyes; dreamy eyes that connected and said, *I've just stepped out of your best fantasy.*

Even from where I was sitting I could see a hint of those mesmerizing peepers I knew from photos I'd seen—blue pools of shadowed mystery I would never forget. Elvis Presley was something else; all my wishes wrapped in one pretty package.

The girls in the audience traded off between swoons and squeals at his gestures; sexy moves, sudden stops, and come-hither looks Elvis used to weave his spell, and we were captured—webbed in his magic.

His breathtaking performance was, for me, like waking up on Christmas morning and finding everything I'd ever wanted and more. Elvis' be-bop, rock-a-billy style literally stole the show. I screamed my silly butt off, in a state of couldn't-help-myself, in a madhouse that left me feeling cheated because I hadn't gotten a piece of him, in a rush that ended so quickly, I was left wanting more of the Memphis Flash.

Daddy was waiting outside for me when the concert was over, and as I climbed into the car, it was obvious he was stewed to the gills. He asked about the show while I silently prayed for God to steer the wheel for my drunk daddy.

We wound up at another of his comrade's and visited for a while. Then, as we headed for the car to go home, Daddy's friends tried to talk him out of driving because he was drunk. So he insisted I drive. I was scared to death and pleaded with him.

"No, Daddy, I don't even know which pedal is the brake and which is the clutch."

But my pleas fell on drunken ears as he shoved me into the driver's seat and pointed to the brake. "That's the brake and the pedal next to it is the clutch. This here's the steering wheel. This thing here is the gear shift. This is first, second, third, and this is reverse. Now, quit acting like a chicken-shit and drive!"

Not my pleas, nor those of his friends, and certainly not my tears, could change my father's mind. He'd decided I was going to chauffeur him and that was the end of it.

By some miracle, I backed the car out of the driveway and started down the road, but two blocks away I ran a stop sign and another car plowed into the side of us. The first thing I heard, even before the sound of grinding metal, was the shouting voice of my father. "Now, look what the hell you've gone and done to our new car!"

The Chevy was messed up bad, but we came through the accident without injuries and the judge excused me from having to attend driving school because of my age. Daddy paid a huge fine, but that didn't bother him. What galled him was the fury of Mama's hellfire sermon. As he put it, he would have rather walked barefoot through hot coals.

True to my promise, I kept my mouth shut about seeing Elvis. After the ruckus the car wreck had caused, I didn't think it would be in my best interest for Mama to find out. Elvis had won her over with his rocking style music, but allowing me to go to a concert by myself, at the tender young age of twelve, was an entirely different matter. I was afraid it might change her mind about my hero and I was not about to trouble those waters. I found it hard to sit on my excitement, though, and was busting at the seams to tell somebody. So I told a few select friends, but no one in my family, afraid it would get back to Mama.

I started cutting out pictures of Elvis from magazines and wallpapered my bedroom with them. I even covered the ceiling. Not only did this hide water stains left by the previously leaky roof that had now been tar papered over, but it also added to the pleasure of lying on my back when I was in bed. I could look up at the ceiling and see my favorite star twinkling down at me. And in this world of mine I wrote the rules, which allowed Elvis to sprinkle me with wish dust that put me to sleep with fantasy expectations.

The double bed I slept in was positioned next to the double windows opposite the door. At the foot of the bed behind a curtain-covered, shelved closet, I stored my Elvis collection; magazines, letters I wrote to him but never mailed, records, pictures, my diary and journals, and my short-wave radio—another of Daddy's drunken extravagances. Beside this closet was one for hanging clothes. It had two open sides and right in the middle was my favorite thing: a four-foot-wide, ceiling to floor, mirror.

That looking glass, my friend and teacher, knew me better than I knew myself. I practiced everything before it; posture, facial expressions, hair styles, walking, wiggling my hips, dancing, and kissing. I learned how to apply makeup and was able to hide my freckles. I could twirl a baton, twist a hula hoop, sing along with Elvis, and play the guitar, all with the approval of the mirror's keen eye.

Across from the bed and to the right of the door sat a dresser with another wardrobe next to it, and in a space between the two closets that met in a corner, I hung my crinolines on hooks. It was here, also, that the red purse resided.

The red pocketbook held my contraband; cigarettes, matches, butts, and ashes wrapped in toilet tissue, and the nasty-tasting sulfur tablets that Mama insisted we take for our blood. I pretended to swallow the hateful pills that were big as horse turds, then I'd spit them into a tissue and stow them away with the cigarette butts till I had a full purse.

Then, very cautiously, I'd take them next door to the vacant lot, dig a hole, and bury the evidence. I was really, really, careful about my sneakiness, because Mama would have flat put the fear of God in me if she'd ever caught me smoking, or lying to her. She'd have danced the jig out of my legs with a switch, then grounded me for a few weekends. I loved Mama dearly for her faith in me and felt bottomed-out-guilty when I knew I didn't deserve her trust.

My bedroom was my personal territory and Mama allowed me to decorate it any way I wanted. Every once in a while she'd take inventory of the clothes piled on top of my dresser and ask, "How high is this heap gonna grow before you do somethin' about it?" This was her way of saying, *Do you want to go anywhere this weekend?* and was the quickest way to stir me into action. But aside from these periodic inspections, Mama didn't intrude upon my privacy. I kind of felt like this came from never having had any when she was growing up in a family of nine children.

E LVIS WAS MY HERO and confidant. I developed a habit of talking to him about everything, and he became the ear for all of my secrets; good ones, bad ones, the ones I could never, never, ever tell anybody, and the ones that helped me escape.

My special picture of Elvis, the one I talked to, sat on a nightstand beside my bed in an eight-by-ten frame that had once held a baby picture of my brother. This photo of Elvis was in color, and what made it my favorite was the way his blue eyes seemed to connect with mine. Sometimes, when I was gazing into those eyes, it seemed as though he could hear my fairy-tale heart. I felt a connection between us, so powerful, the bonding was real enough to believe.

From ceiling to floor and wall to wall, Elvis smiled, sneered, pouted, laughed, sang, and played his guitar for me. I read everything and anything in print about my hero and felt like I knew him personally. I danced to his music in my bedroom before the full-length mirror and took to heart the lyrics of his songs that said all the right things. Things my very soul longed to hear. The way he sang those words was so convincing, like every utterance was straight from his heart to me. He had a special way of communicating. That was the bewitching magic of Elvis. He cast a spell over me that inspired me to kiss his pictures by day and dream of him at night. Dreaming about Elvis tamed the nightmares.

I SHARED A KINDRED SPIRIT with the poor country boy who had been raised in the Assembly of God church. Sometimes I fantasized Elvis coming to visit me at my house. I imagined him accepting, comfortably, our leaky roof, the front screen door with the hole in it, and the sofa that would probably throw him to the floor. I just knew he would love Mama's southern cooking and overlook the chipped and unmatched dishes that the meal was served on. But, more important than any of these things, I knew he would understand my family's religion.

My grandparents on both sides were Pentecostal. Grandma Sheffield belonged to the Assembly of God, while Little Granny Minton went to the Church of God. I never saw much difference myself. It seemed to me they were about the same. They both believed in the baptism in the Holy Ghost with the evidence of speaking in tongues. And their way of dressing was similar; long sleeves, hemlines just above the ankles, cotton stockings, and aprons tied around their waists.

Little Granny, Daddy's mama, wore her thin, white-blond hair brushed back into a bun, while Grandma, Mama's mama, wore her long, thick, dark hair in four braids wrapped around her head. Neither of them wore makeup because it was a sin. They didn't wear jewelry or go to the movies, and dancing was allowed only at church while under the power of the Holy Spirit, or at home under the power of a whipping switch.

People back then who went to Holiness Churches were considered an oddity and joked about. I just knew Elvis had experienced some of the same feelings of being different that I felt.

I loved the music at my grandmothers' churches. It had soul to it, caused, my granny said, by the anointing of the spirit. When the anointing came upon the preachers it excited their congregations. One minute they would be riveted to their seats; the next minute they were dancing and shouting in the aisles. I kind of figured Elvis had some of that anointing on him—that perhaps this was why everybody got so excited over his music.

It seemed to me everything was a sin to Little Granny except dipping snuff, which she carried in her apron pocket along with a hanky to keep her mouth wiped off, and she toted an old tomato can for spitting when she was indoors. Papa Minton used to tease her about finding a way to smuggle her snuff through the Pearly Gates. His reward for the heckling was a smack on his head with a ladle spoon. This made me wonder if Elvis' mama dipped snuff and kept her man in line.

I remember, too, how Papa enjoyed needling Little Granny about her religion and called her a "Holy Roller." But I had witnessed the power at those meetings and even though I didn't understand, it seemed almost like sacrilege not to believe. I sensed that Elvis had this same, reverent fear of God within him. I knew that God was Love and the Holy Spirit engineered that love, so, Elvis being so loving, naturally, I wondered if he had the Holy Ghost.

Even though I had been exposed to the Holy Ghost, and the fear and love of God lived inside me, I was young and didn't really understand everything the Holy Spirit meant. Had I known more about the Comforter, perhaps I would have had more confidence in myself.

A week before school was to start, I took a good long look in the mirror. What I saw made me cry; freckles, eyebrows and lashes so blond they were invisible, and an overall mama's-little-girl plainness I didn't know how to help. I would be the school outcast, never invited to dances. A wallflower. I couldn't stand it. Just the thought of my lonely fate sent me into tears of self-pity, and I fell across the bed and bawled like a baby for a long time.

Finally, cried out and hiccuping, I lifted my head and stared at the wall in front of me. Elvis was smiling. The radio was on, and almost like he knew I needed some cheering up, Elvis' voice came floating through the airwaves.

Well, I don't care if the sun don't shine, I get my lovin' in the evenin' time.

"Lucky you, Elvis." I picked up the framed picture, studied it for a minute, then got up and walked over to the mirror. "Oh, Elvis," I whined in desperation, "help me."

I heard him in my head, faint at first. *Kiss the mirror.*

"What?"

It's me, honey...Elvis. Now, kiss the mirror. Pretend it's me.

I kissed the mirror, then, feeling foolish, fell back on the bed and cried some more. My pillow soaked up the tears till a soggy wet blob lay beneath my face. Then suddenly, Elvis was back in my head and this time he introduced me to the girl in the mirror.

Honey...listen to me. You're gettin' yourself all worked up over nothin'. You have beautiful features; all they need is definin'. You're fair skinned, honey, add some color. It'll enhance your natural beauty.

I stole into Mama's makeup and practiced before the mirror. "How's this, Elvis?" My spirits were lifting already.

Sexy! Now, fluff out your hair some. It looks best when it's long and fluffy.

I followed his instructions, then staring at my reflection, I asked, "Now, what do I do with the rest of me?"

Personally, I like sexy clothes. Somethin' that'll show off your best features. Sexy is a tease, honey. Girls shouldn't show it all. Keep a mystery goin'. Show off your best, in subtle ways.

"I don't know what my best is, Elvis."

Look in the mirror. Your best qualities are your face, your hair, and your legs. You've got great legs, so show 'em off. Bring the eye to them and remove it from the sore...you know, that part of you that's sore to your eye. The part that makes you self-conscious. I like your backside, too. Wear tight pants and skirts with slits. Open-toed heels with stockings or sandals on pretty bare feet look sexy with polished toe nails. I like danglin' earrings or loops. And go sort of heavy on the eye makeup. Show off those perfect teeth, keep brushin' and smilin'. And keep wishin', honey. You're full of dreams and wishes, just like me, and you have the power within you to make 'em all come true. Just believe, and it will happen.

"Oh, Elvis, I do believe." I backed up and studied the girl in the mirror. "This is cool, Elvis, but my name ruins the whole effect."

You don't like your name? Well, that's easy enough. Let's give you a new one! Nicknames are fun. Now, lem'me see...I see you sexy on the outside but innocent inside. It's the most sensuous condition; the best turn on there is! An angel! How about Angela? Like that, honey?

"But, Elvis, they'll call me a prick-teaser if I dress this way...not Angel."

So what? I've been called everything, from too late for supper to Elvis the Pelvis, for cryin' out loud! But listen to me...as long as you know who you are and love and respect your mama, God will watch out for you. Stay innocent, little one, and people will see the angel in Angela.

I liked the angel in Angela and thought it was a pretty name. Unlike, Frances, who in elementary school had been teased for her freckles and called "Frances the Talking Mule," Angela was a pretty blond-haired girl with blue eyes, a perfect nose, and full lips that framed a smile around a mouthful of even, white teeth. Elvis was also successful in convincing me that my long legs, which my kinfolks teased me about, were shapely and that I should dance and proudly show them off.

My identity as Angela was mine and mine alone, shared only with Elvis, my mirror, and a privileged few. My magic looking glass told me Angela was pretty, but I believed it because Elvis had said so. And I was certain...nothing bad was ever going to happen to Angela.

GRANNY MINTON AND GRANDMA SHEFFIELD. CIRCA 1960

2

Young Dreams

1956 - 1957

Being young is not a physical thing. It's a mental outlook, an attitude.

—*Elvis Presley*

The tragic death of James Dean in 1955 left a trail of embers for the right wind to blow. Elvis Presley, already singing up a storm, turned into a whirlwind, blew out of the South on a song, and blazed across the land, a new hero for the rebels. The timing was perfect for Elvis, whose unorthodox performances sent parents, pastors, and community leaders on frenzied campaigns to abolish him, his music, and everything he represented for the youth.

I was glad my mama wasn't on the wagon to ban Elvis: grateful that she was deeper than those shallow people who didn't look close enough to see the polite southern boy who'd been raised in church. Mama saw how happy Elvis made me, and that's all it took for her to like him. One thing about Mama, she let me have my dreams.

I was now in seventh grade at Oak Grove Jr. High School and thought I was Marilyn Monroe, after employing the techniques Elvis had taught me. That is, until Mama caught on to me, had a hissy-fit, and forbade me to wear makeup till I was in the ninth grade. But I got around this easy enough. I simply painted my face while I walked to school, then removed it before I got home.

Another crimp in my crinoline was no dating until tenth grade. But, since I was allowed school functions and Saturday movies, it involved little effort to plot adventures that Mama didn't know about.

By now, Elvis' name was on the lips of almost every girl in school. He may not have had the media exposure artists have today, but his music played continuously on the radio, and more and more of his pictures appeared in magazines, stimulating a hunger in me that could not be sated.

My obsession was a well-known fact among my friends and relatives, whom I suspected thought I was nuts. I talked about Elvis so much, Mama used to say, "I've eaten Elvis Presley for breakfast, dinner, and supper. Do I have to have a bedtime snack, too?"

Seventh grade was merely a prelude for things to come, and I envied the ninth graders who seemed to have it all; boobs, makeup, boyfriends, and dates. I was in my innocence, but being a romantic at heart, I dreamed of getting my first kiss. I'd been practicing on the mirror long enough and felt it was time for some flesh-on-flesh, mouth-to-mouth experience. I suppose you could say I got my first kiss from Kenny, at a school dance, if you called what we did a kiss. I still remember how scared we both were.

I had stumbled through three consecutive jitterbugs with Kenny-the-Square before, humiliated and hot to the point of stifling, I walked outside the cafeteria to catch a fresh breath. Millions of stars expanded a cloudless sky, and a welcome chill from the brisk autumn air clung to my naked arms, cooling me, as I stood alone on another beautiful, wasted night. It seemed all of nature was conspiring with the music that escaped from inside to waltz on the wind, romance the night, and aggravate my loneliness.

Why did my friend Skippy get the best looking guys? I had a crush on Beau, the most popular boy in school, but he liked Skippy. *Oh, who am I kidding*, I thought, *Beau would never look at me.* Guys like him went for girls with big boobs, and mine seemed to be homesteading the A-cup bra they now occupied.

I glanced down at my breasts and spoke to them for probably the hundredth time, "Please grow, you're ruining my life." This was an area where Elvis hadn't been much help. His suggestion to stuff my bra was his only counsel I declined. I didn't think it would be too cool if I got busted while dressing out for gym class, like some girls had.

Completely lost in myself, I failed to hear approaching steps and jumped when I felt an arm, quickly, slip around my waist.

"Kenny! You scared me!"

"Sorry. Who were you talking to?"

Embarrassed, I prayed he hadn't caught me talking to my titties.

"Nobody...just countin' stars. It got so hot inside I had to get some air. What are you doing out here?"

"I'd rather be out here with you, than inside."

Surprising me with a boldness out of character, Kenny tightened his grip around my waist and there we stood: two shy young people pretending interest in stars, while moments of silence ticked anticipation between us like something was going to happen.

"Do you ever wish on stars, Kenny?"

"No, it's foolish."

"Is not," I defended. "But then I don't suppose you'll ever have to worry about such foolishness, because it's only for people who believe."

We fell back into silence. Kenny was a square. He was nice, but square. Why was it, I wondered, I attracted squares? My looks weren't bad. In fact, I was kind of pretty since Elvis had helped me out. It was my darned small boobs. It just had to be.

Kenny broke the silence this time. "Frances, I watch you when we're in history class, but you never seem to notice me. I couldn't believe it when you danced with me tonight."

"You know, Kenny, I said, you'd be okay if you had a little more cool."

Kenny took offense at my audacity. "What do you mean by that remark?"

"Well, like you could wear your hair longer...and maybe grow some sideburns...like Elvis."

"Elvis!" he stormed. "That's all girls think about. Elvis, Elvis,

Elvis! Well I'm sorry! I don't have Elvis' cool. And unlike Elvis, I...ah...oh crap! Frances...I can't grow sideburns, yet, I've tried."

I felt his embarrassment and lifted my hand to touch his un-blemished, stubble-free cheek. "You have a nice face, Kenny, and pretty blue eyes." I couldn't help noticing, too, his beautiful teeth, and his breath smelled like spearmint gum. "Have you ever kissed a girl?"

"Sure I've kissed a girl!" he quickly responded, then defensive-ly added, "Lots of 'em."

Broaching the idea forming in my mind, I stared, breathlessly, into his eyes, and whispered, "Well, I've never been kissed."

"You haven't?" His surprise at my confession was obvious.

"No, I haven't. So I was kinda thinkin' that with all your expe-rience, maybe you could teach me."

Caught off guard, he shuffled his feet.

"What's the matter, Kenny? Don't you want to kiss me?"

"Sure, I wanna kiss you, but...well...I sort of... darn it! Frances, I've never kissed anyone either."

Kenny's confession came as no surprise to me. "Think maybe we could learn together?" I suggested.

We stood frozen, gazing, eye to eye, each waiting for the other to make the first move, while the Platters expressed my muse in the words of "My Prayer." I'd looked forward to my first kiss, imagin-ing I would see stars, hear thunder, float on clouds, and lightening would singe my feet. Little wonder I felt let down when Kenny-the-Square finally leaned closer and pressed his cold, dry, inexperi-enced lips to mine.

Lacking practice, chemistry, and saliva, two tightly puckered mouths met, floundered, smacked a smooch, and created about as much excitement as dirty-sock soup for supper. Quickly forsaking the ridiculous idea that Kenny could teach me anything about kiss-ing, I pulled away from our disappointing flop.

"This is hopeless, Kenny. I think we both need to find some-body who knows what they're doing."

I turned from his red face and was headed back to the dance when I heard him, pleading, "Don't tell anybody, Pleeease."

Glancing back, I thought, *Like I'd want anyone knowing I kissed you.* But I said, "It's, cool, Kenny. Let's just forget about it."

And that's exactly what I was doing when I went back to kissing the mirror and pretending it was Elvis.

I BOUGHT ALL OF ELVIS' MUSIC, even though I didn't own a record player. Mama kept saying, "Maybe you'll get one for Christmas if Santa Claus has any money." *Yeah,* I silently concluded, *and if wishes were records, I'd be in the music business.*

The phenomenon known as Elvis Presley, that wind out of the South, ignited into a blazing inferno. Demand was greater than supply. Magazines carrying his pictures and stories, along with his records, sold "hot off the press." Any time of the day you could turn the radio on and hear Elvis singing.

Ed Bray of WALT radio was, at this time, the most popular disc jockey among teenagers in Tampa. He had a program where we could call and vote for our favorite singer. Elvis, along with other artists of that day, including Pat Boone, Fats Domino, and Little Richard, competed for an hour of uninterrupted spins. Elvis always won.

I loved stretching out across my bed and listening to the hour of Elvis, while I wrote him poetic messages from my heart. I still have a few of those letters and this is one of them:

August 12, 1957

Dear Elvis,

You touch a part of me that is unreachable. You understand me in a way I can't comprehend. You send me your love with a smile that is so unique, it's patented by your signature lip.

Elvis, the words you sing mean everything, they speak to my heart. A song for every season, a song for every reason, they hold the answers to all the questions I am unable to ask.

How do you know the way to show each heart that listens just who you are. You touch a star and my whole world glistens.

*There will never be another you. You grasp the world
then give it back, so generous is your nature. Your love en-
dures forever and I am richer by far, for being a part of
your generation.*

Loving you forever,
Frances Minton

ELVIS' FIRST TELEVISION performance was on the Dorsey Brothers Stage Show in January 1956. I sat glued to the TV, which I
had to fight the rest of my family for, biting my fingernails, shifting
in my seat, eagerly awaiting my hero's introduction.

When the announcer finally said his name, I like to have peed
in my pants. Then Elvis suddenly took the stage in long, quick
strides, wearing a tweed looking coat with dark dress pants.

His attitude when he came to a stop said he knew who he was,
what he was about, and what he was gonna do to us. His feet set
apart, he draped a limp wrist over his elaborately engraved guitar,
conveying enough energy to light up Las Vegas, and I felt the
sparks, sizzling in my blood, making me want...making me need....

The view projecting from the television set allowed me to enjoy at close range what I'd previously seen live, but from a distance. I saw sideburns that seemed to reach armpits, and he was
dangerous, an atomic power with a set of searching eyes that summoned me to wonder; shadowed eyes that made me guess, faraway
eyes that held a mystery.

And he was the biggest flirt I'd ever seen.

It's hard to explain, and was hard to contain, what I felt at that
moment, witnessing the gyrating charisma of Elvis in action, for he
was a man with a secret, one lesser men yearned to possess—how
to make women fall at their feet.

A mysterious individual, his eyes, dark and brooding one moment, searching the next, defied, dared, then quickly warmed to
deliver a joy from the heart that could not be suppressed. A flash of
illumination germinating from his lopsided grin suddenly burst
forth into an openmouthed laugh that made the sun come out. A
laugh that belonged exclusively to Elvis Presley. One that shim-

mered with sun-kissed splendor, spreading to his eyes, lighting up his face, and delivering a promise. What promise? That was for you alone to define, for he was a fantasy come to life.

Elvis demanded attention, if you liked him or not, when he limply bent forward from the waist and spat out like he was chewing his tongue, "*W...ell, get out in that kitchen and rattle those pots and pans.*" His voice, thick with subliminal messages, conveyed an unsophisticated, raunchy appeal, that excited... promised, conquered, and delivered.

He jerked his head, then froze, a slight grin on his face, not really a smile, but more like a beaming, sullen sneer. Then, just as suddenly as he'd frozen, he sprang back into action, shaking his head and commanding his electrifying magnetism to reach through the television and grab me, and I felt like he mysteriously knew from a distance just what I was feeling, and keyed in on my emotions.

He bounced, his searching eyes dashing back and forth, his lips begging me to kiss them, as he shook his shoulders and legs, belting out..."*Flip, flop, and fly—I'm like a Mississippi bullfrog sittin' on a holler stump, I got so many women I don't know which away to jump.*"

Elvis looked over his shoulder at his two musician backups, Scotty Moore and Bill Black, then, tilting his head to the side, he danced backwards, shaking and beating his guitar—then he was back on his song, "Shake, Rattle and Roll," and he tore it up like live fast and die young. Elvis was so, fast, he was through before I could grasp him, and I wanted more. The lingering haunt of his eyes sent me straight to my bedroom to privately ponder his picture.

"It's a personal thing, isn't it, Elvis. You connect with my soul. And someday, when I have the money to put myself in your path, you'll know me by my spirit and respond."

I guess that's why I never joined a fan club. It was like joining a church: I didn't believe it required a church membership to be a Christian, and I didn't feel it was necessary to join a fan club to love Elvis. To me, being a fan was simply loving unconditionally: a personal thing between me and my elusive dream hero, who in spirit encouraged me to believe I could touch him, if only I tried hard enough, if only for a moment...just one fleeting moment to remember for the rest of my life.

Making Elvis and his souvenir-selling manager, Colonel Tom Parker, rich, was high on my list of favorite pastimes. My friends and I went to the dime store and drooled all over the Elvis items displayed on the counters. We hung around that store for hours trying to make our selections. Money was scarce, but I still managed to accumulate a collection of Elvis lipsticks in every available color; plus a billfold, a charm bracelet, photo earrings, a clutch purse, Teddy Bear perfume, and an Elvis Presley felt skirt.

I N THE SUMMER OF '56, we moved to Keysville, not far from my grandaddy's farm, while renting out our house in Tampa. Daddy had taken a painting job in Mulberry and our move put him closer to his work. He painted everything from houses to bridges when, occasionally, he wanted to be home with his family.

Mr. Broadwell owned the house we rented, which was located at the top of a hill on the road that ran directly in front of his combination grocery store/gas station. I climbed that hill on my bicycle every time I went to the store to purchase bubble gum cards with Elvis' picture on them.

The old frame house sat next to the cemetery of the Hard-Shell Baptist church, and I found it a scary effort to pass the graveyard on my trips to the store, but was undaunted in my quest to own the complete set of bubble gum cards. I did question, however, why it was that every house we lived in had some aspect of trepidation about it.

I have a lot of memories attached to the Broadwell house. That was a year of growth for me. I turned thirteen, physically became a young lady, and went to see my first Elvis Presley movie. You might have called it the Elvis year. I saw him eleven times on television in 1956.

Another memorable recollection is my first "real" kiss.

I attended Pinecrest School for most of the eighth grade. The learning facility went from grades one through twelve and I missed the dances I had enjoyed at Oak Grove. There were no organized activities for teenagers in Keysville, so we found interesting ways to entertain ourselves. Parties were the biggest thing. If you've never been to a party in the country, you've missed an experience. Hayrides were a blast, and spin the bottle was a game we took more seriously than kids in the city, who didn't have long, dark, country roads to walk down while they flirted and necked. It was at one of these parties held at the house of a girl named Connie, I received my first "real" kiss from Alex.

My enthusiasm was fever-pitched that night. I had a crush on Alex and I'd heard he was going to be at the party. Actually, you could say it was more than a crush. I was absolutely bonkers over the guy. I was thirteen and Alex was seventeen, and aside from Elvis, he was the sexiest guy I'd ever seen. A gorgeous combination of Elvis, Richard Egan, and Charleton Heston.

I was surprised to find the party in progress when I arrived early. Post office had already begun and I nervously glanced around for Alex. I didn't see him anywhere and asked Connie if he was coming.

"Yes, he'll be here. Don't worry, Frances, he's always late."

How could she be so nonchalant about it? I thought. This was my first party and everyone knew how I felt about Alex. For that matter, so did Alex, but I believed he thought I was too young for him. I knew it couldn't be my boobs this time, since they had made outstanding progress in their development.

They finished playing post office and finally coaxed me into joining them for spin the bottle. As I sat down on the ground in the circle they had formed, Connie explained the rules to me.

"Whoever spins the bottle gets their choice of a kiss or a walk down the road."

The games were held outside around a campfire, and as Connie was speaking, Alex's old Ford pulled up in the yard. He, and another guy I didn't recognize, got out of the car and walked toward the circle.

"Hey, ya'll got room for us?"

I felt my heart leap and hoped he would sit next to me. But he didn't. Alex and the other guy closed in the circle directly across from me. As the game got under way, I became more jittery and anxious, and prayed the bottle wouldn't stop on me until it reached

Alex. God must have been listening, because as it spun in turns, it missed me every time.

Finally, Alex held the bottle. I squeezed my eyes tightly shut, and silently prayed, *Please, Lord, let it land on me.* When I opened them back up and casually glanced toward Alex, he set me to trembling from the decisive look he was sending my way. Then, as though he had control over the bottle, he sent it in a half circle spin and it stopped, pointing directly at me.

Alex stood up and walked over to me. He smiled teasingly, looking straight into my eyes, and offered me his hand. "I wanna take a walk with you."

My pulse raced. I felt a hot blush rush up my neck to my face as I placed my hand in his and let him pull me to my feet. Everybody was hooting and hollering when we left the group and headed down the moonlit dirt road.

We held hands, walking in silence until the campfire was out of view. It was quiet, the only sounds coming from crickets who seemed to be chirping, *He's going to kiss you. He's going to kiss you.* I could feel his eyes on me and glanced sideways at him. He was staring at me through black-lashed blue eyes. They seemed fathoms deep, reflecting a cunning worldliness, and I was certain Alex could make me touch a star with one kiss, even if I was inexperienced and shy. *Send me some magic, Elvis.*

Alex cleared his throat and smiled. "Are you enjoying the party?"

Unable to speak, I nodded my head.

"This your first party?"

Again, I nodded my head.

He dropped my hand, then slipping his arm around my waist, he pulled me closer to him as we continued to walk. He smelled of Old Spice and my heart was captivated. My hands began to sweat. Even with a slight chill in the air, my hands were sweating.

"You're nervous, aren't you?"

I glanced up at him. "How can you tell?"

"You're trembling all over."

We continued to walk and the sorcerous moonlight made everything look promising, but the uneasy silence of anxiety, caused my heart to pump, thumpidy-thump. *Please, send me some magic, Elvis.*

"The moon is out...full one. You know what they say about a full moon, doncha?"

"No."

Then he did the strangest thing. He tickled the palm of my hand with his finger. "Know what that means?"

"No."

Suddenly he stopped walking, bringing me to a halt with him, and turned to me. He tilted my chin up so I had to look at him, while his eyes slowly surveyed my face. "Frances, I'm going to kiss you."

He left no time for me to anticipate his statement, and quickly covered my mouth with his. I melted under his guidance and was lost in emotions so new to me, I just wanted to let go and fall into them. I was definitely ready to explore those heady sensations that tempted to exile me from parents, rules, morals, consequences, and pure common sense, and I delved into the task full steam. *This is how Elvis would do it,* was my last thought, just before I touched the stars.

The kiss was a long one. A really, long one that left no place for anything but feelings. And when it had to end for air, our lips still clung together as we panted out the corners of our mouths, then dove back for more and continued till a sneaky hand brushing near my breast rescued my rational mind from my passion.

Shocked, I jerked back from his lips and just stared at him.

Alex smiled. "You're a fast learner."

"What do you mean by that?" I asked, not ready to admit my inexperience.

Tilting my chin upward again, and looking directly into my eyes, he said, "Frances, don't pretend you don't know what I'm talking about. You've never been kissed like that before."

"How do you know how I've been kissed?"

"Believe me, I know. I knew before I walked you down this road. And do you wanna know why I did it?"

"Why?"

"Because I wanted to be the first. A girl never forgets her first kiss."

And Alex was right. I've never forgotten that kiss nor any of the others that followed. But I knew in my heart, it was Elvis who had really taught me how.

LOVE ME TENDER, which my father took me to see at the State theater in Plant City, was Elvis' first movie. Even though Plant City was a small town, the lines at the cinema were still long. It was wonderful to finally see Elvis on the big screen. He was perfect. The down side was that I had expected technicolor and this movie was in black and white. Also, I wanted to see him kiss his female co-star, Debra Paget, but it was Richard Egan who got her kiss. The worst part was when Elvis died at the end of the movie. I cried, and cried, and Daddy made fun of me for crying. But I was not deterred by these things and saw the movie forty-eight times that year.

My family moved back to our Tampa home in the spring of '57. I was still in the eighth grade and back at Oak Grove Jr. High when I went to see Elvis' second movie. *Loving You* gave us everything we wanted...color, kisses, a happy ending, and lots of songs.

Elvis' third movie, *Jail House Rock*, exploited the rebel side of him which proved to be ultra-sensual. There's just something about a sexy rebel that tends to sweep a teenage girl mindlessly off her feet. Take for instance when Elvis kissed Peggy and she said, *"How dare you think such cheap tactics would work with me?"* And Elvis said, *"That ain't tactics, honey. That's just the beast in me."* This scene became my fantasy. The way Elvis took control and forcibly kissed Peggy made me want to be in that situation just once in my lifetime. It also had girls at school swooning over it and the "really cool" guys took it up in mimicry as a new ploy for instituting the Elvis appeal.

The teenage girl of the fifties now had access to the perfect prince. Every song Elvis sang was just for her. Every grin that lifted his lip to that famous half smile—the one I call his love-me-tender smile, was just for her. I personally savored each and every classic move he made, sitting through his movies many times to relish these gems.

Tall, dark, and handsome, Elvis was indisputably the stuff dreams were made of. So, I took everything he sent me from the big screen; the music, the sensuality, the feeling of being close to him, and I carried the treasures home to fill my nights with sweet dreams—*Be damned the nightmares.*

At age thirteen, I vowed that someday I would meet and talk to Elvis Presley—a monumental goal so far from my reach, I knew I'd need all the help Heaven could give me.

ELVIS POSES IN TRAILER ON SET OF "FOLLOW THAT DREAM." 1961.

3

If I Can Dream

1957-1958

Innocence lets you dream.

—Elvis Presley

The day I made my vow to meet Elvis is fixed like crazy glue in my memory. It was in early fall, which in Florida is like a northern summer, and I was in the ninth grade at Oak Grove. I can still hear the mimicking chirps of the mockingbirds, as they welcomed a new day to a peaceful world outside my raised window. The tantalizing smells of hot oatmeal and scrambled eggs crept through the crack under my bedroom door, grabbed my nose, and made my stomach growl.

"Sister." Mama's soft voice interrupted my thoughts as she tapped against my door, then opened it enough to peek inside. "Time to get up for school." Her voice was sweet and singsongy, her smile cheerful and more comforting than the fresh, white, sun-dried, starched, and ironed sheets I stretched myself into. "Get up, sleepy head. If I have to come back in here you know what I'll do." She closed the door, confident I would get out of bed to avoid being tickled.

Daddy was out to sea and all was as it should be; right, sober, and peaceful. I lingered in bed. Mama's routine wake-up call usually allowed me five minutes before she carried out her threat. Rising up from my pillow, I looked out the window. It was a beautiful day and I inhaled deeply, my share of the fresh air that said, *This is your day. You can make it exciting or you can waste it.*

I wasn't a person to waste anything, although I often wondered what it would be like to indulge. I suppose this thinking came from a hunger to experience everything. I wanted to smell all the roses alongside my path through life. But sometimes I tended to get waysided by the allure of wild scents. I just knew one thing: when my life was over I wanted my tombstone to read—SHE LIVED.

Ah...to smell every flower, see every sight, taste every flavor, sing every song, dance every dance, visit every place, meet every interesting person I could, and feel every feeling except pain. Of pain and fear, I had tasted my fill. Life to me meant taking every lemon fate served me and making a lemon meringue pie, then shoving it back into the face of ill fate. For I was impassioned by my fantasies and meant to dance on four leaf clovers till the magic that filled my dreams sprang to life.

I reached over to the nightstand and picked up my special picture of Elvis and kissed him. "Good morning, Elvis." Then I heard Mama's footsteps approaching and quickly jumped from the bed, put the picture back on the nightstand, turned on the radio, and beat her to the door.

"I was just about to come in there and wake you up," she said.

"I'm up, Mama." I hurried to the bathroom, then headed for the kitchen where Mama, Sam, and Tommy were waiting at the table. As we said the blessing, my hand stole up and snitched a plump, sweet raisin from my bowl of oatmeal.

"Elvis would lo. . .ve your ugly pin curls."

Tommy was in a good mood this morning. At least he hadn't told me to put a bag over my head, yet. Everybody said Tommy was going to be another Elvis Presley. He did kind of look like Elvis, having the same full lips and crooked grin. But, to me he was just my snot-nose, baby brother. The one who got the most whippings. Yes, Mama whipped us, usually with a dog-fennel[1] or peach tree switch, administered to our bare dancing legs. But, I'll say one thing, when Mama was led to whip us she made darn sure we knew what it was for and we always knew we deserved it.

Sam was quiet, as usual, intent upon finishing his breakfast in time to make up his bed before leaving for school. Sam was a neat-freak and rarely got any whipping's but when he did get one, he got the hardest because he was the most stubborn.

Occasionally, Mama stepped from the table to attend to lunches and pour herself another cup of coffee. Her petite figure was hidden under a loose-fitting pink housecoat and her soft, brown hair, had already been brushed out from the pin curls she'd slept in.

"Sister, if you want to you can put on a pot of beans for supper when you get home from school. Then when I get home, we'll make a pan of biscuits and fry up some taters to go with 'em. Mmmm...tater sandwiches and great northern beans...don't that sound laripin' good?" Mama smacked her lips together and popped her tongue. "Then...young lady, you can get your head out of the clouds you live in and get your homework done."

"But, Mama, it's the weekend! I've got all weekend to do my homework."

"Oh...that's right. I declare, I'd forget my head if it wat'n growed on. Ain't Vernie supposed to bring Sandra over this weekend?"

I took a bite of oatmeal while nodding my head. "Um huh, then we're going to the sock hop, remember?"

"Yeah, seems I remember." She smiled. "Sister, I was just teasin' you. I'm sure ya'll have a good time at the sock hop. Just be good girls and don't let them boys dance too close."

"Mama, Frances always burns the beans just 'cause she likes 'em that way." Sam squinted his eyes, then grinned and snorted at me. He was so cute with his red hair and freckles. I was used to his and Tommy's teasing and loved them in spite of their aggravating ways. *After all,* I thought, like the big Ike I was, *they're only children.* Sam was in the sixth grade and Tommy in fifth.

---

[1] A slender weed, with long, soft, limp, needles, that grows in Florida.

I swallowed the rest of my breakfast then, checking the time, rushed to my bedroom to get dressed. Mumbling to myself while I flipped through the clothes in my closet, I decided it felt like an Elvis day and chose my Elvis felt skirt, with a pale pink, short-sleeve, pullover sweater and long-sleeve matching cardigan. A small black scarf, tied choker style around my neck, would give the outfit a "real cool" look.

Next, I reached for my crinolines, hanging from a hook on the side of the closet, and checked to see if Mama had put enough starch in them. *Good,* I thought, *they're nice and stiff.* I'd only need three to get the fullness I desired in my skirt, instead of the twelve it took when they were limp.

I dropped to my knees beside the bed, in search of my black and white saddle oxfords, and as I stood back up, Elvis' voice came crooning through the radio. I hummed along with him while slipping into my clothes.

"I Was the One" was my favorite song. The way Elvis sang it made me feel like it was meant just for me. If I closed my eyes I could feel him right there in the room with me, telling me he was the one. The one who taught me to kiss, and how to touch a cheek, and to cry when I wanted someone under a spell.

I pulled open the top dresser drawer and took out a black patent-leather belt. The belt would need a new hole punched into it soon and I puzzled over where I could fit another one. I wore it so tight the eyelets ripped and this one was already a graveyard of holes. But how else could I make my waist look twenty-one inches? That was the popular size. Twenty-three was my old waist pincher's limit. I hated my waist. I could never get it small enough.

Checking the time again, I quickly removed the bobby pins from my hair. I needed to hurry if I planned on having enough time to stop at the Sugar Shack. I hated the way my hair looked in the mornings. The curl was tight and made it look shorter than its shoulder length. It always looked the best at night, after having loosened up during the day. I started for the bathroom to put on my makeup and Mama stopped me.

"Frances! Did you shrink that sweater on purpose?"

"Only a little bit, Mama."

My exaggeration did not escape her observant eyes. "It looks like you painted it on." She emphasized her disapproval with a you-should-be-ashamed-of-yourself look. "I bet if you was to raise your arms over your head that sweater would bust wide open, then your everything would be shinin'."

I smiled at her attempt to lecture me with a joke, then slid past her and continued on my way to the bathroom. Sam and Tommy were ready to leave for the bus stop. I peeked around the door and watched Mama hand them their lunches and kiss them good-bye. We might have a drunk for a daddy, I mused, but God had more than made up for it when He gave us Mama. Mama was the best.

I gathered up my books, planted a kiss on my favorite picture of Elvis, rushed into the living room and gave Mama a kiss, then dashed out the front door. When I reached the end of the street I stopped by Dinah's house. Sometimes we walked the two miles to school together. She was just coming out the door as I approached the steps.

"Hi, Frances. I'm ready...let's go."

Dinah was a sweet girl from a large family. She was the oldest of eight children and being as her responsibilities were so many, there was never any time left over for fun. We headed down the narrow, tree-lined, paved road, carrying our books.

"Dinah, are you gonna go to the sock hop tonight?"

"No. Mama and Daddy are going out. It's their wedding anniversary and I'm babysitting for them."

"Don't you get tired of takin' care of your brothers and sisters all the time, Dinah? I mean, the same old rut...doesn't that just drive you crazy? Make you wanna get loose and do something...I don't know, sort of...dangerous and exciting?"

"No, thank you. I like my safe little ole life just like it is. You're wild at heart, Frances. I'm not like that. I want to go to college and make something of my life."

I glanced sideways at her, taking note of her cute figure that seemed to go unnoticed because of her serious personality, and shook my head.

"Not me. No wasted years in college for me. I want a husband who looks like Elvis and lots and lots of babies."

I skipped along beside Dinah. "Isn't it a beautiful day? Just feel the crispness in the air. I can almost hear it crackle. I love it!

Mmmm...and smell the pines. Don't they smell good? Makes me feel like somethin' special is gonna happen. Like maybe Elvis will appear at my door...and haul me away to a place I've never been. Then I'll have him aaall to myself." *And I'll be safe in his arms.*

Dinah shook her head, "You're the biggest dreamer I've ever seen."

I didn't appreciate the skeptical way she was looking at me. "I know I'm a dreamer. But one of these days, Dinah, something special is gonna happen to me. I just know it." I giggled, "Who knows, maybe Elvis'll send his houndog to sniff me out, and if I'm high-class enough, he'll lead me straight to Elvis' front door and we'll get married."

Dinah rolled her eyes in disbelief and I giggled. I loved messing with her head.

"Well, if its high-class he's looking for," she was wearing a smirk, "that houndog may sniff the straw behind your ears and pass you by."

"I ain't no bumpkin."

"I know. You just talk that way for the fun of it."

Dinah was one of the few people, besides Mama, that I couldn't have the last say with.

"Are you going to the dance tonight?" she asked.

"Yeah. My cousin...Sandra Polk is coming over to spend the weekend with me and we're going to the Hop together. The last time she went to a dance with me she met this guy named Chuck and I think they're kinda sweet on each other now. Anyway, Sandra's supposed to meet him at the dance tonight."

"Do you have a date?"

"No. All the cute guys are taken and I'd rather go by myself than with some goofy-looking square. I hope I don't get stuck with one hanging around me for a dance tonight. The only good part about going stag is you get to dance with whoever you want."

We continued to talk while we walked to school, but when we reached the Sugar Shack, Dinah kept on going. She didn't hang out with this crowd who smoked cigarettes, wore black leather jackets, and rode motorcycles.

The Sugar Shack (as we called it, coining the phrase long before the popular song of the same title was written) was a small Mom and Pop store located next door to the school. The elderly couple who owned it befriended the teenagers who hung out there and had fixed up a room in the back of the store, next to the juke box, with sofas and overstuffed chairs. There used to be a whole lot of smooching going on in the Sugar Shack. Matter of fact, that's how it come to acquire its name.

We hung out here before and after school; talking, drinking Cokes, smoking our cigarettes, smooching, playing the juke box, and dancing. Flipping for pennies was the rage, but an outrage to the school board when it carried over onto the school grounds. So, we flipped our pennies at the Sugar Shack and if I was lucky, it meant a new Elvis record.

As I started to enter the Shack, I heard my name being called and turned in the direction of the voice.

"Frances, wait up."

Holly was my best friend. She was sexy looking with a reputation for being wild. Maybe that was why I liked her so much. Holly thumbed her nose at gossip and did what she pleased.

"What's up?" Holly's big, flirtatious smile revealed her gums as she approached me; then leaning near while holding her books, she bumped me with her shoulder. "Frances, you look so damn silly in that Elvis skirt."

"Holly! How can you say that? You know you like Elvis, too!"

"Yeah. But I don't go around with his face plastered all over me looking like some mooney-eyed ninth grader. Next you'll be wearing Howdy Doody." She laughed as we walked into the Sugar Shack together.

We found us a seat then pulled out our cigarettes and lit up.

"Frances, I know this cool looking guy and he's got a friend. They want us to double tonight. Maybe see a movie...or something."

"Oh, Holly. I'd love to go. But Sandra's coming over tonight and we're going to the Hop. Then she's staying at my house till Sunday night."

"Those dances are sissified shit! Why do you like all that stupid school-shit, anyway?" Holly took a long, slow, drag on her cigarette, then blew the smoke in my face.

"They're fun. And they're not sissified. You never go to the dances...so how do you know what they're like?"

"Well, it sure as hell ain't 'cause I can't dance." Then she pranced her wiggly butt over to the jukebox and dropped in a coin, while everybody backed off and made room on the small dance floor for Holly to put on a show. She played "All Shook Up" and did her sex kitten bumps and grinds till the school bell rang.

The first bell indicated it was time for us to gather up our books and head for class. It was Friday, and on Fridays the halls were lined with colorful posters, meant to rev up our school spirit for that evening's sock hop.

The school day progressed as usual. Nothing exciting happened, but the feeling was still with me. I'd been wound up all day and now it was time for my last class. I had a big crush on this guy who sat across from me in civics. His name was Cliff, and he looked so much like Elvis, it was hard for me to concentrate in class.

Cliff's resemblance to Elvis went beyond his looks. He had a warm, southern, good-ole-boy charm that attracted lots of friends. His charisma and mannerisms were amazingly Elvis. But what really caught my attention were his full, soft-looking lips that I'd have bet anything would kiss just like Elvis'. I studied those lips hard enough that if they had offered a Cliff's Lips class, I would have made an A plus. I was always looking for Cliff to show up at one of the dances, but I never saw him there. When I finally asked him about it, he told me he lived in Lutz and had a problem getting a ride into town.

When the last bell rang, I hurried home and put on a pot of beans to cook. Then I turned on the radio and started straightening up the house. Mama was fair. If I did my chores, Fridays and Saturday nights were mine. I checked the time and it was four o'clock. Time for the Elvis hour. An uninterrupted hour of music by Elvis the Pelvis, as the disc jockey called him.

I went to my bedroom, turned on my shortwave radio, and stepped out of my crinolines while the deejay rambled his ads. Then I took off my shoes and fell across the bed. Lying on my stomach, I reached over to the night table and picked up my favorite photo. As I studied Elvis' picture, the deejay put on a record and Elvis started singing "Anyway You Want Me."

"Oooh...I want you, Elvis." I closed my eyes and let him into my head. *Just you and me, Elvis, that's how I want you.* The song ended and was followed by "Too Much."

"Elvis, how much is too much? I mean, how far do I go with a guy and still keep it innocent? I like the kissing part, you know, the romance and all. But I don't like it when their hands start to roam."

That's because you're an angel.

"I...don't think so, Elvis. I don't know why, but I feel like I'm bad. And you still ain't told me, how far should I go?"

First off...you're not bad. Keep it above the waist. That's the limit. But it's safer above the neck, honey. If a guy likes kissin', then he likes kissin', and if he likes it enough, he'll never get enough of the thrill of a kiss. Even if he has to keep his hands to himself. You see...the mystery... that's what gives the kisses life. It's a turn on that lives and breathes on its own—the mystery.

Now Elvis was singing "I Want You, I Need You, I Love You" in his smoldering, come-hither voice that transported me to Paradise a la Elvis.

"Why can't they all be like you, Elvis?" I lay on the bed staring at his picture and he stared back. His eyes were piercing, soul-searching, and I just knew he could hear me when I talked to him. I experienced all the feelings his music conveyed. His voice had arms to hold me, lips to kiss me, and words to comfort me with understanding. Moved by my emotions, I kissed his picture, then told him about my day.

"This is a special day, Elvis. I've felt it since this morning. But nothin' exceptional's happened so far."

That's when it struck me. It was up to me to make it special. Elvis' eyes were burning into mine and suddenly, I knew. I knew that no matter what it took, or how long it took me, someday I was going to meet Elvis. I knew it with a certainty way down deep inside me, and to seal it, I held his picture before me, alone in my bedroom with the radio on, and Elvis singing "Heartbreak Hotel." I was embraced by an echo of haunting sensuality—touched by a voice that felt me. And I made a vow.

"Someday I will meet you, Elvis Aron Presley[2]. Do you hear me? I'm not talking about sittin' at the back of a concert auditori-

---

[2] Elvis spelled his middle name, Aron, until after he became famous, at which time he changed the spelling to Aaron.

um. I mean we will talk, you and me. We'll just talk, talk, talk. I promise you, Elvis. I vow to you, one of these days we'll meet and we'll talk and who knows, I might even write a book about it. I want to be a writer, Elvis. It's like I've got all these words inside me, you know, just bustin' to be put down on paper. Only I don't know which side of the comma they go on. Some writer I'll make, hunh? Oh, well, whether I write about you or not, I'm still gonna meet you. That is a promise. And I promise you my loyalty, too. Forever, Elvis. I don't care what people say about you or what you do." I meant that vow, as much as a bride speaking her wedding vows to the man she loves.

After I made the vow I could have sworn Elvis' eyes were saying, *And I'll be waiting.* Now I knew why this day had seemed special, and I would reflect back on it, many times, in the years to come.

S ANDRA MADE IT in time for supper. I thought the scorched beans were delicious, but my brothers complained.

"Oh, you boys quit fussin' and eat," Mama told them, "and be grateful you got it."

"I'm grateful, Mama," Sam piped up, smirking from ear to ear.

"Me, too," Tommy aped, while he played with his food, "Come on burnt bean, stay on my fork so I can eat you."

"Use a spoon, Tommy," Mama said. Then, turning to Sandra, "What's your mama been up to lately? I ain't visited with Vernie in a coon's age. Why didn't she come in when she dropped you off and eat supper?"

"She was in a hurry, Aunt Artie Mae. She's been sewing ...staying busy." Sandra looked at me, pursed her lips, and raised her eyebrows. "Frances, we better start gettin' ready for the dance, doncha think?"

We excused ourselves from the table and went to my bedroom to start our primping ceremony. The door to my room had barely closed before I snatched Sandra by the hand and dragged her over to the bed where we could sit down. Then I told her about my vow.

"Today's a memorable day, Sandra. So don't forget what I'm gonna tell you, okay? Today, I made a vow to Elvis that I was gonna meet him." I hesitated...waiting for some kind of reaction...but she just sat there looking at me like I'd lost my last marble. I told her all about my vow and my feelings. I poured my heart out. I was so excited. I couldn't understand why this revelation hadn't sent her to the ceiling, made her scream, or show some kind of emotion other than the scowl she was directing at me.

"Yeah, so when do you get to the good part?"

"What do you mean the good part? That is the good part. I just told you I'm gonna meet Elvis Presley and talk to him and kiss him and get to know him and you don't consider that the good part? Are you nuts or somethin'!"

"Yes, indeed, so nuts, I think I'll do the same. Oh...but you're gonna marry Elvis, right? Guess I'll have to settle for marrying his cousin."

Her mockery didn't set well with my serious convictions. Sandra was bitchy and high-strung, but good-hearted, and had a re-markable sense of humor when she applied herself. Although we had our differences, we agreed on one thing. We both loved Elvis.

"Smart aleck. You can make fun, but just you wait...I'll show you."

The dance, held in the lunchroom, was in full swing when San-dra and I arrived. We were thirty minutes late and Chuck was ready to have a conniption when we walked in. Buddy Knox's "Party Doll" had jitterbuggers heating up the floor. Girls used to dance the fast ones with each other until the guys loosened up. I left San-dra talking with Chuck and joined some girlfriends who had gath-ered out on the floor.

We were dancing, cutting up and acting silly, when this drop-dead gorgeous, cool looking daddy-o sauntered over to our group and asked me to dance the next slow one with him. He said his name was Sabino, and he was tall, well built, and had a face to die for. I couldn't believe he'd picked me!

We danced to "The Great Pretender" by the Platters, so close, I practically rode his lead leg. He told me he had come with a friend and that school dances weren't his usual style.

"But then I didn't know they attracted cuties like you."

He appeared to be Spanish and combed his dark hair into a ducktail. His black leather jacket and blue jeans made him look dangerous and out of place at a school dance.

"Where's your friend?"

"Oh...he's around here someplace."

He asked me for a date. I wanted to tell him yes, but it wasn't that simple. I wasn't allowed to single date. We'd have to double with another couple or meet at the Springs Theater. I stalled, waiting for the right opening to tell him.

I danced every dance with Sabino and felt on top of the world, until later, when I told my friends about my vow and they all looked at me pathetically, and said, "Good luck, dreamer." *They're just like Sandra,* I thought, *a bunch of faithless butt-heads.* Then I worried, *Is that all it is, just green stamp wishes and bottle top dreams?* But their disbelief made me more determined. I would make it happen, then they could eat their words and I wouldn't even offer them ketchup.

Sabino had gone out to the car for a cigarette and Sandra was dancing with Chuck when I strolled outside to cool off. *Why,* I thought, *are my so-called friends so negative about my vow?* Their smugness irked me and I declared aloud, "I'll show them. I'll show them all! I'll show everybody who's ever hurt me!"

"Who you gonna show what?" Sabino surprised me. I told him about my vow and expected him to laugh, too, just like everybody else. Instead, he slouched sideways in a cool Marlon Brando imitation, lazily tilted his head and said, "That's a big order you got wished up for yourself."

"It's not just a wish," I told him, "it's a fact!" Then I turned heels and hightailed it back inside where they were playing the last dance. Sabino followed me, then pulled me into his arms and whirled me out onto the dance floor, first into a slow jitterbug then a dirty-waltz, while Pat Boone sang "Ain't That A Shame."

"Don't be so down, baby. And quit telling those creeps about what you feel inside. Believe me, they don't give a shit. If you believe it that's all that counts. So just believe it and do it. But don't be mouthin' off about it, 'cause they'll only laugh."

Something about him made me think of Elvis. "Sabino, where are you from? I can see that you're Spanish but you sound like you're southern...with a Spanish accent thrown in." I watched his face and puzzled over his expression.

"I'm Cuban. But I was born in Florida. Now, don't ask any more questions 'cause that's all you're gettin'." He nuzzled his face around my hair and kissed my neck, then whispered, "Unless you want some sugar and that I can supply."

My skin sprouted goose bumps and I pushed against his chest, just enough to give me breathing space. "I usually go to the Springs Theater on Saturdays. Maybe you could meet me there sometime."

"I get it. Your daddy won't let you date." Sabino was perceptive.

"Not my daddy. My mama."

He smiled, letting his cockiness show, and said, "Mamas I can handle."

The song ended and too soon the dance was over. It was time to go home. Mama would be waiting outside for Sandra and me. "Well, I gotta' go." I started to walk toward where Sandra and Chuck were kissing good-bye, but Sabino grabbed me by the hand and stopped me.

"I don't know your name."

I hesitated for a moment...staring into his questioning, brown eyes, before answering. "Angela."

He smiled, "See you around, Angela." There were more words in his exploring eyes that trailed up and down me, than just see you around.

That night, after we got home from the dance, Sandra and I were sitting up in bed talking. "So...I've just been dying to ask you, who was that guy you were dancing with most of the night?"

"His name's Sabino. I don't know his last name, he never did tell me. But ain't he cute?"

"Cute! Cute's not what I'd call him. Trouble sounds like a better description." She giggled, "He sure could dance good, though. You two were dancing so close, I was afraid he was gonna rape you right out there on the floor. So what's he like, huh? Come on, spill...I want all the details."

"Well, there ain't any details, yet. But he asked me for a date."

"So, what are you gonna do, meet him somewhere?"

"I told him he could find me at the Springs Theater on Saturdays. We didn't make any definite plans, though, so I hope he goes."

"Well, sorry to disappoint you, but we won't be there tomorrow because I told Chuck we'd play golf with him."

"Golf! Who plays golf? I don't know how to play golf, Sandra ...furthermore, I don't care to learn."

"Chuck's family lives on the golf course. His father's bringing him over tomorrow to pick us up, then he's gonna teach us to play golf." Reading the look on my face she gave me no chance to beg off before saying, "You owe me one."

"But what if Sabino goes looking for me tomorrow and I'm not there? He might never go again and he's soooo cute."

"Tough titty. Tomorrow's mine. We had a deal, remember. I covered for you last time, kiddo, so you double with me tomorrow."

There was no way out of it, so I went golfing. What a waste. I destroyed the greens, but at least I survived the weekend. The only good thing about it was my debt was paid and next weekend belonged to me.

CLIFF DENISON. 1961

4

They Remind Me Too Much of You

1958

Being cool is knowing how much to let things show, and how much to keep 'em in.

—*Elvis Presley*

The weekend following the golf catastrophe with Sandra and Chuck, I went to the Springs Theater dressed in pink and black, Elvis' favorite colors, hoping to see Sabino but he was a no-show. When the movie was over and I walked out in front of the theater, it was raining, not hard, but nevertheless it was wet. I asked around to see if I could get a ride, but most of the people I knew were in the same predicament as me, and that meant walking in the rain.

On my way home from the picture show, the streets glistened from the soft, drizzling mist, and suddenly, there was Sabino, stopped for a light. He sat in his Ford revving the engine. The car radio was playing "Don't Be Cruel."

Sabino leaned out the window and shouted, "Hey, doll!" I stepped from the curb and approached his car. He threw open the door, "Hop in, beautiful."

I climbed into the car and he reached over the back of the seat and tossed me a towel. "It's too wet to be walking, don't you think?"

"What other choice did I have without wheels?"

"Good lookin' chick like you should be able to get a ride easy enough."

I smiled. "And I did."

I hummed along with the radio while fluffing out my hair. "Do you always carry a towel in your car?"

He smiled, "I'm a guy who's always prepared."

I shifted in my seat and went back to humming. Had he been driving up and down Nebraska Avenue waiting for me to come out of the theater? If that were true, then why hadn't he just parked outside the movie house? The traffic light changed to green and Sabino stepped hard on the gas, causing the car to slide on the wet road.

"Where are we going?" I asked.

He glanced sideways at me and patted the seat next to him. "Move over here closer, pretty thing." I scooted over near him and he draped his free arm around my neck. "Would you light us up a fag, baby?"

I reached for the cigarettes lying on the dash, tapped the open pack against my palm, then lit two and handed him one. I took a puff and blew smoke at him. My feelings were high. Sabino hadn't been sitting at that light by chance. I felt it, I almost knew it, and if I'd been a betting person, I would have bet twenty good wishes on it.

"You still haven't told me where we're going."

"I thought we could just hang out at the Spinning Wheel for a while. You hungry?"

"I could go for a hamburger and a vanilla Coke."

He looked at me with one eye on the road. "I could go for you, sweet thing."

I let my eyes roam boldly over his handsome face. Sabino was good-looking. His dark hair and full lips reminded me of Elvis. But his eyes were dark brown instead of blue.

We stopped for another red light. He looked at me again and let his eyes travel slowly up and down, then flipped his cigarette out the window. I knew he was going to kiss me. I wanted him to kiss me. I put my cigarette out in the ashtray and turned my face up to his. There was no hesitating as Sabino quickly locked his mouth over mine.

Nothing turned me on like a good kisser and this guy definitely held the key. His expertise drew me in. I was a sucker for good-looking sweet talkers with full, soft lips, and hot sensual bliss flamed the fires of my desire, leaving a trail of twinkle dust along the way.

The sound of a honking horn interrupted our first kiss, but Sabino was in no hurry. A second blast from the car behind us ended our middle-of-the-road passion, and pulling away, he smacked his lips. "Mmmmmm...I want more. You got a mouth made for kissin', Angela." Then he quickly threw the car into first, made a right-hand turn, and took off down Florida Avenue.

The Spinning Wheel was buzzing. Music blared from the outside speakers as Sabino pulled in, shut off the engine, and reached for me. The Platters romanced the moment, singing "Only You."

"Take your order?"

Sabino's face had a what-next look on it when he turned to the car hop and gave the order.

The curb-girl left and he leaned toward me, gently sucked on my lower lip, and nose to nose stared into my eyes. "You're some kind of sweet, soft somethin'," he murmured. Then he took my whole mouth and I surrendered. Someone punched "Heartbreak Hotel" on the jukebox and Elvis crooned through the speakers while we kissed. I could almost believe it was Elvis kissing me, but that didn't seem fair to the genuine feelings I had for Sabino, who was showing me he could carry his own.

A low moan escaped him as he drove his tongue into my mouth. Finally, we ended the kiss on heavy breaths.

"You like Elvis?" I asked, smoothing my hands over the front of his white T-shirt.

He shifted in the seat and stretched his back. "Who don't like Elvis?"

"Well, some guys feel threatened by him, you know, 'cause girls dig him so much."

"Then they got a problem. I don't got a problem and I don't feel threatened, 'cause Elvis ain't here. But I am." And with that said, he kissed me again, long, deep, soft and good.

"Hey, Sabo."

I opened my eyes and glanced over Sabino's shoulder.

"What's a spick like you doing on this side of town?"

The guy with the voice resembled Frankie Avalon, and was watching us through the open window. "Miguel! Hey, baby, this is my friend, Miguel. Hey, man, what you up to? You by yourself?"

"No, I got Holly with me. She just stepped into the bathroom and I saw your car parked over here. Hey, who's the good-looking chick with ya?"

"This ain't no chick. This here's my lady." Sabino winked at his friend. "And her name's Angela. Hey, Miguel, you on your bike, man?"

"Yeah, man. You know Holly. She'd rather ride the cycle any day. Don't matter to her if it's raining or not." I started to get a funny feeling about this Holly when suddenly, Miguel hollered out, "Hey, Holly, over here." I looked in the direction he was shouting and sure enough, heading toward us wiggling her butt in skin-tight, short shorts, and wearing wedge mules and a leather coat, was my friend Holly.

"I don't believe this!"

"What's that, baby?" Sabino had a strange look on his face, one that made me feel like he wanted to laugh.

"Excuse me." The curb girl had arrived with our food, and as Miguel stepped back, she hung the tray on the window.

"Frances!"

"Holly? I don't believe this."

Sabino paid the check and the curb girl left. "You two know each other?" Sabino still had that funny look on his face.

I looked at Holly and she was wearing the same expression. They were up to something. "Miguel, what's going on here?" I asked. Miguel shrugged his shoulders, "Don't ask me." Then, all three of them busted out laughing.

"Frances," Holly squeaked as she talked through her laughter, "Sabino is the guy I tried to fix you up with last weekend, remember?"

Sabino hugged me up to him, "Yeah, and when you turned me down for a school dance, that's when I decided to check out the sock hop. Holly showed me your picture and the rest was a snap. You kinda threw me for a minute, though...when you said your name was Angela. But, what the hell, if my name was Frances I'd change it to Angela, too." Sabino was still laughing.

My face turned red. "What's wrong with Frances? It's my name...and I don't appreciate what you just said."

Sabino couldn't stop laughing, so Miguel spoke up. "Sabino's sister is named Frances."

"That's right, baby, and she-is-a-nag." He laughed some more. "So...do you mind if I call you Angela?" Now Sabino stopped snickering and poked out his bottom lip. "It fits you, baby." Gazing into my eyes, he gave me a quick wet peck on the lips, "'Cause you look like an angel." Then grinning, he turned his head back to the open window. "Hey, you guys wanna hop in the back seat? I'll flash for the curb girl."

"We've ordered already," Miguel said. "But...just a minute, I'll go tell her to bring our food over here."

Holly got in the car, then Miguel came back and jumped in beside her while Sabino fed me french fries. "Holly, why didn't you tell me Sabino was so cool?"

Holly chuckled her deep, sexy, Marlene Dietrich laugh. "Why bother? You were more hep on going to a shitified school dance." Glancing toward Sabino, she said, "Frances digs all that school shit, you know, dances, football games, all the old alma mater bullshit. Give me the wind in my hair and a bike out on the open road, any day...with a Budweiser in my hand."

"Well, I'd just like to know what's wrong with liking school? And what does it have to do with motorcycles? I like motorcycles."

"You like motorcycles, Angela?"

"I love motorcycles, Sabino."

"I've got an idea. Why don't you guys take my car and Angela and me, we'll take the bike and meet you at Supertest?"

"Sounds good to me," said Miguel. "What do you think, Holly?"

She looked at me, her eyes challenging, "You sure you want to ride the bike with Sabo?"

"Sounds like fun to me."

The curb-girl brought Holly and Miguel's food. Miguel rolled down the back window for the tray, paid the girl, then passed Holly a Coke and burger.

"I gotta go make a phone call, you guys. I'll be right back."

I went to the phone and called Mama. I told her I had met Holly at the movies—"and when her mom picked her up she invited me to go with them to Supertest." I felt guilty for lying to Mama, but my conscience was quickly numbed when I thought of the evening ahead.

After clearing everything with Mama I went to the bathroom, then back to the car. Holly and Miguel were polishing off the last of their burgers and Sabino had retrieved a black leather jacket from the trunk of his car.

"Put this on, Angel. It gets chilly on the bike after a rain."

"But what about you? What will you wear?" His jeans and T-shirt didn't look like they'd serve as any buffer against the weather.

Holly and Miguel drove from the parking lot as Sabino and I walked over to the motorcycle. He gave me a quick, knowing grin. "Guess you're gonna have to keep me warm." Then he straddled that big, dangerous looking monstrosity of a machine and held out his hand to me. I stepped forward and took it, then threw my left leg up and over and boosted myself into a comfortable position behind him. It was a tight fit, but one that lent me a feeling of safety.

Sabino revved up the motor. "Hang on, baby, you're in for the ride of your life."

I wrapped both arms around his middle and did as he'd ordered, hung on for dear life.

The wind, colder than I had anticipated, felt good whipping through my hair. A fragrance of fresh rain in the early night consorted with the strong, dark scent of Sabino to seduce my senses. I buried my face into his back and hung tight when he reached Gunn Highway and leaned the Harley into the curves. I loved it. I loved the way riding a motorcycle made me feel free.

After a while he slowed down, pulled over to the side of the road somewhere near a cow pasture, and cut the engine.

Sabino climbed off the cycle then reaching over, gave me a peck on the lips then pulled me up close to him. "Warm me up, baby." He was shivering against me when I held open his jacket and made room for him to run his arms around me and into the warmth of the coat.

Early night lights of southern stars and moonglow lit up the sky when a sudden burst of color streaked the heavens.

"Sabino, look! It's a shooting star! Quick, make a wish!" I squeezed my eyes shut and wished, with all my belief in wishes, that my vow to Elvis would come true.

When I opened my eyes and looked up at Sabino, he plastered me to his length and kissed me a long, fiery kiss that made me feel things I knew I shouldn't be feeling. Dangerous things. But as long as his hands stayed under control, I smothered my doubts and shared his passion, while sparks ignited and blazed through me. It was Sabino who finally ended our kiss on a heavy breath, the desire in his eyes shining full as the moon.

"Angela, baby, do you know what you're doing to me?"

"Probably the same thing you're doing to me."

"No. I don't think so. I don't think you have any idea how it is for a guy." I was puzzled by his quick mood change—let down when he stepped to the motorcycle and climbed back on. "Come on, baby. They're probably waitin' on us at the park by now." He grasped hold of my hand and hoisted me up behind him.

"Did I say or do something wrong?"

"No, we just gotta get going."

All the way to the park I could feel the heat from his body. I kept my face pressed tight to his back and knew I was falling for this sensitive guy who only looked dangerous. I could almost believe I was in love. But, even if I was in love, I would never say it. I was too afraid of getting hurt. Elvis was the only one I could utter those three words to, because he would never hurt me.

When we reached the park we found Holly and Miguel at the concession stand buying cold drinks and cotton candy. We spent the rest of the evening riding the rides, kissing on the caterpillar, laughing, joking, and almost forgetting the time. Mama was strict about my curfew, and I knew I'd better be home by eleven and not two minutes later.

It was ten-thirty when Holly told the guys to drop us off at Smitty's, a small restaurant and bar on the causeway where her mother was waiting for us. Holly's mom was cool and covered our sneaking expeditions from Holly's dad and my mother.

When they dropped me off in front of my house at eleven, Mama was waiting up for me. She smiled her usual sweet smile and asked if I'd had a good time. Then, in my typical manner, I related the evenings acceptable events.

That's how I met Sabino, and he filled many of my weekends for the remainder of ninth grade. Mama never met him and I never learned his last name. Neither did Holly know Miguel's. It was like an unspoken agreement among us. Not knowing last names made everything exciting and the secrecy lent a mystery.

Sabino and I saw Elvis movies and went for long rides on his Harley, the one that had sat at home out of the rain on that first day. We met at Lowry Park, often, and sat in the gazebo and talked for hours. But we never pried into the other's privacy. Throughout the entire time we snuck around together, Sabino never overstepped my boundaries—limits set by fear. I was lucky and I realize it more today than I did back then.

MAMA FILED FOR A DIVORCE from Daddy while I was in ninth grade. I was happy about it. Daddy had never been at home much anyway, and when he was, his drinking and fighting upset our otherwise peaceful home. I figured we could do just as well without him, if not better.

This was the summer of '58: the summer before I started tenth grade and Elvis was in the army. Our last movie from him until his return from overseas was *King Creole*. To me, this is Elvis' best picture. I loved to read and Harold Robbins was my favorite author at that time. When I found out *King Creole* was based upon the Robbins book *A Stone for Danny Fisher*, I knew it was going to be Elvis' best role yet.

The day *King Creole* opened at the Tampa Theatre, Sandra and I were waiting at the front of the line. She'd spent the night at my house, and in order to get this spot near the front of the line, we'd gotten up early, packed some tater sandwiches and a thermos of iced tea, and caught the bus downtown.

I never went to see Elvis' first runs with a date. Guys wanted to smooch through the movies and I wasn't willing to share my concentration with anyone but Elvis.

Waiting in line for the theater to open at 12:45 p.m., we took great delight in drooling over the marquee pictures that covered the front of the theater and filled the entrance walls. There was something magic about standing in front of a theater back then, before miniplexes and multiplexes took over.

Music from the movie blared in front of the building, loud enough to be heard four streets away. The line grew and grew, until it wrapped around the block and down another street. Sandra and I ate our sandwiches while we stood in line.

When the movie sold out and people were left standing, they continued to wait till the next showing. Theater management had a real problem clearing out the place to let in the next crowd. Kids from the first presentation didn't want to leave. Sandra and I were experts at hiding on the floor behind the seats until the new crowd began to file in, then we lost ourselves among them and found new places in the balcony.

We screamed through the movie till the salty popcorn made our throats raw. It was impossible to hear all the dialogue, the shrieks were so loud. In our excitement, we threw popcorn down on the heads of people below us and soon had a corn melee cooking. We stayed in that theater all day, watching Elvis till it was time to catch the last bus home.

My favorite part of the movie was at the very beginning, when Elvis sang "Crawfish" with a New Orleans street vendor. That balcony scene, when he leans forward over the rail and kind of bounces while he's singing, well, if they'd had VCRs back then, I would have worn the thing out doing rewinds on that scene.

I saw *King Creole* every day for the two or three weeks it played the Tampa Theatre. Not just one time a day, but over and over, every day. I saw that motion picture so many times the weirdest thing happened. One night I dreamed the entire script, word for word. If you think this is strange, I can still top it. How about going to see Jerry Lewis in *Sad Sack* fifteen times, just to see the previews of Elvis' newest movie!

ELVIS AND IRA JONES IN GERMANY. CIRCA 1959.
(FROM THE COLLECTION OF IRA JONES)

5

G. I. Blues

1958 - 1961

The Military is an excellent experience. It lets you find out how other people think and live.

—*Elvis Presley*

I embraced my high school years from tenth through twelfth with genuine love. Chamberlain High had one of the best football teams Tampa had ever seen. Our graduating class brought forth future sheriffs of Hillsborough and Pasco counties, Cal Henderson and Jim Gillum, and model/actress Lauren Hutton, better known to her classmates as Mary Hall.

Mary (Lauren Hutton) was naturally pretty. Friendly and smart, she sowed her dramatic seeds as a thespian before going out into the world of glamour to blossom as a model, then bloom into an actress. I remember Mary because she was popular. We had the same lunch but didn't personally know each other. We ran with different crowds. I was a wild thing and Mary was an achiever. But we had one friend in common, Cliff. I always had the impression Mary didn't notice her popularity any more than she noticed the next breath she took. And I admired her for it.

I loved everything about high school but I missed Elvis. He'd been inducted into the army in March of 1958, and toward the end of his basic training in Texas, his mama passed away.

On August 14th, according to the radio, Gladys died of hepatitis. Then, the news turned around and reported she'd had a heart attack. I didn't know what had killed her, but I felt his pain and grieved with Elvis. Perish the thought... *What if it was my mama?*

September 19, 1958, Elvis left America on the troop ship U.S.S. Randall, to join a tank unit in West Germany. By the summer of fifty-nine, it seemed like he'd been gone forever and I thought almost constantly about him. I was envious of pretty frauleins who lived in Bad Nauheim. Selfish stuff; I knew that. But, jealousy plays hard on lonely heartstrings.

I SPENT A LOT OF TIME at Lowry Park that summer. Having nothing to do at home after the house was cleaned, I hung out at the snack bar near the boat ramp and listened to the jukebox, sometimes dancing with friends I met there. When I wasn't at the park I was home writing letters to Elvis and actually mailed a few of them.

I worried and fretted that Elvis might like Germany and want to remain there when his tour of duty was up. Even though there was no basis for my reasoning, I was still stressed over the possibility. I thought of Elvis in Germany, then of Elvis in Paris on leave. Always Elvis, but from a distance. It just didn't seem fair for the army to send him so far away. Elvis belonged to America. To us. To me.

Sabino and I had dated pretty regularly during my freshman year at Oak Grove, but it wasn't what you'd call a steady thing. The last time I saw him was close to Christmas in fifty-eight. We were at the Springs Theater when he told me he was moving to Miami. *Jailhouse Rock* was playing.

I remember I was wearing a pair of skin-tight spandex pants. They were turquoise. And I had on a sweater the same color. Sabino was sporting his basic black leather jacket and dark denim jeans with a white T-shirt. I loved that jacket and so did Sabino. It was just like the one Marlon Brando wore in *The Wild One*. Anyhow, there we were, cuddled up close together in our seats watching the movie, and every once in a while, when he could steal my attention away from Elvis, we would kiss...long, deep kisses, fifties style. Then Elvis did that scene with Peggy, the one I put myself into so many times. Sabino watched me watching Elvis kiss Peggy.

"What do you dig in that scene?" he asked. "I mean...why's it drive you so crazy?"

I leaned forward, crossing my arms over the back of the seat in front of me, and sighed. "Oh, Sabino...I don't know. It's just everything, you know. Everything! The way he looks at her so sexy, the way he acts so sexy, the way he shocks her when he snatches her to him and kisses her. And that look he gives her when he says, 'That ain't tactics, honey. 'That's just the beast in me.' Oh, Sabo, if Elvis was to ever kiss me that way, I'd...I don't know what I'd do...Yeah I do! I'd make it count...good enough to last a lifetime."

Suddenly, Sabino reached forward from his seat and grabbed me. He kissed me, hard, his version of what he'd just seen Elvis do on the screen. I must admit Sabino's kiss was a real toe curler, shooting stars of fire all through me. When he withdrew from the kiss, he stared straight into my eyes and raised the side of his upper lip, like Elvis, and said, "That ain't tactics, honey. That's just the beast in me." I bounced up and down in my seat, he did it so good. But, alas, he wasn't Elvis.

Sabino said he was moving to Miami. He'd gotten a job offer that was too good to pass up. When the movie was over we kissed good-bye and that was the last time I saw him.

Being without a boyfriend was the worst state to be in as far as I was concerned. I hated it. And I hated that Elvis had to be so far away. I remembered crying when the army cut off his gorgeous hair. Just before they did it, I had thought, *Will he look like a square now? Will he lose his charm, his mystery, his charisma?* I vowed my loyalty no matter the outcome, which in the end showed Elvis still had IT—even without the hair and sideburns.

I was down in the dumps, depressed, and sick of settling for blind dates that Holly kept setting me up with. So, I went to my hero for advice.

"Elvis," I said to his picture, "I went out tonight with this guy who's a buddy of one of Holly's boyfriends.

You went out with Buddy Holly?

"Nooo, Elvis, not Buddy Holly...I said a buddy of Holly's boyfriend. Yuck...I hated the way he kissed. His teeth kept gettin' in the way and he moved his head back and forth so fast, I thought he was havin' a convulsion. Then, you know what the damn fool did?"

Angela! Angels don't cuss.

"I'm sorry, Elvis, but right there at the drive-in movie, he hops out the car and howls at the moon! Made me so embarrassed. Holly and Lee thought it was funny. But I sure didn't. That guy made me madder'n a piss-ant."

Sounds to me like he enjoyed himself.

"Yeah...well, somebody enjoyed it. Look at my mouth. Looks like I was mauled by a teenage werewolf. And it didn't get past mama. I'm grounded again."

Angel, why did you let him kiss you if you weren't into it?

"I was lonely, Elvis."

Honey, never settle for less than you want.

I moaned and groaned to Elvis about being dateless, until I met David: my first official, wear-my-ring-around-your-neck, steady beau. Unlike Sabino, David was not an Elvis type. Oh, he had full lips and blue eyes, but that's where the similarities between him and Elvis ended.

I met David on a rainy day under the pavilion that housed a juke box and snack bar at Lowry Park. I was sitting on a bench, one foot propped up, smoking a cigarette and daydreaming. He rode up to the pavilion on a motorcycle, cut the engine, then pushed the bike under the shelter and out of the rain. The park was almost vacant except for the bald headed man who ran the snack bar, me, and this cute guy I'd seen around the park a time or two with some other guys I knew. I looked at him, all wet, and was reminded of a puppy I once had. Curly Wolf had always been getting into water.

As I stared at him, I didn't really care what he might think. I moved my foot from the bench, drew on my cigarette, inhaled, then blew circles with the smoke while I surveyed him. He pretended not to notice and walked over to the juke box, dropped in a coin, and punched "I Was the One."

It's fate, I thought, when the song began to play. Rain beat against the tin roof like a symphony doing backup for Elvis, and my heart beat fast, then fluttered...faster, then fluttered. *He played my favorite song. Is it a sign? Is he the one sent to take away my loneliness?*

I watched as he walked back over to the bike, bent down, and did something to the motor. He had blond hair and was shorter than me, but he filled out his jeans and T-shirt in all the right places. I took a deep breath and started to say something, then paused, trying to decide whether or not I should speak.

He turned his head and captured my eyes with his. Then he smiled and walked toward me. He didn't say a word, but simply held out his hand and I took it. I rose to my feet and was pulled into the arms of a stranger. Just that word, s-t-r-a-n-g-e-r, excited me. Then we danced while the thundershower rendered romance all around us. A pure crystal essence of rain and wet earth mixed with the river's flora and summoned my senses. I sucked in my breath...closed my eyes, and let the magic take over.

The song ended, and in silence except for the still-drumming rain, he walked back over to the juke box and played it again, and we slow danced, heads together, while the wet from his clothes soaked into mine. And then he kissed me.

His soft mouth, the weather, and the words in the song combined to blow my mind, and I knew he would be my next boyfriend. Elvis had taught me so well that within a week, David's class ring hung on a chain around my neck. We took walks along the banks of the Hillsborough River. We fed each other ice cream and we saw movies together. And we rode his bike.

Two days before my junior year started, we were traveling at warp speed when we hit a pot hole and crashed on his chopper. Unfortunately, I'd been wearing short shorts when I bounced from the seat and straddled the exhaust pipe. I was cooked to that machine and suffered a large, third-degree burn on a sensitive portion of my upper inside thigh.

Mama took me to the doctor but like most people back then, we didn't go to the hospital unless it was absolutely necessary. So, Doc sent me home with medicine and orders to stay in bed and keep the wound clean. It hurt like Hell, but not as bad as it did a week later. That's when I knew I'd have to get saved before I died. If Hades was half as hot as this burn, I didn't want to go there.

When we got home from the doctor's office, Mama told me she had met a nice fellow that afternoon. She said he'd be coming over to visit the next day. I was shocked! Even though she was a really pretty woman, Mama never dated. She'd had plenty of offers but she used to say, "All I need are my kids and the good Lord above."

Mama said his name was Sandy. He was a Korean War veteran. I was curious about Sandy but at the same time, I had my doubts about any man that mama would have shown interest in. I figured she'd used bad judgment with my father and I sure didn't want another one like Daddy around. So, I planned on checking this Sandy out, and if he survived any of the trials I figured on putting him through, I'd make his life even more miserable if he ever failed to live up to my mama's love.

David and the gang came by to see me that evening. Mama stepped into my bedroom to say I had company. "Sister, there's a bunch of fellows out there wants to see your burn. I figured I'd charge 'em a quarter apiece to look at it, considering where your burn is. What do you think?"

"Mama!"

Her face broke into a great big smile, then she laughed till she cried. "Well, I just thought I'd make me a little change." She cackled so hard her eyes became squints on her face.

When she started out the door, I said, "Okay, Mama, but I'm holding the sheet like this." I pulled the crisp white material up to reveal my burn.

"Frances! You keep that cover up on you." Then she quickly turned to the closet, pulled out a robe, and tossed it to me. "Here, put this on and crawl back up under them covers or there won't be nobody coming in here to see nothin'." She was grinning when she backed out of the room to get David.

While David and I visited in my bedroom, Mama had a straight-shot view of us through the open door from the kitchen where she stood at the stove cooking. I wanted David to kiss me and make my pain go away, but I was afraid Mama would see us.

Finally, she went into another room, but if I knew Mama and I did, she wouldn't be gone long enough for us to hardly pucker. Still, unwilling to pass up a risky thrill, we stole a hasty kiss.

Later that night, after the gang had gone home and I was alone in my bedroom, I talked to Elvis.

"Elvis, Mama's got a boyfriend. He was in the army just like you. She said he lost his arm and his ankle in combat. He must be nice, doncha think?"

Honey, I'm certain of it. Your mama ain't no fool. If she agreed to see him...he's okay.

"But Elvis, she married my daddy and look at him."

Trust me darlin'. Your mama won't make that mistake again.

MY COUSIN BETTY came to visit me that summer and during her stay she and I got into a quarrel. We were always fussing over some trivial thing or another. Anyhow, I said her family was rich because they always had paper towels and bananas in their house. Betty wanted to know what paper towels and bananas had to do with being rich and I told her, "Cause they don't last long. Least ways not in our house. Sam and Tommy don't stop bein' monkeys till the nanners are gone. And paper towels? Tommy, the little bugger, ain't never give a fiddler's fart whether his hands were clean or dirty. But, just one look at them paper towels and all of a sudden he's as nice-nasty as Sam and gotta wipe everything."

Betty didn't see the jest of my funny and accused me of picking on her family. One thing led to another, and pretty soon our bickering had generated a hair-pulling scuffle, which later prompted Betty to get her revenge by painting nail polish across Elvis' mouth on the picture I talked to.

When I found her mean-ass handiwork, I was mortified. I tried to take the polish off with remover, but of course this took away Elvis' entire mouth. I squalled for days over his mutilated lips, but I kept on talking to the picture.

"Poor Elvis," I sobbed, "your pretty mouth is all catty-wampus now."

His eyes were still intact and Elvis used them to reach me.
Angela. Get up and kiss the mirror.

"What?"

You heard me. Kiss the mirror. You haven't done it for a long time.

"But, Elvis, I know how to kiss now. I don't need to practice on the mirror anymore."

Would you just shut up and get up and do what I'm ordering you to do?...NOW!

I jumped to my feet and faced the mirror and suddenly, everything was alright. I saw Angela and everything was alright. I pressed my hands to the smooth glass, then flattened my mouth against its coolness. And I kissed the mirror.

What did you discover?

"I didn't discover anything but that the mirror was cold."

Not so, honey. You saw Angela. And everything was alright.

CHRISTMAS CAME and went. Santa had finally scraped up the money for my record player. That it solely played forty-fives was cool with me since the small disks were all I owned anyway. Every day after school, David and I spun our favorite tunes on my musical gift and danced around the living room, necking while Elvis sang "Don't." But David felt self-conscious about being shorter than me, so we eventually broke up.

I DATED A LOT in my junior year. No more going steady for me. The freedom to go out with different guys was what being young was about. And I didn't want to miss out on anything.

And neither did Richard.

Richard was a drummer in a band, but his dream was to go to New York and become an actor.

We had a class together and, like me, Richard loved Elvis. He dressed like his hero, whose humble beginnings and rise to fame were the inspiration that drove him to pursue his goal of acting. I told him about my vow to meet Elvis and he understood and encouraged me to make it happen. Just like Sabino had. Richard kind of reminded me of Sabino in some ways. I suppose it was their similarities to Elvis I was seeing.

TAMPA, FAMOUS for its Cuban cigars and Cuban bread, offered another Cuban commodity for its teenage girls. Cuban boys.

Spanish guys were the coolest. Dark haired, g-o-o-o-d lookin' sweet talkers. My Spanish craving was a guy I'll call Frankie, because he was a dead ringer for Frankie Avalon. Man, could he kiss. Dance and kiss. Those were his specialties.

I MET BRUCE while he was on six weeks vacation from the seminary where he was studying to become a Southern Baptist preacher. He was staying with some relatives who lived down the street from our house. We went to church on our dates. Bruce was a nineteen-year-old, handsome hunk, looking for a wife, and I had illusions of filling the job. But our courtship was short lived when he delicately told me he didn't think I was cut out to be a preacher's wife.

CLIFF WAS REALLY POPULAR in school by now. Voted best personality and on the football team, he had no problem getting the girls. I still had a crush on him, big time. Cliff was my second love, coming after Elvis. Of course, he never knew this because I never told him.

I enjoyed going to Colonial Beach for many reasons. It offered all the enticements of a weekend outing for me and my friends: swimming, volley ball, or dancing to platters spun by our favorite disc jockeys. On Saturday nights there was usually a live band playing in the pavilion. Quite often, Cliff showed up.

One night Cliff and I entered a jitterbug contest.

He was a good dancer, easy to follow, and deliciously romantic when he sang in my ear. Which makes it really funny when I remember that contest. Cliff dropped me on my head. We were doing the jitterbug and I got tickled. Cliff told me to get serious so we could win, then he flipped me over his head and dropped me on mine. His first reaction was typical Elvis. He laughed. I know he was concerned about if I was hurt, but he laughed the whole time he was helping me get on my feet.

Later, we laughed about it together as we walked outside and strolled along the dark pier that extended out into the water. When we reached the end we stopped and talked. I was all goose bumps from being with Cliff in this romantic setting. And if it wasn't the knot on my noggin then I must have been struck by moonlight, because all of a sudden, Cliff was Elvis.

"Cliff," I said, with fresh dawned awareness, "I just can't get over how much you remind me of Elvis. I mean...it's in your looks, and your voice, and your laugh, and...you know, you really do laugh like Elvis." Then I took a deep breath, "I'll bet you even kiss like him."

Cliff looked at me with interest in his eyes and a grin just like Elvis' on his lips. I'd wanted to try out those lips since ninth grade and thought, *This night is too right, dear Cliff. You're getting kissed tonight.*

And then, like magic, he kissed me. His mouth, soft as a downy cloud, fit mine just right and I closed my eyes...and let the magic take me. I was Angela and he was my prince. Cliff's kiss was romantic: a soft magnificence, floating my head while electricity charged helter-skelter through me.

I remember thinking, *Elvis, I hope you can kiss as good as Cliff, 'cause he's got some natural magic.*

Our kiss was a long one, neither of us wanting it to end. But oxygen is a necessity so we came up for air, then instantly dove back in for more of the tender, breathtaking feelings.

When our soul-searching kiss ended, I suddenly understood that damned fool Holly had once set me up with. The one who'd bayed at the moon. I felt a howl coming on. Quickly stifling it, I asked Cliff to sing me a song. He soothed the savage beast inside me with "Young and Beautiful," in a natural voice so much like Elvis', I swooned and almost fell off the dock.

Cliff's laughter broke free.

"Oh, you think it's funny, Hot Lips?"

"Hot Lips?"...Man...Frances, you make my head swell."

"You kiss better than anyone I've ever kissed, Cliff...I mean, Hot Lips. Of course I haven't kissed Elvis, yet. But I plan to...one of these days."

Cliff laughed, "I'll bet you'll do it, too." Then he said, "You really think I've got hot lips?"

"Absolutely. And I'm sure I'm not the first girl to think so. You really know how to kiss, Cliff."

"Yeah, really...well you're a pretty terrific kisser yourself."

IN 1959, AMERICA'S teenagers were bopping to the latest hits by artists other than Elvis, until we got a couple of new songs from him. "I Need Your Love Tonight" and "A Fool Such As I" were a welcome treat for fans of the King.

I was sixteen when Mama and Sandy got married. I remember Mama gathering my brothers and me around the table for a family talk. She was thirty-five at the time.

"Sandy has asked me to marry him. But I told him he'd have to get each one of your blessings. That means if just one of you says no, then we'll stay like we are...'cause you kids are my life and your happiness comes first. I couldn't be happy if you weren't...but re-member this, if you say yes and he moves into this house and helps support you...you will respect him. I won't be caught in the mid-dle. Do you understand me?"

We all three nodded our heads.

"Tommy, do you understand?"

"Yes-um."

"Sam, do you understand?"

"Yes, ma'am."

Mama looked at me. "Frances, do you understand that if Sandy changes a few rules, you're gonna have to abide by them?"

I hesitated for a moment.... "Yes, ma'am."

"Okay, now that we all understand, I want you to think about all this. Give it some serious thought. Because, if I get married things will change. They can't help not to."

I'd had plenty of time to get to know Sandy and was thorough-ly certain by now that he loved my mother and was a good man. And so, not having been raised to be selfish children and out of concern for Mama's happiness, we gave them our blessings, and with our unanimous approval, Sandy became our Pap.

The day Mama and Pap got married was a busy one for me. Their wedding took place somewhere around noon, at the home of Mama's best friend, Marian. As soon as the wedding was over, I left for the television studio to be a guest on *Teen Time*, a local teenage bandstand type show.

The idea of being on television was exciting, yet the only thing I remember is kids hogging for the camera while they were dancing and my partner and I winning a jitterbug contest. We received records for the prize. Mine was "Cat Walk."

THE FIRST SITUATION to test Pap and me after he and Mama got married was when he changed my curfew from eleven to ten o'clock. We butted heads on several occasions over this one and my rebellious attitude just dared him to hit me. But he didn't. I don't know how he tolerated me. But he did. Even though we were rarely in agreement on matters, Pap, consistent in his loyalty, ultimately came to my defense every time I needed him. Like the time Mama told me I had to wear my eleventh grade formal to the senior prom and was adamant about it.

I'd already picked out the dress I wanted. It was the prettiest one I'd ever seen: strapless, floor length, mint-green, with yards of ruffles, lace, and netting. I talked about it constantly around my family. I pleaded and begged for the dress till Mama said she'd had a bellyfull and didn't want to hear any more about it.

So, I told Elvis about the dress.

"Baby, don't cry. Your mama won't let you down. I think she'll give in before the dance...have faith.

Then, a week before the prom, Pap came home from work toting a large dress box. Mama looked at him funny, then asked, "What's that, Sandy?"

"Now, don't get on your high horse. I've been rat-holing my lunch money to buy this dress for Frances." Pap understood me and his heroic acts of love and rescue endeared him forever in my heart. His tolerance for Elvis earned him a place in my special persons' hall of fame.

Another time Pap came to my rescue was during the summer between eleventh and twelfth grade. I wanted to go and work on a tobacco farm in Simsbury, Connecticut, with a work program that required under contract the full summer's stay. If you broke the agreement, you were responsible for your own way back home.

Mama, taking into consideration that I'd never been away from home before, warned me. "What if you get homesick, sister? You ain't never gone off this far for so long. This is an entire summer you're talking about. Do you realize this? I'm not paying your way back home if you change your mind in midstream. Can you make that kind of commitment and stick to it?"

"Yes, ma'am," I answered. Like any normal teenager, it was my first opportunity to get away from home and I would have promised anything.

Our camp took trips to places like West Point Academy, Bear Mountain, Sturbridge Village, and New York City. Although I had seen much of my country while traveling out west as a child, this was new and different and I found it delightful to experience, first-hand, America's north east coast.

Two out of the three girls I roomed with loved Elvis. The other girl was a Pat Boone fan and we made her life miserable. We short sheeted her bed, picked on Pat, and did other mean and contemptible things. Our greatest bond was Elvis and soon enough she got the message and traded rooms with an Elvis fan.

Now we all loved Elvis and talked about how we could hardly wait for his return to the states. But we kind of missed the Pat Boone fan. It had been fun having somebody to pick on.

About three weeks before the summer was over, Cousin Sandra, who had gone to Connecticut with me, decided she'd had enough of the fieldwork and wanted to go home early. It sounded wonderful to me. I had suckered, strung, and sewn tobacco till I was burnt.

When I called Mama, she said, "You know what the deal was, Frances." But a couple of hours later Pap called me back and said he would send the money.

That trip home was a dream-come-true adventure for two love starved girls who hadn't had a date all summer. Sandra and I were the only females on a bus filled with sailors. I made friends with one of them and we wrote letters to each other for over a year.

G.I. Blues premiered about three months after I got home from Connecticut. It was a fun kind of movie and again the lines were long. The theater gave out paper soldier hats as promotional souve-

nirs. Elvis was devastatingly handsome in his uniform and I recon-
firmed my vow to meet him.

E LVIS WAS PROMOTED to sergeant before his discharge from the
    army. March 3, 1960, he stopped over at an airfield in Scot-
land while flying back to the U.S. from Germany. On March 5th,
he was released from the army at Fort Dix, New Jersey, then he recorded his first song in almost two years, "A Mess of The Blues."

May 12, 1960, was the day Elvis fans had been waiting for.
Elvis was a guest on the Frank Sinatra special, taped at the Foun-
tainbleu Hotel in Miami, Florida. We had him back and he was
better than ever; a lean, mean, singing sex machine.

ELVIS ON SET OF "FOLLOW THAT DREAM." 1961

6

Follow That Dream

1961 - 1962

Dreams tell us truths that we've got to be smart enough to interpret.

—*Elvis Presley*

I was seventeen when I graduated from high school in 1961. Mama wanted me to continue living at home and attend the University of South Florida. She was high on education. But my dreams lay elsewhere and I was ready to pursue them. Besides, I was tired of living by the rules at home and wanted to try my wings, alone.

Mama and Pap had planned a trip to Cape Cod that summer, to see Pap's family. Rather than go with them, I accepted my aunt and uncle's invitation to come to Ocala for a visit with my cousin Betty.

Betty worked as a waitress at the lunch counter of the Liggets Rexal drug store at the Pine Street Shopping Center. She suggested I come to work with her instead of staying at the house by myself. "Who knows, Frances? Maybe somebody'll quit or drop dead from overtime. And if you're right there...handy, there's a good chance you could land a job."

This sounded good to me. I liked Ocala and I loved the hundred-mile distance it put between me and home.

I found it easy, acquainting myself with customers and the job duties of a waitress, while hanging around during Betty's eight hour work shift. And within the first week there was an opening and I was hired on the spot. I was tickled to tears, thrilled with my new job and the independence it provided me. I worked vigorously, trying to prove I could master everything at once. But when I made my first banana split, I realized the folly of this thinking.

I'd taken the order during the dinner rush. The other waitresses were too busy to give me any instructions, so I attacked the job, confident in my ability to know how a banana split should taste. I was proud of my loving effort that boasted a pretty topping of three puffs of whipped cream, cherries, and nuts, and wore a big smile on my face as I strutted around the counter carrying my masterpiece to its owner.

I set the customer's order in front of him. "You're lucky," I said. "This is my first day on the job and beginners do it best." Then I winked and left him to enjoy.

I never checked back with him until he was finished. Then, when I went to give him his check, he said, "Next time you make me a banana split, do me a favor. Put a banana in it." He winked and added, "I like 'em that way."

I'd been working about two weeks when my parents returned from Massachusetts. I told them I'd found a job and wanted to stay in Ocala. Mama said, "No!" She didn't cotton to the idea of her little girl living a hundred miles from home and pressed her point. "What about college?"

"Mama, you're the one that wants college," I told her, "not me!" We argued our differences, but arguing never did work with Mama. So I changed my approach and pleaded my case, eventually winning.

I had been with my aunt and uncle for close to a month when I decided to move in with another of Mama's sisters, Aunt Ernestine, and her husband, Uncle Charlie. I didn't want to wear out my welcome with any one relative before I found an apartment of my own.

Although Mama and Pap would have liked me to move back

home, they still wanted me to succeed at whatever I chose to do. They knew I was handicapped without a car and remedied the situation by giving me Pap's old, 1950 red Ford.

Betsy, that's what I called my first car, had a stick shift, and my few experiences with driving had been in an automatic. But this did not abate, to any degree, the thrill of having my own automobile. *Hey,* I thought, *I have wheels. How difficult can a stick shift be?* Of more concern was getting the driver's license I needed before I was allowed to take possession of Betsy.

Uncle Charlie drove me to the highway patrol station to take my test in his automatic. I passed all the written part, but when it came to actually driving, I was sorely lacking in everything and flunked.

I was starting to feel at home in Ocala, but not with relatives. I was eager to be out on my own, so I started looking for an apartment. When the news got back to Mama she tried to change my mind, but she knew I was hardheaded and determined, so in the end she accepted what she couldn't change.

I found an apartment close to work. The rent was ten dollars a week or forty a month. It was located a block from Silver Springs Boulevard, across the street from the Commercial Bank and Trust Company of Ocala.

My tiny kitchenette apartment was a block structure with bare cement floors that stood between the telephone company and the landlord's big house. When you walked in the front door you almost bumped into the foot of the double bed, which took up most of the space that served as a living room and bedroom. Straight ahead, a small gas stove, a sink, and an apartment-sized fridge offered the hint of a kitchen, and off to the left was a shower and toilet.

Even after I had my own place, Betsy stayed parked over at Aunt Ernestine's house. "Orders from your mama," she said, "until you pass your driving test."

Uncle Charlie was kind enough to take me every time I asked him. But unfortunately, I'd been car-shy ever since I'd wrecked Daddy's new Chevy six years earlier and wasn't as prepared as I should have been for taking the test. So I continued to scare the crap out of the patrolman and justified my failures by wondering how a person was supposed to learn without the use of a car. I soon grasped, too, that Mama was right when she said, "Walking ain't crowded." I seemed to be the only one doing it.

I had a habit of going into work early every morning. It provided me time to set up for breakfast, then kick back and enjoy my cup of coffee and Long John donut over the newspaper.

One morning, I picked up the *Ocala Star Banner* and almost choked on a sip of hot java when I read the headlines. ELVIS DUE IN OCALA FOR FILM. I dropped the coffee in my lap, screamed, then grabbed a towel and continued to read.

Elvis will be in Ocala this Saturday and Sunday to film sequences of his next motion picture, Pioneer Go Home, a movie based on the Richard Powell novel of the same name.

I was so excited, I'm sure I'd have swallowed my snuff had I dipped. Then I closed my eyes, took a deep breath, and continued to read...and discovered the filming was to take place across the street from my apartment! Straightaway, I had illusions of grandeur and fantasized Elvis coming into the drug store and ordering one of my famous bananaless splits.

Vi, the manager, was in the back kitchen.

"Vi!" I hollered, "Vi!" then took off in a run toward the good smells of roasting turkey and found her up to her elbows in dressing, busily preparing the lunch special.

"Vi...oh, Vi!"

"What is it? What's the problem?"

"Can I have this Saturday and Sunday off, huh, can I, can I?"

"What's the matter with you? No, you can't have the weekend off. Who died anyway?"

I was beside myself with excitement and it had never occurred to me she might say no. No was like the end of the world. No wasn't even an option.

"Vi, Elvis is coming to town to make a movie and I've just gotta have the weekend off. Pleease?" I begged.

"You got a part in the movie or somethin'?"

Her sarcasm was starting to irritate me and I matched it. "No! I don't have a part in the movie." Then I softened my tone to a plea. "I just wanna see Elvis. Please, Vi. I'll do anything. I'll work doubles when he's gone. I'll work late shift on weekends. You just gotta let me off. Please."

"The answer is no. If I let you off then the rest of the girls'll think they gotta have off. No...I ain't changing the schedule and that's the end of it."

You'd have thought she was my mama. "But you ain't my mama," I gritted through my teeth as I walked back to my station and started setting up for breakfast.

"The old fart," I mumbled aloud. She wouldn't stop me from seeing Elvis. She could just take this old job and stuff it in her dressing. I could sure look for another one. With that resolved in my mind, I felt better. I wouldn't tell her anything. I'd work up until the weekend, then I wouldn't show up again till Elvis left town. And since I didn't have a phone, she couldn't call me. Boy, that'd make her biscuits rise.

I eagerly counted off the days till the weekend. On Friday, Uncle Charlie took me to the highway patrol station for another try at my driver's license, but again, I failed. Uncle Charlie said it was because I had a case of Elvis on the brain. I supposed he was right, but knowing I was going to lose my job didn't exactly help matters.

I was up early on the morning of July fifteenth, slipping into my cutest pale-pink shorts outfit and brushing my hair into a ponytail. Then I grabbed my trusty old Brownie camera and together we made our way to the sidewalk across the street from the Commercial Bank and Trust.

The Mirisch Company of Hollywood had set up their lights and cameras in front of the bank. There was a trailer parked beside it and the filming area had been roped off. I was one of the first of approximately 3,000 fans to line the street that morning—all hoping to catch a glimpse of their rock and roll idol.

The wait seemed like eternity but about 9:45, a 1960 Cadillac drove up the alleyway next to the bank building and Elvis stepped out of the car and immediately went into the trailer. It happened so fast, I scarcely got a glimpse of him.

Shouts of "Elvis! Elvis!" rang through the air, and in a trance, I held my position behind the ropes and waited for him to emerge from the mobile dressing room.

When he finally stepped out and headed straight toward us, I had my camera ready and started taking pictures. I remember being in awe of breathing the same air as Elvis Presley, and was unable to take my eyes from him as he moved closer to the street in front of me. My brain, having difficulty handling all it was taking in, said adios and left my heart to think for me.

The crowd squealed, sighed, and shouted messages to Elvis, while respecting him and the police by staying behind the ropes. I screamed right along with them and like to have tore up my throat trying to be heard above everybody else.

It was a differently dressed Elvis viewed by his fans that day. The role he played called for jeans, a blue shirt, and tennis shoes. His hair was its natural color, slightly bleached from the sun, and he was sporting a beautiful, soft, Florida tan. I know jeans were not Elvis' favorite choice of attire, but I love jeans, and he looked absolutely scrumptious in them. Good enough to eat.

I waited for a lull in the noisy crowd then leaned forward, pressing against the ropes, and hollered.

"Elvis, you're the prettiest thing I've ever seen! I love you, Elvis!"

Wonder of wonders, he heard me and looking my way shouted back, "I love you too, honey!"

"Oh, my Lord, he said he loved me!" I turned to the girl standing beside me, "Did you hear that? Elvis said he loved me!"

"Yeah...he sure did! I heard him. Gosh-o-mighty, look at him! That man's so handsome I could eat him alive."

"I was just thinking the same thing," I told her.

When the filming commenced, the frenzy of the crowd switched to a more subdued curiosity. Elvis climbed into a seasoned old roadster and closed the door. Ann Helm, Elvis' co-star who played Holly, took her position on the sidewalk. No one seemed to be paying any attention to her. All eyes were trained on Elvis.

We watched as the cameras began to roll. Action! Elvis drove the old car down the street in front of us while the cameras rolled along beside him. Ann Helm walked down the sidewalk in search of a parking meter that still had some time on it. She stopped beside one and hollered, "Toby, fifteen minutes left."

Elvis nodded, then pulled into the parking space, got out of the car, and walked over to join Ann. They headed for the bank entrance and then the filming stopped. The scene was shot a number of times until the director was completely satisfied with the take. They had a problem with the fans' reflections appearing in the glass windows of the bank. I found it fascinating to watch the actual filming of a movie, but it was more interesting to look at Elvis. My, my, that man was pretty.

By now the temperature had reached ninety-four degrees, but with the crowds pushing it felt more like a hundred and ninety-four. When the outdoor filming was done, the cast and crew continued their work inside the bank. My friend Richard, was a member of the Marion Players, an amateur theatrical group in Ocala, and had landed the part of a movie extra in some close-up shots. Much to my envy, he was allowed entrance into the bank. All I could do was stand outside popping off shots with my camera, while Elvis took all the action inside where Richard was. Then I waited, an interminable length of time, before Elvis appeared again.

When, finally, he exited the bank, Elvis was rushed back to the trailer and out of our view. I considered camping outside the front of that mobile unit but was discouraged by the Ocala Police Department. So, I went home to dream about how close I'd been to him that day and of the possibilities tomorrow held. And I did dream of Elvis—*In shimmering sunbeams of light, we made love in a bed of ruby red roses, amazingly untouched by thorns.*

The next morning I was up bright and early, refreshed, and very optimistic from my most pleasant dream. I planned to outsmart them all by waiting as close to the front of that trailer as I could get. But when I arrived at the bank, I couldn't believe what I saw. It appeared everyone else had the same idea as me and I was the one who had been outsmarted. Rats!

The parking lot behind the bank building must have held a thousand fans, all waiting for Elvis to make his appearance. With a determination akin to an army tank, I bulldozed my way through the crowd. But after pushing and shoving as far as I was conniving-ly able, I finally reached the limit. Everybody was holding their positions like solid granite.

I thought I was going to pass out before Elvis finally emerged from that trailer. Then, everyone started to rush him. But security was everywhere and the crowd was restrained. I raised my camera to snap a picture and he looked straight at me, like he knew I'd never reach him through the press of the crowd.

When Elvis headed for the other side of the building everybody ran around to line up behind the ropes. I made it to the front and held my place with a growl of determination, while Elvis went inside the bank.

I sighed my disappointment and, with hope in my heart, continued to endure the heat. I knew one thing. The unattainable Elvis was in that bank, and like the hunter who has his prey cornered in a hole, I knew he'd have to come out sooner or later. All I had to do was wait.

People talked among themselves, while fanning the heat, and I learned the title of the movie had been changed to *What a Wonderful Life*.

When the filming inside was finished for the day, Elvis made his exit and headed for the trailer. We hastened around to the back of the bank to meet him. When we got there, he was encircled by the press and his stogie-chewing manager, Colonel Tom Parker. They held us back, but I treasured every glimpse of Elvis I was afforded from where I stood, enviously, watching him give autographs to some who were close enough to get them. I tried to work my way up closer and had my camera ready. I almost made it to him but then he turned and started for the trailer.

I called out to him, "Elvis!"

He looked toward me and our eyes locked for just a moment and I heard him say, "Next time, honey," then he turned and stepped into his dressing room. I pushed my way up closer to the door, which was standing open. People were crowded around talking and I saw my chance. I snapped a picture of him inside the trailer before the door was closed. Then I thought about the way Elvis had looked at me when he'd said, "Next time," and I smiled. It seemed as though he was sending me a message, like the final title of the movie, *Follow That Dream*.

I felt a sense of loss when the filming was all over, like the day after Christmas. I was as disappointed over not getting a kiss and an autograph from Elvis as a kid with no batteries for his (or her) new toy, and I wondered if I was ever going to make my dream come true. But instantly my heart said, *yes. You will do it, Frances.*

Sometime, somewhere, someday, it will happen. Just like magic. It will happen.

I took my film to be developed and was confused when I got the pictures back. Some of the shots I recognized, while others were foreign to my memory. I wondered if the people who did the developing had mixed up some of the photos. I'm sure they had a lot of Elvis pictures that weekend. But, I figured somebody's loss was my gain and treasured what my money had paid for. Especially since it appeared some of my pictures were missing.

Elvis was gone and the facts of life had a way of bringing me back down to earth, fast. Faced with bills and no job, I humbly went back to Liggets on the chance they would be shorthanded. Luck was with me. It turned out I was not the only one who'd abandoned her job for Elvis, and Vi was at her wit's end, trying to take care of everything by herself. When she saw me standing near the register, she said, "Don't say anything! Just get behind this damn counter and get busy."

The following day I earnestly committed to passing my driving test...and I did! Perhaps because the highway patrolman feared for his life and was unwilling to climb back into the car with me again. Not unjustly though, since I was stopped three times by one policeman on the day I received my license. The first time, my car was smoking from my failure to release the emergency brake. The second time, I made an unlawful U-turn in the middle of downtown. The officer, who had already seen my license and knew I'd gotten it that day, stopped me and shook his head.

"That was a mighty pretty U-turn you just made. Would you like to tell me why you did it?"

Feigning innocence, I smiled at him, "Yes, sir. Because I was going the wrong way."

"Oooooh, you were going the wrong way," he said, while slowly nodding his head. He decided to show mercy and let me go with just a warning. Then he went back to his car and waited for me to pull out. But, not having mastered the stick shift yet, I put it in reverse and backed into the police officer's patrol car. When I stuck my head out the window to see what was wrong, he was already approaching my car. He threw up his hands and said in exasperation, "I know! You were going the wrong way."

*F*OLLOW *THAT* *DREAM* premiered in Ocala on April 11, 1962. It starred Elvis Presley with Arthur O'Connell, Ann Helm, Joanna Moore, Jack Kruschen, Simon Oakland, Gavin and Robert Koon, and Pam Ogles. While traveling through Florida in an old jalopy, the Kwimpers run out of gas, and when the governor parades through the next day, they tell him they are homesteaders. They start up their own business renting out fishing poles, bait, and eventually boats. Others move in to homestead along with a trailer of gamblers. Toby (Elvis) is elected sheriff to keep the peace, which he does in his own way. Miss Claypole (Joanna Moore), who works for state welfare, is scorned by Toby when she tries to seduce him, so she sets out "to give him what hell ain't got no fury like," and take the orphaned children away from his pop. But the judge rules in favor of the Kwimpers. The movie ends with Toby kissing Holly for the first time. *Follow That Dream* is a comedy and in my opinion was one of Elvis' best movies. But then, maybe I'm prejudiced.

A few days after Elvis left town, I met my first serious boyfriend. I was back working at Liggets when this guy came up to the register. It was closing time and I had the drawer open counting money. He was about five-foot-eight, good-looking with brown hair and sincere eyes. A real clean-cut, moral-looking guy. Paul (not his real name) had come to pick up Lydia, a girl I worked with. Lydia and Paul were dating, but Lydia was seeing other guys and Paul eventually asked me out.

On our first date, Paul picked me up in his 1957 red and white Chevrolet. We stopped at the Chicken Ranch drive-in and sat in the car sipping Cokes and talking. He told me he had been in the army, stationed in Alaska, and had not been home long. We talked for a couple of hours, then he drove me home. When we reached my place I invited him in.

This was the first time I'd asked anyone into my apartment and there was no place to sit but on the bed. Naturally, I was leery. But I felt something else, too. I suppose you could call it temptation.

We sat down on the edge of the bed, side-by-side. I had turned the bedside lamp on, but now Paul turned it off. I could see him in the dark. Flickering lights from a neon sign across the street danced through the thin fluttering curtains at the open window and settled on his face. I felt a chemistry going on between us as we talked, and a lump rose in my throat, then stuck there. And he kissed me. *Oh, no...soft, full lips!*

Paul pushed me back onto the bed and we kissed up a storm. He was trembling. I felt like lightning had struck me. Suddenly, through the raging tempest, I heard Cupid singing and told Paul I loved him. He was shocked. I was shocked. I'd never spoken those three words to any guy before. I had thought them, but never said them, and I'd just met Paul.

I think Paul was flattered by my words. He said, "It wouldn't be hard to love you."

He didn't say he loved me. But he'd said enough. Elvis had taught me well and I was confident I could make Paul love me.

Paul introduced me to his best friend, Bradford, and I liked him right away. He was funny. A real hoot to be around. Paul and Bradford were the oddest twosome. Paul was the straightest guy I'd ever met, and so serious that when he did express himself in some unexpected way, I dug on it. Valene, Bradford's girlfriend, had a personality a lot like Paul, while Bradford was more like me—outspoken and daring.

Paul said he didn't like me living alone in "that bedroom," referring to my place, so Valene and I rented an apartment together.

From the first time I saw that big house, surrounded by motel units on one side, and new cabins being added one at a time in the back, I was somehow reminded of a hard-working laborious mother trying to support young ones, while all the time continuing to become pregnant and adding to her brood. The owner's family occupied the lower level of the main house. Our chamber was one of two upstairs in the large two-story that sat facing Silver Springs Boulevard. The enormous living-room/bedroom combination held a wrought-iron double bed that sat catty-cornered next to a wood-framed, push-up window. The floors were cherrywood, clean and polished, with pretty rugs scattered around. Another window, across from the foot of the bed, allowed the sun out of the west to send beams of light filtering through and bouncing off the shiny floors.

At the other end of the suite, we had a huge eat-in kitchen with a chrome dinette set sitting in the middle. And centered between the kitchen and bedroom was a big bathroom. We used to have to walk through the bathroom to get to the kitchen. Unless we went out the kitchen door, down the hall, and back to the living room.

We kept the windows open when we were home. I remember sitting there in that open window, with a mirror propped between my knees for the best angle of light, and piercing my ears. An act of independence, I'm sure. I'd always wanted them pierced, begged Mama, but she never gave in. "No. When you get grown and gone, you can put holes in your ears, nose, or whatever," she said, "but as long as you live under my roof and I pay the bills, the answer is No!"

I fell hard for Paul and thought he felt the same. He said he loved me and we talked about getting married. He treated me like I was precious to him and gave me the respect every good girl expects. And all the kisses she desires. He preserved my virtue with chaste hands, like I was a nun or the Madonna herself.

Paul was twenty-three and I was nearly eighteen. Perhaps it was the difference in our ages that made him so protective over my virginity. He needn't have worried about it; Mama's face always materialized in my mind before anything had a chance to get out of hand.

We necked a lot though, and according to Bradford, Paul was forever taking cold showers. But I was on my own private cloud: one of those pink fantasy ones where I wore rose-colored glasses and felt secure in words. Deceptive words like *I love you, too*—spoken by the one I loved.

We'd been dating a few months when Paul started to change toward me. He didn't spend as much time with me as he had in the beginning, and he talked about wanting to sleep with me, but acted like he wouldn't respect me if I did. It was all very confusing to me.

One night we were sitting on the steps in the hallway. Bradford and Valene were in the apartment and the door was open. Music drifted down the stairwell, softly reaching our ears. "I'm In The Mood For Love," had me in the mood for romance. Paul held my hand. He had just kissed me and I was sensing something. Something so disturbing, I really didn't want to know.

Staring intently at the tips of his shoes, he said, "Frances, we need to talk." I didn't understand at first but Paul very quickly made himself clear.

"I think things are moving too fast. Maybe we should see other people for a while."

My world tilted. My heart was ripping. Everything was coming apart. This wasn't the way love stories ended. We were supposed to live happily ever after.

Paul saw the effect his announcement had on me and he kissed me. His gesture was kind, but that was all. I think he was afraid of me and the problems he sensed were buried inside me. Things I refused to deal with. Stuff that stemmed from the secret memories and nightmares.

During the next two weeks Paul's visits tapered off until finally, he told me, "I think I'm still in love with a stewardess I met while I was in the army."

He might as well have stuck a knife into my heart. My self-worth was crushed beneath his feet. He didn't want me!

Bradford and Valene had gone to the country to visit Valene's family. So when Paul left, I was feeling dumped, depressed, lonely, and by myself. The events that followed went beyond my understanding. The mind is a strange thing, a place where secrets are given over to the subconscious. Here the secrets sleep in dark corners, absorbing silent things, like a cat in the night stealing breath from an infant. Sometimes, unpleasant things happen that arouse the silent mind, not completely, but just enough to spur destructive emotions.

I drove to the Chicken Ranch and sat in my car, drinking a Coke, listening to the jukebox, and crying. I had a headache, so I flashed for the curb girl and asked if they sold any tins of aspirin. She said they had bottles, but no tins. I said a bottle would be fine.

"Oh, Paul, why?"

The sound of his name spoken aloud made me feel so alone. "What's wrong with me?" I asked the windshield. My head was pounding and I heard voices...*you're not good enough for him.* The headache continued to throb, more fiercely.

I remember taking two for the pain, and five minutes later when it hadn't eased, I took the whole bottle, which contained a hundred tablets. I didn't think about what I was doing. I didn't want to die, I loved living too much. It was like someone else was out to get me. Someone inside me who wasn't me. Someone who lived in a bottle of suicide and wanted me dead.

According to Valene, I was out of it when she and Bradford got back from the farm. I have no memory of driving home from the Chicken Ranch. Valene said she found the remains of my suicide attempt and that I had taken a half bottle of tranquilizers, on top of the aspirin, before they found me. Then she said I jumped out of our second-story bedroom window, right in front of them. Lucky for me the ground was soft. Bradford carried me back upstairs, then Valene forced me to drink some raw milk she had brought home from her parents' farm. The milk induced vomiting and probably saved my life. But my friends still took me to the hospital to have my stomach pumped.

I was bedridden with side effects for a week. The newspaper got hold of the story and titled it, *Girl Who Wants Boyfriend to Feel Sorry Changes Mind*. I was humiliated. I didn't want Paul to feel sorry for me and I, for sure, didn't want to die. I tried to tell Paul it wasn't like he thought, but he was appalled by my actions. He said I had head problems and he was sorry, but he couldn't see me anymore. As if this were not enough, Mama found out. It just about killed her.

"Why, Frances?"

"I don't know." But no one understood my answer. Of course, I couldn't blame them. I didn't understand it myself.

The last time I saw Paul was at the Big D drive-in. I spotted his car when he pulled in and parked. He was alone. I couldn't stand the thought of him believing that newspaper story. I wanted to explain things to him and apologize. So I got out of my car and walked over to his.

"Hey, Paul. I saw you parked and wanted to tell you I'm sorry about everything."

If looks could kill, I would have been lying beside his car, prostrate on my back, holding a lily over my chest. "Frances, I'm gonna make this as plain as I can for you. I don't ever want to see you or speak to you again. Never!" He rolled up the window, cranked up his car, and drove away. *What a shallow person*, I thought.

There is a funny side to this story. Ten years later I happened to be in Ocala, saw Paul's name in the telephone book, and decided to call him. Innocent enough. After all, it had been ten years. Who carries a grudge ten years? I dialed his number and Paul answered.

"Hello, Paul? This is..."

I barely got out "Fran," when he said in a fierce voice, "I told you I never wanted to speak to you again!" Then he slammed the receiver down. I laughed so hard I almost peed my pants. The way I figure, he must have cared an awful lot to remember my voice and maintain all that anger for so many years.

After Paul and I broke up, I packed up and moved my wounded heart back to Tampa to heal.

LAUREN WITH GUITAR. CIRCA 1967.

7

Live a Little, Love a Little

1962 - 1969

Life and living aren't the same thing. Life is more than just drawin' breath.

—*Elvis Presley*

I moved back to Tampa without letting my family know I was in town. Cliff let me stay at his place for a week or two until I found a job, then I moved in with his cousin and two other girls. I'd been working at the snack bar of Grandway Department Store for a couple of weeks, when Mama walked up to the counter one day and surprised me.

"Sister...why?"

I saw the sadness in her eyes and then she started to cry. Oh, Lord. Nothing hurt me worse then to see Mama cry and know I was responsible for her pain. But, thinking like the young person I was, I still wanted to be on my own.

I quit my job at Grandway about a week later and went back to Ocala. But things weren't the same. And I was constantly running into Paul. I don't think he ever saw me though, because I tried to hide. I wasn't into suffering any more humiliation from him.

When I told my friend Margo I was going back to Tampa, she

wanted to leave Ocala and go with me. So we left together and rented a cheap apartment in Sulphur Springs; then we both landed curb-hop jobs at Dee's Dog-n-Suds on Nebraska Avenue.

About a month of slave scrubbing let me know I'd never be able to work with the owner. She was a hard taskmaster, a perfectionist, and I wasn't mature enough to appreciate the work it took to meet her constant demands for cleanliness. So I gave her two weeks notice, and thought, *You're lucky to get it.* And do you know what she did? She fired me. Right there on the spot she told me to hang up my apron. Margo had already been fired and didn't seem to be in a hurry to look for work.

Unconcerned about how we were going to manage with both of us unemployed, we soon found ourselves in dire straits and were evicted from our apartment. Of course, Mama and Pap would have welcomed me back home, but I was independent, shortsighted, and stubborn.

That night, we spent the last of our money on a motel room that, in the light of the next day, turned out to be about three blocks from Papa and Little Granny's house. My dad's brother, Uncle Heyday, had moved his family in with Papa and Little Granny so they could help his parents in their old age. Uncle Heyday had the old house torn down, then built a new one large enough to accommodate both families.

I told Margo, "Let's walk over to their house and feel out a welcome. Till we can think of something else."

Hinting for an invitation to lay over a few days with my kinfolks was unnecessary. They welcomed us with open arms. And it was while we were staying with Uncle Heyday and his wife, Aunt Bernice, that I met my first husband, Lauren.

The day after we arrived, Lauren, who lived across the street, came over to speak with my aunt. She'd gone to the store and Margo and I were alone in the house, contemplating our circumstances, when he knocked at the door. You can imagine my surprise when I opened it and in walks this handsome man, without even being invited.

He had sideburns and was over six feet tall. It was the sideburns that got me! He asked if Bernice was at home. I told him no. Then he wanted to know who we were.

"Well, who are you?" I asked.

He looked straight at me with big brown eyes and said, "I'm the man you're going to marry."

Margo and I traded glances back and forth as if to say, *What's he talking about?* Then she made some remark that I can't recall now, and he looked at me and said, "I'm talking about you. I'm Lauren. And what shall I call you, my bride-to-be?"

Something about Lauren made me think of Elvis and I told him so. He said I reminded him of Marilyn Monroe.

When he left, Margo and I joked about his marriage proposal. She said, "Well, this could be a way out for you, Frances."

"That's your way of thinkin', Margo, not mine. When I get married it will be for love and not as a convenient way out of a situation."

We stayed at my aunt's house for about two weeks and during that time, Lauren did everything imaginable to capture my heart, till I finally realized he was serious. He played the guitar and sang to me all the time. Every day, here he would come, Lauren and his guitar, looking like Elvis. And at night, he serenaded me from right outside the bedroom window. I was eighteen and Lauren was the same age as Elvis, eight years older than me and a practiced flirt.

Aunt Bernice told me he'd recently come home from the hospital, where he'd been rehabilitating for the past year and a half from a twenty-eight-foot fall he'd taken while working on a construction site. Lauren had busted his head wide open on the concrete pavement that stopped his fall.

The ambulance attendants drove him to the hospital, believing he was dead. Then the doctor examined him and sent him into surgery on a "gut feeling." After the operation Lauren lay in a coma, with a tracheostomy, for six months. When he finally awoke from the long sleep, he faced the seemingly insurmountable task of learning to walk and talk all over again.

It took a year and a half of in-hospital therapy for Lauren to accomplish this feat. And when it was time to go home the nuns called him "The miracle boy of St. Joseph's Hospital."

Lauren's accident left him with some childlike sides to his personality. He laughed at inappropriate times, and he did what he felt like doing, without any regard as to how it was received by society. In other words, he had an innocence that was intriguing and made me laugh. He did outrageous things, I believe sometimes just to stagger people. And sometimes to shock me.

Before he was employed by the construction company, Lauren had been a sergeant in the marines. From the way his family told it, he'd had a mean side to him that was replaced after the fall with the sweet and teasing forthrightness that became the best part of his personality.

During his stretch in the marines he'd been involved in another accident that left him unable to father children. Having babies and being a mama had top priority on my must do before I die list. And I was bothered about giving up this deep natural need in me when I found myself falling in love with Lauren. But as the young think, so went Frances. After all, a miracle could happen.

Lauren was from a large family. He was the fifth of twelve children. His father was a Dutch/French migrant worker who spoke no English, while his mother was a school teacher from a well-to-do Michigan family.

Lauren spoiled me every way possible. He did silly things, like pulling me to a fancy restaurant in a little red wagon, then serenading me with his guitar in front of all the diners. I was soon won over by his unique charm and romantic nature, and I accepted his proposal of marriage.

On September 28, 1962, Lauren and I stood in my mother's house before a Nazarene minister and said our vows. I wore a knee-length, white wedding dress with a shoulder-length veil. Both our families were there to celebrate the occasion, and when we tried to slip away from our reception early, they told us, "You'll never forget this special night so enjoy it while you have it and don't be in a hurry to leave. You have the rest of your lives to spend together." Funny, the part I never forgot was my wedding night.

We spent our first night as man and wife in the furnished apartment we'd rented and moved our clothes into the day before. Lauren was very patient for an eager groom.

I was experiencing all the emotions one feels when every "taboo" you've been programmed all your life to just say no to suddenly becomes not only permissible, but lawful and expected.

Facing it from love's perspective, I battled the demons of fear and anger that unexplainably attacked me, and overcame my first thought, which was, *I'm just supposed to lie down for this?*

I loved Lauren, and it was through love's eyes that I saw my husband. He was this tall, dark, and handsome man who reminded me of Elvis. And he'd promised to love and cherish me for the rest of my life. A hot-blooded Frenchman who would have moved Heaven and Earth to give me the sun, moon, and the stars if it was possible. And I took a deep breath...closed my eyes, and surrendered to the magic.

LAUREN LOVED SPOILING ME better than he loved himself. He pampered and powdered my butt like I was the royal baby of the Queen of England. And he took me to see Elvis' movies and sat through them for as many times as I wanted.

When we went downtown for the new releases, I noticed the lines weren't as long anymore, and I couldn't understand what was happening. It was almost like I'd gone to sleep and awakened in another generation. I think this was probably the first time getting older bothered me. Girls were into the Beatles and Tom Jones.

I remember this sixteen year old girl saying to me, "Elvis is out of it. He's old stuff. Now, Tom Jones...he's hot! He's the sexiest man alive."

I couldn't believe my ears and told her that Elvis would still be around when Tom Jones wasn't even a memory. Now I liked Tom Jones, so don't get me wrong. He was all those things people said he was; sexy, good-looking, and he had an incredible voice and stage presentation. But he wasn't my pretty Elvis.

Lauren bought every magazine he found that had a story about Elvis in it. And boxes of chocolate candy for me to eat while I pored over the latest word on my hero. He made sure I owned all of Elvis' records, too, and bought me a beautiful console stereo to play them on.

Sometimes Lauren imitated Elvis. He said the way it excited me turned him on. With his guitar hanging from a neck-strap, he'd rest his left hand against the strings, flatten his right hand with his fingers spread wide apart, and rub it down the side of his pants leg and start shaking all over, fluttering his arms like Elvis, and he'd give me one of his Elvis sneers and say, "You know I'm better than Elvis. I know you'd throw rocks at him if he ever tried to do this to you..."

He cooked my breakfast and brought it to me in bed, washed and ironed all the clothes, and put me through beauty school. Lauren even polished my white shoes, every day. It became like my symbol. No one at beauty school wore whiter shoes than me. Lauren literally spoiled me so rotten, Mama said I stunk. I was his princess and he called me by my first name, Nellie, his precious love. And whatever Nellie wanted, Nellie got. Alas, except children.

His family thought I took advantage but Lauren didn't agree with them. I could do no wrong in his eyes and this remains true even to this day. Loving me makes Lauren happy.

Man! Did we ever get into some in-law fights over this. Me against his whole big family. But I hung in there. I know now that we all loved each other but I'm not sure we realized it back then.

The only real threat to our marriage was the absence of children and my need to bear them. I just couldn't stand the thought of leaving this world without ever having experienced childbirth and motherhood and was absolutely obsessed with wanting a baby of my own. I remember when Lauren, trying to hold on to me, told me to just go out and get pregnant. Only, don't tell him about it. Just come home from the doctor one day and announce we were going to have a baby.

I was shocked! "Lauren, are you crazy? First of all I wouldn't do it! I don't believe in adultery. Second, even if I was to do it, it wouldn't work! Everybody in your big ole family, twelve of them, Lauren, twelve of them; your brothers, your sisters, and...your mama makes thirteen. No, let's not forget about your gossipin' mama! They all know you can't have kids. And they're just waitin' for me to fall. The only one who won't give me hell is your daddy 'cause he's dead."

"Love, you're paranoid."

"And you're blind as Mr. Magoo."

My obsession with wanting a child eventually led to a divorce.

I'd had three and a half blissful years with Lauren and now it was time to let go and move on. I had goals to reach and dreams to fulfill.

I was twenty-two when we separated, employed by Reynaldo's Hair Styling Salon in Temple Terrace, across the street from Busch Gardens. After my divorce was final, I moved in with a customer of mine who'd become a close friend.

Several months after my divorce, I started dating Fred. A patron of mine introduced us. Fred was a master sergeant in the air force, stationed at MacDill Air Force base. He brought out the best in me. I don't know how he did it but somehow Fred inspired me to believe in myself.

I was always at my best when I was with Fred. I looked my best; my makeup constantly on and never a hair out of place. I watched my weight, which had a tendency to go up and down, and I tried not to bite my nails. I acted my best; stayed out of trouble and visited Mama pretty often instead of worrying her into a panic. And I felt my best; who doesn't feel great when they're in love, looking good, and on solid turf with their family?

Fred was eleven years older than me and had a way of getting me to do what he wanted while making me think it was all my own idea. It was definitely his personality that attracted me. And with it he was able to wrap me around his finger.

I remember a funny incident that happened when Lauren found out I was dating Fred. Lauren knew who Fred was, I don't know how, but Fred didn't know this. Fred knew who Lauren was; he'd seen his pictures, but Lauren didn't know this. Fred worked a second job outside the air force as a salesman for Western Auto. George was the manager of Western Auto and he knew all of us; Lauren, Fred, and me.

One evening, Lauren went into the store while Fred was working and approached him as a customer. "I'd like to see some guns," he told Fred.

"What kind of gun are you interested in? A rifle...a BB Gun?" Fred asked.

Lauren probably looked him in the eyes wearing an expression similar to one a cat wears when he's playing with his mouse, just before the kill. Anyhow, he told Fred, "I'm looking for a gun to shoot my wife's lover."

Even though Lauren and I were divorced, he still considered me his wife. Fred excused himself for a minute and went to the back of the store where he recounted the incident to George.

"That big, crazy galoot, wants me to sell him a gun to kill me with!"

George laughed. "Lauren's harmless. He just wants to set you on edge."

Well, Fred didn't take it so lightly, and later when he told me what had happened, I had a hard time convincing him that George was right.

Fred was married and had three children but he'd been separated from his wife for over a year before we met. Our courtship was perfect, except for Fred's ongoing battles for the custody of his children. Fred was a father, first and always. And even though I respected this rare quality in a man, one year of his family complications and I got fed up with being stood up and came unwrapped. I'd been too spoiled by Lauren to take second place, so with my I'll-show-you attitude, I did something really stupid. I married a man I hardly knew. I'll call him James (not his real name).

Reason does not always count for what we do. I've done things without knowing why. I just did them. Serious stuff, like marrying James. He said I used him for legal stud service as a means to get a child. If I did, I wasn't aware of it.

James and I were married on January 12, 1967. We were strangers who I figure, by fate, were destined to cross paths so that our daughter, Jolynn, might come to be born. The ensuring lure? You guessed it. Blue eyes and soft, full lips. For James, I can only guess. When I think of our marriage, it just seems like a long ago short dream in which we wedded...we bedded...then our eyes were opened and I woke up pregnant.

We were a total mismatch. James was bossy and domineering. He said the same about me. He was rigid in his opinions and he for darn sure didn't share my obsessive love for Elvis.

Jolynn was conceived on our wedding night. I know this because I woke up sick the very next morning and stayed nauseated for the next nine months. I really didn't plan it that way, although James thought I did. We lasted six or seven weeks. Then I moved back home with my parents and filed for a divorce. But it didn't become final until after the birth of our daughter, Sandy Jolynn.

I lived with my parents while I carried Jolynn. Sometimes I went to Ocala and visited relatives in an effort to break the monotony of the seemingly endless pregnancy. I was in Ocala when Elvis and Priscilla's wedding made the headlines. The news was shocking at first, but then I figured it was about time. After all, I looked forward to seeing Elvis' genes passed down, ensuring his immortality. I did worry if his taking a bride would get in the way of fulfilling my vow. But, something in my spirit reassured me that Elvis would never cut himself off from his adoring fans.

His marriage to Priscilla and the birth of Lisa Marie nine months later put him back in the news. Photographers wanted pictures of Elvis the family man. Magazines wanted interviews and people speculated if it would last.

I was pleased with his choice of bride. And amazed at their striking resemblance to each other. I remember thinking, *She looks like Debra Paget. Ah...but they're perfectly matched...like they were made for each other.*

Priscilla was beautiful when Elvis married her. Let me rephrase that. Priscilla has always been beautiful. I personally adored the fashions Elvis was so fond of on his wife. I thought they were absolutely the coolest for puttin' on the ritz. And I loved her hair. After all, I was a stylist during that time and therefore had a fine appreciation for the labor that had gone into her high-stacked curls and big hair.

Jolynn was born October 10, and Lauren and I were remarried, December 11th. Nineteen sixty-seven had been a very busy year.

Lauren and I seemed to have everything we wanted in our second marriage to each other. I had the child I'd longed for and I loved her better than life. Lauren adored my daughter and doted on her, if you can believe it, even more than he did on me. That young'un stunk from spoiling, worse than I ever did!

I kept on working at Reynaldo's and life was good. I had the best of both worlds; as a wife and mother, and as a hairdresser.

Lauren had bought a small, two-bedroom frame house on 30th Street in Tampa, while we'd been divorced. He got it for five thousand dollars. Fifty dollars down and fifty dollars a month.

"It's only temporary," he said, "till we can save up enough money for a better one. It won't be long, love. I know how to work and cut corners. All I care about is loving you and taking care of you and making you happy. Keeping the nightmares away."

Then in sixty-nine, we got a break. One of the girls I worked with said her husband was looking for a husband and wife team to manage a trailer park he'd just bought. The position came with a big, rent-free house, in addition to the salary. We were told that if we wanted to buy our own vending machines, we could make some extra money from them.

We rented out our house to my newly married brother Sam, and his wife, Nancy and moved into the one provided by the trailer park and took over the position of manager. Investing in the beverage and candy machines brought us sizable profits and paid for themselves in a short time. Then, the returns allowed us to buy new furniture for our dream home, which was becoming more of a reality since we no longer had to make house payments.

By 1968, Elvis' movies had become almost predictable. Even though I still enjoyed them, I longed for the unpredictable Elvis. The Elvis who had said, "That ain't tactics, honey. That's just the beast in me." I was thinking about this while looking through the movie part of the paper one day. Then, just as though Elvis could read my mind, an article in the TV guide section leaped up in my face. Singer was presenting Elvis' 1968 comeback special!

What a show! Elvis showed 'em all that the King still had it! Of course, I'd always known that. But seeing it again was wonderful beyond words.

JULY 20, 1969, IS A DAY that clearly stands out in my mind. Sam and Nancy had come over that day to have dinner with us and we were watching television when Neil Armstrong took his first steps on the moon.

During their visit, my brother said they'd like to buy the house they were now renting from us. Lauren and I had just been talking about asking them if they wanted to buy it. So this was like an answer to prayer.

They paid us cash, and with the money we'd already saved, we now had the down payment for our new home. It was on Dartmouth in Tampa, not far from the Hillsborough River, and not far from Elm Street, where I'd grown up.

I loved our new house with its real fireplace: one of the requirements of my dream house. The Mediterranean furniture we'd selected looked like it had been custom made for the rooms. You would have thought my life was perfect now. Right?

Wrong. I still hadn't reached Elvis and the longer I prolonged it the dimmer it got. Sometimes it seemed so far out of my reach, I almost abandoned hope.

But hope wouldn't let me.

Lauren, trying to pacify his princess, took me to see Elvis' movies every time they played anywhere in Tampa. One night we were at the Fun-Land Drive-in when a funny incident happened. The theater was running an all-night session of Elvis' movies. Lauren and I were parked behind a car the same color and model as ours. I'd needed to go to the bathroom for quite some time, but I'd been putting it off because I didn't want to miss any of the movie. Finally, not being able to wait any longer, I headed for the restroom with my eyes locked on the screen the entire time. It wasn't intermission, so the lights were out and the bathroom was empty. In my rush to get back to the flick, I got my zipper stuck.

Unwilling to waste time fiddling with the zipper, I grasped the sides of my pants, held them together, and rushed out the door, keeping my eyes glued to the screen as I backed all the way to the car. Still holding my pants together, I opened the door and jumped in, quickly sliding across the seat and up close to my husband, never taking my eyes from the movie for a moment.

"Honey, can you get this stupid zipper uncaught?"

A deep, strange voice laughed and said, "I think you've got the wrong honey."

I looked up into the unfamiliar face and panicked. "Oh, my God! This isn't my car!"

Then scrambling out of there as fast as I could, my pants slipped and dropped to my knees, tripping me, and I fell forward onto the ground. I was one pissed-off, red-faced young lady when I reached the car.

Lauren had been watching the entire episode and was in tears by the time I threw open the door and got in. He laughed even harder when he saw my broken zipper. I told him to kiss my ass. And he said, "Gladly."

THE OWNER OF THE TRAILER park had found someone else to manage it after Lauren and I moved out. So I went back to work for Reynaldo. I liked my job as a hairstylist. I used to refer to putting up all those curls that were so popular back then as "build-a-hair-do," because it took a great length of time and effort to back-comb all that long hair, then stack to the ceiling those big blown up curls that we sprayed with lacquer then dried with a blow dryer till they were stiff enough to last for a week or two.

I remember all the jokes that flew around the beauty shop in the big hair days. Like the one about the lady who hatched roaches in her beehive. Or the one about wives not giving their husbands any poontang, 'cause it'd mess up their hair.

I enjoyed sharing my life stories with customers and they loved hearing them. Some even said if they hadn't liked the way I did their hair they'd still have come to me, because my life was like a soap opera and they didn't want to miss the next segment.

One of Reynaldo's customers was talking with him one day and I overheard her say she was Col. Tom Parker's daughter-in-law. I curiously walked over to where Reynaldo was rolling her hair up in a wet set and asked, "Did I hear you say Col. Tom Parker is your father-in-law?"

"Yes," she said. Then she unsnapped her purse and pulled out some pictures of her children with the Colonel. I asked if she ever got to see Elvis, and again she said, "Yes." I found this very interesting and banked it in my memory for possible future use.

Shafter Miles Sheffield
and Ora Sheffield
(with child).
Circa 1923

Papa
David Minton

Sam and Tommy, Seattle
1948

Ora Sheffield
and Allie Minton

Mama (on right)
and best friend
Circa 1942

Me and Mama,
1945

Mama and Pap, 1959

Frances and brothers
Sam and Tommy, 1949

Frances and Sandra,
Circa 1947
(I can't believe there
was a time I was
shorter than Sandra)

Cliff Denison
(Doesn't he look like
Elvis here!)

Artie Mae Minton
1957

Husband Eddie

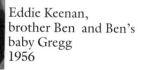

Eddie Keenan,
brother Ben and Ben's
baby Gregg
1956

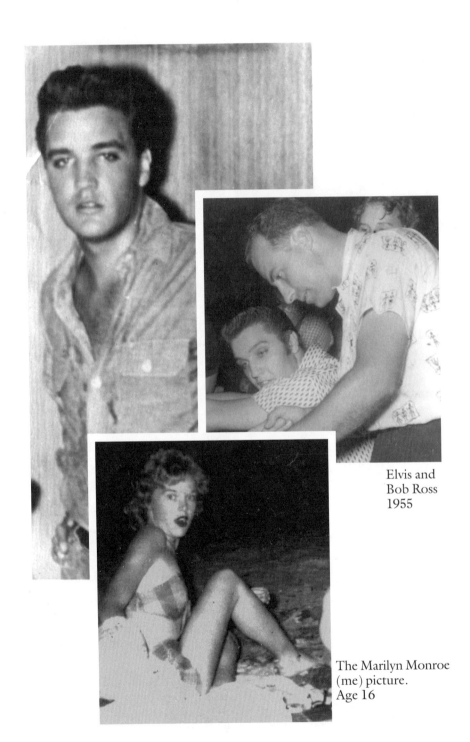

Elvis and
Bob Ross
1955

The Marilyn Monroe
(me) picture.
Age 16

Elvis in Germany

Elvis in Germany with Ira Jones
1958-1959
(From the collection of Ira Jones)

Elvis and
Nancy Sinatra

Mama and Pap (Sandy).
Wedding photo, 1959

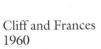

Cliff and Frances
1960

Lauren and Frances' wedding
1962

Cousin Betty, Frances and
Aunt Geneva

"Follow That Dream" movie set, Ocala, Florida, 1961

Birthday greetings to Bob Ross from Elvis
(on toilet paper) with the Colonel's face
stamped on it.
July 15. 1977
(from the collection of Sandra Ross)

Ed, daughter Patti
and Frances, 1988

Darlene and Frances, 1974

Frances and Aunt Maggie at
Sam and Nancy's wedding
1968

Frances and
Jolynn
1971

Vester Presley with
Frances, Jolynn and
Jessica, 1979

Frances wrapped in fur

Me, Lauren and his
mother Maxine

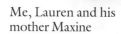

Frances with big hair

Sylvia Shemwell, Estelle Brown, (Sweet
Inspirations) and Sandy Jolynn, 1970

Hal Wallis "Loving You" cast party. 1957
(from the collection of Sandra Ross)

Frances, Jolynn, and Jessica,
1975

Frances and Jolynn, 1972

Sam Minton
(my brother)
and family
1974

Frances wearing
red outfit Elvis
liked.
Las Vegas

Eddie and Frances' wedding
January 29, 1977

Billy and Jessica

Billy and Frances,
1974

Billy and me, Jolynn
and Jessica

Tampa International Airport–
Frances and Jessica. Home from
Las Vegas and happy to see my baby.
1975

"Elvis in Concert"
1970–1975

Frances, 1975

Sylvia Shemwell and
Frances, 1971.

Colonel Tom
Parker in his Palm
Springs office.
(from the collection of
Sandra Ross)

Frances
the year Elvis
died
age 33

Frances
1977

Bob and Sandra
Ross' wedding,
with Colonel
Parker's wife,
Marie

The Sheffields (my mama's side of the family) from left:
Aunts Bethine, Inez, Maggie. Uncle Oliver, Grandma Ora, Grandaddy
Shafter Miles Sheffield, Bride Aunt Geneva, Uncle Vivern, Aunt Colleen,
Mama Artie Mae and Aunt Ernestine (far right). 1961

Tom Minton, 1983

Sandra and Eula Mae

Uncle Vester Presley,
Jolynn, Jessica
and Frances,
1979

Kenneth Ross and
Jolynn, 1982

Eddie Keenan, 1980

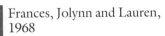
Frances, Jolynn and Lauren, 1968

Mama and Tiffany, 1986

Eddie playing the guitar

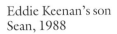
Eddie Keenan's son
Sean, 1988

Frances, Jolynn
and Jessica
1978

Frances, 1988

Tiffany
(my
granddaughter,
1994

Billie Jessica,
Author's youngest daughter.
1994

Sandy Jolynn,
Author's eldest daughter
1985

Joe Esposito and Frances, 1994

Frances and friend "...taking care of business" in Memphis

Sweet Inspirations singer Myrna Smith with Frances, 1995

Frances and Ira Jones, 1994

Sylvia Shemwell,
Frances, and
Nancy Minton
at Graceland.
1996

Sandra Ross and
Frances, 1995

Mike McGregor, me,
and Dick Grob
1994

Frances with
Trent Carlini,
Las Vegas,
1997.

Betty
Zogob,
Trent
Carlini,
and
Frances,
1997.

Frances in
Las Vegas,
1997

Peekaboo.

Ed and Frances at
home, 1997

Frances
and Aunt
Inez at
family
reunion,
1993.

Part 2 1970-1995

EULA MAE AND SANDRA. 1971.

8

Viva Las Vegas

1970

Without a song, the day will never end.

—Elvis Presley

My Las Vegas fever began in the spring of 1970, when cousin Sandra married a man in the military who was stationed in Washington State. The wedding was held in Tampa, then he had to report directly back to the base. Sandra had bought a new compact car before she got married and was going to drive it to Tacoma. She rented out her house and readied herself, her young son, Kenneth, and Omar their Siamese cat for the long trip.

Not wanting to drive across country by herself, she enticed me to go, with vivid descriptions of places and things we would see along the way.

"Come with me, Frances. All it'll cost you is your plane fare back home. I'll cover the rest."

The icing on the cake and deciding factor for me was, of course, Las Vegas. I knew Elvis had played there recently and I was hoping, against the odds, that he'd be in town when we got there.

I'd been talking to the old picture a lot lately. Elvis' pretty, smeared mouth reminded me of bananas and paper towels and the

senseless fuss Betty and I'd had that summer in fifty-nine. I smiled
and lightly kissed his wounded lips.

"Be there for me Elvis. Please."

*I don't know, baby. I might be booked somewhere else when you
get to Vegas. But have fun while you're there and pretend I'm with
you. And...honey...never give up your dream.*

LAUREN WAS SWEET about letting me use my vacation time to
make the trip with Sandra. My ex-landlady, I called her Nan-
ny, had a daughter who lived in Las Vegas. Eula Mae was eager for
us to stay a week with them. So, Sandra and I loaded up her tiny
car, packing two kids, a cat, and a litter box, and headed out on
our long journey.

Our trip turned out to be quite an excursion. We went to New
Orleans, Carlsbad Caverns, and the Grand Canyon so Jolynn and
Kenneth could spit in it. When we reached Hoover Dam, our
nerves were more then a little bit rattled from fighting with kids, a
cat, and each other. But by this time, Sandra and I had pretty
much given up our own bickering. We'd determined that our combined efforts were mandatory if we wanted to keep our sanity. Still
so, it didn't help matters when I nearly refused to cross the dam. It
was so high it scared the dickens out of me and I started whining.

"Sandra, I'm sooo scared. I can't do this. Plea...se, just let me
out of this car. I'll walk across the dam and you can wait for me on
the other side. I'd feel more in control of the situation if I could
just cross over by foot."

"Are you stupid, dip shit, or just plain ignorant?"

"Both, if I don't get outta this car...now!" I tried to get the
door open but Sandra, losing her patience, snatched me by the
shirttail while I screamed.

"Shut up, Frances, or I'll blindfold your ass! You're making me
a damn nervous wreck and I've gotta drive this car!" I pleaded
with her to drive slower. "The car won't go any slower without
stopping."

In the meantime, a line of traffic was backed up behind us, with
drivers blowing their horns and yelling out of windows. This lasted
the entire time it took us to cross the dam, which, at five miles an
hour, was a lot more than the locals wanted to put up with.

We finally made it to the other side of the dam, then stopped to take a breather and settle our nerves. Unfortunately, we forgot to dump the litter box during our respite, and it wasn't long after we got back on the road before the smell of our oversight became obvious.

Sandra accused me of stinking, I accused her, and the kids got the blame while Omar hid. By the time we reached Las Vegas and pulled into a gas station, we all stunk. We checked the back seat of the car and found the litter box had dumped over. But the kids seemed healthy and happy. So, we cleaned up the mess, then went to the restroom and freshened ourselves up as best we could.

Finally, we started our search for Eula Mae's house. It took us longer than we thought it would to locate their place and by the time we found it, we were exhausted and in desperate need of baths. Thank goodness, Eula Mae was wonderful about everything and made us feel right at home.

She was a pretty lady, probably around thirty-eight. She had blond hair and wore it stacked up high on top of her head in fashionable curls.

After we'd had our baths, Eula Mae exclaimed, "Wow! You look like different people!"

She fixed us something to eat, then we sat around talking and just getting to know each other. Eula Mae and her family were our kind of people and we all felt like we'd known each other forever.

Then, Eula Mae said she had a surprise for us.

A girlfriend of hers, who was a friend of a friend of the president of the International Hotel, had said she could get us good seats for the Tom Jones show. Elvis wasn't in town at the time and I was disappointed. But since I really hadn't believed he would be, I figured I'd get the details on when he'd be back, then make my plans. Anyway, Tom Jones was at the same hotel where Elvis played and somehow that made me feel closer to him.

Feeling refreshed from our baths and nourished from the delicious meal, we finally relaxed after having put the kids to bed. Tired as we were, Sandra and I were still excited and ready to go when Eula Mae suggested a ride down the strip. Her son, Bobby, volunteered to watch the kids for us.

She took us in her 1956 Chevy, on a route that approached downtown from the back side. I remember when she made that turn onto Freemont Street. It was like an unexpected, overwhelming smack in the face. Those dazzling, splashy lights of glitter-gulch hit me like looking at a twelve-carat diamond on black velvet beneath a big, brightly lit Christmas tree. It was an exciting, gaudy breath-taking, emotional experience that stirred my blood much the same way Elvis did, and it was love at first sight for me and Las Vegas. I thought, *What a perfect playground for the King.*

We rode through town then headed for the strip while Eula Mae instructed us on proper Vegas protocol. Number one lesson: Always carry money for valet parking. "Makes you feel important, right, and we want to feel important...right?" She laughed. "Even if we are driving a clunker, right? It's the only way to get the true impact of Las Vegas."

She took us on a trip she called hotel hopping. We drove up like big shots, under the lighted entrances in front of the hotels, then left the old car to the valet and went inside to play slots and look around for movie stars.

The minute we stepped inside the first casino, my unaccustomed ears picked up its excitement: sounds from slot machines ringing and clinking as they spit out coins, flashing lights, jackpot sirens, dealers calling the dice rolls, "Coming out," and the excited shrills from gamblers on winning streaks. All filled me with the sheer delight of Las Vegas.

I stared bug-eyed at everything around me. I'd never seen so much money, elegance, lushness, or just plain-out extravagance in my life! And the clothes! People wore outrageous stuff, like mini-skirts that literally showed their butts, and long slinky dresses with necklines that plunged down to their belly buttons. And the furs and jewels. I'd never seen so many. Vegas made me feel like a star while we played slots and drank a couple of drinks in the lounge. But my and Sandra's tails were dragging the ground, so we went back home pretty early to get a good night's sleep before we pounced upon an unsuspecting Las Vegas.

The next evening found us dressed early, eager to begin our first big night on the town. We drove over to the International Hotel, did our parking thing, and as we walked through the casino en route to the showroom, I was overwhelmed, blown away, and just had to stop and think about it. The very fact that Elvis had stayed in this hotel!

Since we were early, I told Sandra and Eula Mae, "Come on ya'll, let's explore this joint." We checked out the expensive dress shops and "ooed and aahed" jewelry till time for the seating to start in the showroom.

Our seats were right down front and one away from the stage. Two men had the stage chairs and I was jealous and without giving thought blurted, "It's a damn shame they'd give those good seats to men."

Both gentlemen instantly responded, "You want our seats?"

"Yes, I do."

They traded with Sandra and me and Eula Mae moved up one, next to me. We ordered champagne and when the waiter brought it to our table, he poured a small amount into my glass.

"Is that all I get?" I asked.

Sandra was embarrassed by my ignorance and gave me a kick under the table. Shocked, I bellowed out loud, "Stop kicking me!"

She gave me a dirty look then primly said, "You're supposed to smell the bouquet." She swirled the golden liquid around in her glass then sniffed it, took a sip, smiled at the waiter, and said, "Very good."

"Well, la-de-da...hotsy-totsy and cha-cha-cha. Ex-cuuuse me, for not knowing anything about wine!" Then looking to the waiter I told him, "Just fill 'er on up." Needless to say, I had not started my night out well with Sandra.

The thing I remember most about this performance was when Tom Jones came to the edge of the stage where I was seated. I'd drunk several glasses of champagne by this time and was ready for action when Tom leaned over pretty close to me and started talking.

"Where are you from, love?" he asked.

I told him Tampa, Florida, and he called me Tampa as if it were my name. Tom was exciting but he wasn't Elvis. I remember thinking, man, that guy wears his pants tight. If he bent over we'd be looking at his moon. They made me think about what Mama had meant by her expression "painted on."

Girls in the audience were really making it known they wanted a kiss from Tom. So I sat on the edge of the stage, struck a toe to knee, palm to nape, pin-up pose, and that's when suddenly and to my surprise, he leaned down, took me by the hand, pulled me up, and kissed me!

My stupid response was spontaneous and totally misrepresented what I really meant to say.

"That was a lousy kiss. I'll bet Elvis kisses better."

The audience roared and Tom said, "She thinks Elvis kisses better." He smiled as he gallantly finessed his way out of my blooper.

It really wasn't a lousy kiss. I honestly don't know where that remark came from.

I was the only girl to get a kiss that night, and when I sat back down in my seat, I said to Eula Mae and Sandra, "Oh, he kissed me! No one is going to believe this!"

"We're witnesses! We saw it!" But what they couldn't believe was what I'd said to Tom after the kiss.

"Frances, it came out over the microphone! Everybody heard you!" Sandra scolded me with a humor she couldn't hide.

The rest of the evening went famously. We left the showroom and crowds of people gathered around us. "She's the one, the one he kissed. Touch her!"

Sandra, just joking, asked if anyone would like to drink champagne from my shoe. Some guy told her he'd like to drink from her shoe. Lucky for him it was a new shoe because she pulled it off, filled it with champagne, and true to his word the man drank from her shoe.

We went on to explore several other hotels, and I felt like a bigger big shot when we met Jan Murray (he used to host a television show called *Treasure Hunt*) and he invited us to sit down and have a drink with him. While we were talking he asked for our phone numbers. Said he'd give us a call when we got back home. Sandra and I thought, yeah, right. But he did! He rang us up on a conference call about a week or two after I'd returned to Tampa and Sandra to Tacoma.

At another hotel, we saw Dean Martin having a drink with a

friend and we said hi and talked a few minutes. I couldn't get over how friendly and accessible everyone was.

Eula Mae said, "Well, it's probably because they've never seen anyone quite like you, Frances. I've lived here long enough to tell you, most people are not as up-front with the stars as you are."

We saw Frank Sinatra, too. I remember grabbing Eula Mae and Sandra by the hands, "Come on, ya'll, it's Frank Sinatra!" But they were chicken and stood back to watch as I bravely pranced up to him, waving my hand in the air. "Hi, Frank Sinatra!" He looked at me strangely, then shook my hand.

Sandra and Eula Mae were laughing their butts off when I walked back over to where they stood watching me. Sandra was quick to inform me, "You looked like Lucille Ball in *I Love Lucy*, when she went to Hollywood."

"Laugh if you want to, but I shook Frank Sinatra's hand."

"Yeah," said Sandra, "and I got to watch a horse's ass, first-hand."

We went from hotel to hotel throughout the rest of the night. It seemed like everywhere we went, someone had been at Tom Jones' performance and had witnessed my memorable stage kiss. The celebrity status this seemed to have afforded me accelerated my taste for Las Vegas and sort of went to my head.

We stayed with Eula Mae five days and saw four of Tom Jones' performances. Some incidents that happened were really wild. Like the time Tom put his tie around my neck and people near our table were offering me money for it. One fellow wanted it for his girl-friend and flashed a hundred dollar bill in my face. I could have used the money and was tempted to barter the souvenir, but since we weren't allowed to have cameras in the showroom, the necktie was tangible proof of this night for my memory box. So I refused to sell and still have it to this day.

Another night, we were sitting at a center table next to the stage and I was feeling quite mellow from several glasses of champagne. Tom was singing "Try a Little Tenderness," and as I sat there watching him in the spotlight, through the darkness, it was as though no one existed but the two of us.

I picked up a note I'd written to him and, in the middle of his song, climbed on the table, stepped up onto the stage, and walked right up to him and kissed him. The action that followed my stunt, happened fast.

One minute I was kissing Tom. The next minute another girl in the audience had climbed on stage and started pushing me aside. She was rude and in an unkind voice she told me to let her have a turn at him. Then she jabbed me in the ribs with her elbow.

I'd turned and started back to my seat when it dawned on me, I hadn't given Tom the note I still held in my hand. I spun back around and when I reached him, the girl pushed me again. *Who does she think she is?* I thought, and returning the shove I said in a too loud voice. "You hit me again and I'll slap the dawg shit out of you."

Security guards came rushing from each side of the stage to escort us off. I told the guard who'd grabbed me, I could make it to my seat by myself. That's when I tripped at the edge of the stage, did a half somersault and landed right in the middle of the table, then...I rolled off and into the chair. I felt like the proverbial meatball.

When I straightened up in my seat, the first face I saw was Jane Russell's. I felt the heat from embarrassment flame through me. She was smiling, the audience got off on it, and Tom Jones was laughing so hard he was about to choke on the words to his song. I guess it did add a lot to the show. I think Tom started looking forward to seeing me after that, because he'd speak to me from the stage, still calling me Tampa.

Sandra didn't know whether to be mad at me or not. She was laughing while trying to scold me and it just all kind of got mixed up together.

"Frances, do you realize everyone in here heard you tell that girl you'd slap the dog shit out of her? What's the matter with you? You act like you're from Dogpatch. Didn't you see that mike in his hand?"

I hadn't realized what I'd said. When Sandra pointed it out to me, I was mortified. Why did I always put my foot in my mouth and embarrass myself to the point of wishing a trap door would open and let me fall in? I hoped God hadn't been looking and almost didn't go back for another show. But I did. Lucky for me, I get over myself.

During this trip I met Alex Shoofey, president of the International Hotel. Eula Mae faked our way into an introduction.

"It's easy" she'd said, while directing me toward Mr. Shoofey's office where the door was open. We stopped in front of the doorway, looking at Mr. Shoofey sitting at his desk, and Eula Mae said, "Excuse me...Mr. Shoofey, my name is Eula Mae and I live here in Las Vegas and I have my friend," she nodded at me, "here with me. Frances is from Florida and she's vacationing with us and she wanted me to introduce her to you."

Mr. Shoofey smiled. "How can I help you, Frances?"

I asked him when Elvis would be doing another concert and he told me, "August and the first part of September."

"Do you think I could get a good seat, right down front and up close?"

"Will you be staying at this hotel?"

"Yes, sir."

"Then I think we can do something about getting you a good seat."

I made up my mind then and there, I was going to be at Elvis' next engagement. Sandra wanted to see Elvis, too, and said she'd fly out from Washington and meet me at the hotel.

It was hard saying good-bye to Eula Mae. We'd become good friends over the previous five days and looked forward to seeing each other again in August.

Sandra and I left Las Vegas and headed across the desert toward "The Biggest Little City in the World." I liked Reno but after the grand sparkle of Las Vegas, it seemed like a little chip diamond. We left the kids with a babysitter and went out on the town. We saw Barbara McNair sing and got her autograph. She had starred with Elvis in *Change of Habit*.

We left Reno and continued on to Washington, still vacationing along the way. When we finally reached Tacoma, I couldn't wait to explore Seattle, where I'd lived when I was a child. Over the next few days we visited with relatives and drove around the areas I hadn't seen for so many years. Everything had changed. Interstates had taken over where our house on the hill had been. And Georgetown Elementary School seemed to have shrunk since I'd attended the first, second, and third grades.

Our visit soon came to an end. Jolynn and I had been gone for about a month now and it was time to bid Sandra and Kenneth farewell. They saw us off from the Seatac Airport and we boarded the plane for home.

I was really looking forward to my upcoming trip to see Elvis. I started planning for it as soon as I got back to Tampa. Lauren had a vacation coming up and wanted to go with me, so the trip was settled and the first thing I did was call and make reservations at the International Hotel. I meant to spend all my time in the same building where Elvis resided.

I also intended to employ every trick I could think of that might better my chances of meeting Elvis while I was in Vegas.

Considering what gimmicks I could use, a conversation I'd overheard in the beauty shop between Reynaldo and the daughter-in-law of Col. Tom Parker dawned on me.

The next time she was in the shop getting her hair styled, I asked if she thought her husband might be able to help me get an introduction to Elvis Presley. She didn't offer much hope, but still gave me a phone number to call.

That evening, as soon as I got home from work, I called the number. Bob Ross answered. I introduced myself and told him how I'd gotten his number. I went on to explain my reason for calling, then asked if there was anything he could do to help me. He said he'd like to meet me at the Temple Terrace Lounge. I told him I was married and didn't think it would be a good idea. He reminded me that he was married, too.

"But what do our marriages have to do with you seeing Elvis?" he asked.

I declined his invitation, anyway.

"You have my number if you change your mind," he said.

The next item on my list of preparations was to make a scrapbook for Elvis. I went through all my old pictures and put together such a good one, I almost hated to part with it. That scrapbook contained the best of my Elvis collection. I cleverly included a picture of myself inside the front cover. This was my sneaky way of trying to get Elvis to recognize me when I was sitting in the front row seat I was determined to have. I designed and made a couple of new outfits for the trip and Mama agreed to keep Jolynn for me. I was ready to fulfill my long-awaited dream. I was going to see Elvis! And this time I intended to meet him.

About three weeks before we were to leave, Lynn, an elderly friend of Lauren's and mine, said she'd love to go out West with us. "I've always wanted to go to Las Vegas," she told us, "but I didn't want to go by myself. If it's all right with you guys for me to tag along, I'll pick up the tab."

So it was agreed. Lynn would accompany us.

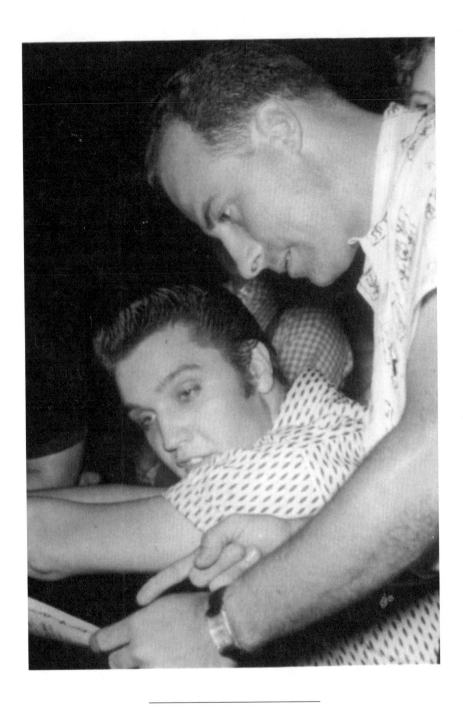

ELVIS AND BOB ROSS, STEPSON OF COL. PARKER, AT LOUISIANA HAYRIDE. CIRCA 1955.
(FROM THE COLLECTION OF SANDRA ROSS)

9

Trying To Get To You

1970

Curiosity is...the head light that keeps us from losin' our way.

—*Elvis Presley*

We arrived in Las Vegas the day after they finished filming *Elvis, That's the Way It Is*. From the moment we got off the plane, I felt like Dorothy in *The Wizard of Oz* when she stepped out of Aunt Em's house after the tornado. Only I wasn't in Oz. I'd landed in Elvisland and the Emerald City couldn't hold a candle to the big sparkle of Las Vegas.

Banners and signs, posted everywhere, announced the Elvis Summer Festival. From the airport where cabs and buses carried his image, all the way to the International Hotel, Elvis smiled and sang along the desert roadside from eye-catching billboards.

When we reached the hotel it was crowded. Fans from all over the world dashed about in their Elvis clothes, wearing happy smiles permanently fixed to their faces. Everybody was talking about *Elvis, That's the Way It Is*. Many of the people we met had been in the movie, and I regretted that I'd missed out and was pea green with envy.

By late afternoon we'd finished checking in and went up to our rooms. My and Lauren's was plush: all velvety in soft shades of blue and beige. I fell on the bed, kicked my sandals off and my feet in the air, and just gloried in the feeling of being under the same roof as Elvis Presley.

"Man, I could get used to this."

Lauren lay down beside me on the bed. "I'm happy you're happy, love. It tickles me to see you this excited."

"You're so good to me, Lauren." I touched his face and sent him a heartfelt thanks with my eyes, then quickly jumped from the bed. "We gotta get dressed. I don't wanna miss one show while we're here."

I bathed while Lauren shaved, then decked myself out in my prettiest tight, black, sequined dress. Lauren slipped up behind me and wrapped his arms around my waist and nibbled on my neck. "Mmmm...I better keep an eye on you or Elvis will leap right off that stage and steal my treasure away."

"In my dreams."

"Love, how can you say that?"

I kissed him and patted his cheek. "I'm only teasing." But I don't think Lauren believed me.

By the time Lynn knocked on the door we were ready. I grabbed the scrapbook I'd made for Elvis and the three of us went downstairs and headed directly for Mr. Shoofey's office, only to find he was gone for the night. There was nothing we could do but get in the long line that already wrapped forever through the casino. Lauren made me mad while we waited in line. He kept saying stuff like, "I'm gonna show Elvis who your man is. You know I can do it too, love."

"Lynn, will you make him stop that? Don't let him embarrass us."

"What can I do, Frances? He's your husband."

I was fit to be tied and prayed fervently for Lauren not to do something outrageous.

When we finally reached the maitre'd', he told us the show was sold out. I couldn't believe it. And I refused to accept it.

"But, love," Lauren said, "they're sold out so we'll have to wait till tomorrow."

"Lauren, please...just let me handle this, okay?"

"Well, all right, but you'll just be making a fool out of your-self."

"Is that what you think? I'm gonna make a fool outta myself? Like you've never made one of yourself? Well...watch me."

I stepped back over to the maitre'd', who'd said his name was Emilio. Then, throwing my shoulders back like I was somebody important, I told him, "Mr. Shoofey promised me seats when I was here before, if I stayed in this hotel. Well, I'm here." Then reaching into my evening bag, I pulled out my room key and displayed it in front of his face. "For three weeks."

Emilio alluded to capacity and something about fire laws, then frowning like he was at his wits' end, he called a waiter over. "Find a place for them." Turning back to us, he said, "It will be in the back. I'm sorry, that's the best we can do for you tonight. Make your reservations early tomorrow."

The waiter motioned for us to follow him and we were ushered to a table near the back of the audience.

The room was packed. We were late. And the opening acts were finished and Elvis was about to come on stage. It was dark and the theme from 2001 sent chills rushing up and down my spine. The seats were arranged in such a way that I could see the stage. But it wasn't close enough for me. I experienced the same mixture of frustrations I'd felt at that first concert, when I was twelve and had to sit in the back row. Still, my heart stopped beating and leaped into my throat when Elvis suddenly made his entrance, reached for his guitar, and started tearing up "Johnny Be Good."

He was wearing a sexy white jumpsuit and a magnetism that reached right across that vast room and snatched me right up against his chest. That feeling hit me in the pit of my stomach like a triple shot of straight whiskey, and I sat on the edge of my seat, straining for the best view possible while screams pierced the air.

I was shaken and in awe of Elvis' performance. Lynn said my mouth hung open and I never batted an eyelash through the first song. He was so pretty. Not in my best fantasy had he ever been so pretty.

When Elvis sang "Tiger Man" the strobe lights flashed off and on, off and on, in rhythm with him like the pulse of my heartbeat ...beating...thumpidy-thump, right along with his hips and shoulder rolls.

Lauren watched me. "You like all that wiggling, love? All that hoochie-coochie stuff he's doing?"

"Hush...Lauren. I can't hear."

"I can wiggle my butt better than that...I think I'll go up there on the stage and show you."

"Lauren...please!"

"I know...you're afraid all these women in here will attack me." I rolled my eyes and he laughed. "I'd make 'em throw tomatoes at Elvis."

"Lauren, stop it! I thought you liked Elvis, so why are you acting this way?"

He saw he was making me angry. "I'm sorry, precious. I won't say nothin' else."

Lynn seemed to be more involved with our bickering than she was with the show.

Elvis continued to belt out one song after another, while I vocally whined.

"Oh...I wish I was closer."

Then he started singing "Love Me Tender"...and kissing the girls seated near the stage! Envy leaped on me like *The Blob*, sucking and draining all my common sense, while I watched women from all over the room leave their seats and head down front for a kiss from Elvis. And I looked at Lauren with determination in my eyes.

"Go on down and get a kiss, precious." I hurried to get up and Lauren reminded me, "Don't forget the scrapbook."

Grabbing the gift I'd made for Elvis, I rushed away from the table and straight toward the crowd that was growing fast at the foot of the stage. When I reached the edge of the multitude, I felt like the ninth little piggy on an eight-tit sow, rooting my way to fulfillment. I was determined. And I think everyone in my way got the message because I made it through and suddenly, Elvis was in my face and on my lips!

Wonder of wonders, I didn't die on the spot! As he started to back away and go to the next waiting pucker, I remembered the scrapbook.

"Elvis, I made a gift for you!"

He glanced down at the book I was holding out to him and

said, "For me?" I nodded my head while my heart fainted. Then he took the book and said, "Thank you, dear," and gave me another kiss. This one was better than the first. I tasted the tip of his tongue as he pulled back from the kiss and placed a blue silk scarf around my neck.

"What's your name, honey?"

"Frances."

"Thank you for the scrapbook, Frances. Where are you from?"

"Tampa, Florida."

"Thank you, again," then holding up my scrapbook for the audience to see, "for the gift, dear. It's beautiful." He handed the book to Charlie Hodge, his right hand stage man, then continued kissing girls and handing out scarves.

I returned to my seat in a trance. I savored the flavor of Elvis on my lips: a unique taste seasoned with soul and myth. The tease of Elvis' tongue served as an appetizer and now I wanted a full-course meal—one I could gorge myself on.

I found it hard to believe my good fortune. I'd received two kisses and a scarf from Elvis Presley, in the flesh, and was paralyzed for the time it took that knowledge to sink into my brain. Then I deviously smiled, and thought, *This is only the beginning. I'm gonna get me a big bite of that sweet potato before I go back home, or stage the biggest show this town's ever seen, trying.*

The next day I woke up with a determination probably unsurpassed by anyone else in the hotel. I was going to have a good seat for the next performance and my sights were set on the one right at Elvis Presley's feet.

I called Eula Mae and we made plans to meet downstairs in the coffee shop for breakfast. Lynn had her own room and Lauren and I would be sharing our double with Sandra when she arrived. Hopefully, she'd make it in time for the late show.

When I thought of seeing Elvis again, I was anxious about what to wear that night. I wanted to look extra special. Blue! That's what I'd wear. I laid out for the evening my silk sleeveless dress, with a lace-trimmed scoop neck, that was blue as Elvis' eyes. Mama had made it for me so the dress hugged my curves in all the right places, but with a decent fit. I decided it would look chic with my hair up in curls.

I showered and dressed for breakfast, then went down to the coffee shop to meet Eula Mae. She was already seated in a booth when I got there, drinking coffee and waiting for me.

We put in our orders and talked over coffee. I told her about the lousy seats we'd had the night before. "But I got two kisses and a scarf from him."

"We'll go over to Mr. Shoofey's office when we're through eating. He did say he'd help you get good seats last time you were here, right?"

After breakfast we took off for Mr. Shoofey's office, next to the entrance of the big showroom. When we got there, the door was standing open and we waved at Mr. Shoofey before entering to talk. Chris Karamanos, the public relations person for the hotel, and two glamorous women were in the office with him. Eula Mae introduced us for the second time and I talked a mile a minute, telling Mr. Shoofey how much I loved Elvis, and reminding him of the stage-side seats he'd promised me the last time I'd been in Vegas.

Well, to make a long story short, we stayed in that office somewhere between two to three hours, talking, laughing, and just having a good ole time. Then Mr. Shoofey told Chris, "Give them my table for the dinner show. Take down their names, Frances and Eula Mae."

Mr. Shoofey leaned back in his chair, clasping his hands under his chin, and just looked at me. Then I said something funny and he cracked up laughing. I was glad he was smiling and returned a big grin back at him.

"Mr. Shoofey, would it be possible for me to go backstage and meet Elvis after the show?"

For a second I wondered if I'd pushed my luck. Then he laughed, and looking at Chris he said, "I like this girl." He looked back at me, "I've never met anyone like you. And glancing at Eula Mae, he said, "She's for real, isn't she?" Then he wrote down a phone number and told us to call at three o'clock for confirmation. I was amazed at how nice everyone was to me and expressed my feelings to Eula Mae after we left Mr. Shoofey's office.

She said, "I keep telling you, Frances, it's your personality. They've never seen anything like you...unless it was on stage."

"Do you think they will remember us, Eula Mae? Do you really think they will give us a good seat and introduce us to Elvis?"

"I don't know. We'll just have to wait and see."

Waiting for three o'clock would be nerve-wracking, so we browsed around the casino for a while, stopping to watch gamblers and taking time to notice the styles people were dressed in.

I asked Eula Mae about the miniskirts. "How do they dare wear them that short? I mean for heaven's sake, their backsides are sneakin' right out from under 'em."

"They wear G-strings under them, Frances."

"What's a G-string?"

"A pain in the ass."

Soon, Eula Mae had to go back home. She said she'd see us in our room that evening before the dinner show, then Bobby would meet us later for the one at midnight. "Call me after you talk to Chris and get a confimation, Frances."

When I met up with Lynn and Lauren back at the room, they wanted to go sightseeing and make reservations for the Charo show that was playing at another hotel. They liked Elvis, but weren't interested in devoting three weeks exclusively to him.

Lynn played the slots at Caesar's Palace. She won three hundred dollars and split it with Lauren. Then he hit for seventy. We had lunch at the Tropicana, made their show reservations, and still got back to the hotel before three.

I remember feeling like maybe I'd missed out on something while we were away from the hotel. I just didn't want to miss it if Elvis decided to come down to the casino. I'd heard that he did this once in a while.

When I called the number Mr. Shoofey had given me, Chris answered and confirmed our table. He told us to stop by Alex's office that evening and someone would take us through the guest line.

"Then after the show we'll have you escorted backstage to meet Elvis." *Oh my stars,* I thought, *this is really happening!*

I called Eula Mae and told her everything was set, it was for real, we were going to sit at Mr. Shoofey's table.

That evening after we were dressed, Lynn, Lauren, and I sat around talking until Eula Mae arrived, then she and I went downstairs to Mr. Shoofey's office. I wanted to get there in plenty of time tonight.

When we arrived at his office, he informed us that two front-row seats were reserved for us at the dinner show and four for the late performance. We'd told him about Bobby and Sandra, and I guess he decided to extend this courtesy to them, also.

Anyhow, we were on cloud nine as we went through the guest line, and while we were being led down to our table, my eyes grew larger with each row we passed on our way to the front. Our seats were center ringside! Right up next to the stage!

I told the waiter who seated me, "Hot damn!...Oops."

He laughed, then informed me I had the seat all the girls wanted. Like I hadn't figured that out. But once we sat down it really hit me, the view these seats afforded. It was absolutely mind-boggling. I was right in front of the mike. I remembered sitting this close in this very same showroom for Tom Jones. But that experience hadn't grazed the impact of what I was feeling now. And I knew that another longed-for dream was about to come true. So I closed my eyes...and photographed the memory and the magic.

"Can you believe how close we are, Eula Mae?" I placed my hand on the stage. "Elvis is gonna stand right here when he sings! I'll be able to reach right out and touch him!"

Eula Mae, tuned in to the same station as me, was surveying her panorama when the waiter came around. He introduced himself as Maurice, then took our orders. The menu held four choices: prime rib, roast capon and wild rice, New York strip steak, and lobster. We selected the prime rib, then were served crab salads on hearts of romaine.

Souvenirs of Elvis had been placed on the tables; pictures, calendars, even the menu was a souvenir. While we were eating our salads, Maurice came by our table and stopped to tease me about having the special seat that was coveted by all the girls. He winked, then smiled while he encouraged me.

"Have a good time. Elvis likes to play with the audience and he always kisses the girl in your seat."

I drifted to fantasyland. *Is this heaven or what?* Entranced, I placed my elbows on the table, propped my chin on my knuckles, and stared at the stage. It was huge. *Wonder how many yards of fab-*

ric that curtain took to make? I thought. I loved the bold, red velvet that covered the seats of the booths. *That must be where the rich and famous sit.* But I liked my seat better. I glanced back to the stage, then reached out and placed my hand on it. *I really will be able to touch him! There'll be no one seated between me and him!* Excitement boiled my blood and I felt like a whistling teapot, about to go off.

In an effort not to squeal, I glanced around the large showroom, studying the Cupid statues that protruded from the walls and ceiling, while I nibbled at my salad. My eyes scanned over the people taking their seats. Women of all ages filled the room. The waiter brought our food, and as we ate, I spotted a few familiar celebrity faces and my excitement pitched to hype.

"Eula Mae, do you feel it?"

"Feel what?"

"The purpose flowing through this audience. Like everybody is here to get a little piece of Elvis."

After dinner, The Sweet Inspirations opened the show with "Creole Lady Marmalade," followed by several other songs. Sammy Shore was next. His stand-up comedy was hilarious, but I was anxious. I knew Elvis would be next.

Finally, the moment arrived! The lights dimmed, my eyes expanded, and I held my breath and watched the side curtain from where I knew he'd soon emerge. Every nerve in my body waited as a chilling buildup of horns accompanied by a heavy drum broke the silence in the dark room. My heart beat; boom, boom, boom, in time with the kettle drums, and the spine-tingling music of Also Sprach Zarathustra crescendoed, introducing the entrance of Elvis Presley—the King of Rock and Roll!

Intensity increased when the music switched to an electrifying fast tempo. Then Elvis magically appeared before my eyes and was quickly handed his guitar, and he struck a pose, sending the audience into a trance.

My breathing stopped and I froze. It was one of those golden moments you try to memorize on the spot. Elvis was right in front of me, bigger than life, and so handsome it just had to be a sin. He had on a clinging white jumpsuit that caressed his perfect body, and a macrame belt with silver decorations sexily embraced his hips.

Being eye level with his feet, I focused on the tips of his bell bottoms, dancing across his white boots. *Wow! His feet are big!* I thought. Then he moved to center stage in a rhythmic sweep, wailing "See See Rider." He looked out at the audience then glanced down at me, smiled, and mouthed me a kiss. I was blown away. The hairs on my arms stood on ends and I was captured, my heart stolen away by the arresting powers of Elvis Presley.

Paralyzed, I basked in the moment, wishing it to never end. Elvis was beautiful. He was perfect. He was the King lovin' his audience and I was the nearest member of that assembly to him. I felt like every song he sang throughout the show was just for me. I relished every pout of his beautiful lips and every drop of sweat that fell from his brow. I knew I had the best seat in the house, but the impact of his presence at such close range amplified it even more. Only an Elvis fan could understand the total bliss of this spectacular view.

My emotions were uncontainable. I gawked, I stared, I shook, I trembled, and then a scream tore from my throat. Elvis glanced my way and delivered a quick, teasing lunge right at me, smiling through the words of his song. I was lost to the people around me, caught up in a world that held no one but Elvis and me, and he met me where I was at.

He ended the song by charging right on forward with a medley of his hits from the fifties. Then he karate chopped his way through some other songs and he was my dream hero come to life. Sweat rolled down his face and I handed him my linen napkin from the table. He reached over and took it, blotted the perspiration from his neck and face, then grinned and wiped the cloth under his armpits and handed it back to me. I stuffed the priceless treasure into my bra and said, "Elvis...I'll keep it forever."

He laughed, then continued to play around on stage with his band. Suddenly, Ronnie Tutt did a drum roll. Elvis started with shoulder rolls, then his whole body took off and purred like a new motor, turning our adulation into a love affair. He was the lover and we were his mistresses.

The room took on a glow when he started to croon "Love Me Tender." Then he paced the edge of the stage slowly, like a panther, teasing in a way that seemed to say, *Who gets the first kiss?*

Reading the message carried by my outstretched arms, he dropped down to one knee and planted a kiss on my eager lips. It was a quick, sweet kiss, electrified because it was Elvis', and if my hair hadn't already been up in curls, that kiss would have curled it. As he moved on to the next girl in the unending line, I licked and tasted my lips, savoring the memory and the thrill of Elvis' kiss, and the way his face looked when it was right in front of mine.

Adonis, Elvis, how beautiful you are, I thought. I knew I wouldn't be satisfied though, until I got a "big ole kiss" from my beautiful, gorgeous, handsome, good-looking, pretty hero. Elvis was addictive. The more I got, the more I craved.

I slowly gravitated back to reality and glanced over at the smile on Eula Mae's face. She'd fallen under Elvis' spell and was now somewhere off on her own planet. I smiled and thought, *No woman is immune to Elvis' charisma.*

The memorable performance eventually came to a climactic close with Elvis singing "Can't Help Falling in Love." The gold lamé curtain dropped, the house lights lit up, and I was already looking for a way backstage.

Maurice brought our check, stamped *complimentary*, and told me to sign my name and room number. I asked him who was taking care of it and he winked at me and said, "I don't know. Perhaps, one of the big wheels?"

I talked to Maurice about going backstage, explaining the promise I'd received from Mr. Shoofey. He said he'd check into the matter. A few minutes later he came back with another waiter and told me to follow him. Eula Mae asked if she could go.

"Just the two of you?" he held up two fingers.

"Yes!" We both answered at the same time.

He led us on a confusing journey backstage through halls filled with smells coming from the kitchen, and as we walked, I dug into my purse for some Clorets gum, popped three into my mouth, and chewed fast and hard.

We got on an elevator and finally arrived at Elvis' dressing room. Our escort knocked on the door. I took the wad of gum from my mouth, and finding nothing to wrap it in, I panicked and stuck it in my purse.

Joe Esposito, Elvis' road manager, answered the door and the waiter handed him a note while conversing in a low voice. Then suddenly, the door shut so abruptly, it felt like a stab of rejection and I thought, *Is this the entrance to Heartbreak Hotel?*

"What's wrong?" I asked. "Ain't we gonna get to see Elvis?"

"Yes", the waiter said. "He will be out in a moment. Just wait here for him." And then he left.

Eula Mae and I stood looking at each other, nervous as two setting hens, wondering if this egg was ever gonna hatch. Then I looked up and saw the door opening.

I was paralyzed, taken aback by the tallness and the Elvisness of the man approaching me. I looked up into familiar blue smiling eyes that matched perfectly the blue, casual, lace-up jump-suit he was wearing, and he extended his hand to me and said, "Hello, I'm Elvis Presley."

As though I didn't know who he was!

Standing frozen to the floor, I stared at him, surrendering to my eyes all the love and fascination in the world. Loving feelings, like stars in my stomach, twinkled up to my head then tickled back down to sting my toes as I held onto his hand, mesmerized and speechless. I thought, *He's more breathtaking, more handsome, than I've ever seen him.*

He was slim, in the best shape of his life. His black hair was styled beautifully—not a hair out of place, and his sideburns were big. His complexion appeared flawless and he was taller than I'd imagined. His lashes were dark and long, his nose perfect and straight, his hands clean with slender tapered fingers that held several diamond rings. A bracelet that spelled out ELVIS in diamonds wrapped around his wrist. He had a rich-clean, look, about him, and I wasn't even thinking money. It was like the clean look that lots of money can buy.

Finally finding my tongue, I introduced myself. "I'm Frances Commee...and this is my friend Eula Mae."

"Nice to meet you, Frances...Eula Mae."

Even with Eula Mae standing beside us, it felt like we were alone. There were no crowds pushing, nor mobs of girls vying for his attention. Just me and Elvis outside his dressing room, where I was drinking in all his magnificence. My legs threatened to fail me as I stood spellbound, staring into deep blue eyes that out-sparkled his diamonds. I trembled under their hypnotic power and all I could say was, "Elvis, I've waited a long time for this. I hope I get a big kiss and your autograph."

He smiled.

I melted.

And before I knew what was happening he gave me a big kiss. His mouth, soft and wet, tasted like he'd just brushed his teeth and drunk water. He French-kissed me, fifties style, soft and wet, and when our tongues touched, I saw stars, heard thunder, floated on clouds, and lightening singed my feet.

I felt like I'd climbed Mount Everest; breathless and exhilarated, and inhaling a deep breath through my nose...I let the magic take me....

I moaned in his mouth and slumped in his arms and Elvis held me up, until he ended our kiss.

When I opened my eyes he was staring down into them and I thought I was going to die right there on the spot. I could see the headlines: GIRL DIES IN ELVIS' ARMS. Then he smiled at me, so pretty.

"Big enough? That was for the scrapbook, Frances. I liked your picture."

"Ooooh, Elvis." I was breathless. "You've been my fascination for sooo many years."

His loving smile at my admission spoke more to my heart than all the beautiful words in Webster's dictionary could have ever expressed. And I thought, *Elvis remembered my scrapbook.*

We talked for a bit but it's hard to remember what we discussed. Elvis' kiss had left me foggy headed.

Watching him, in a daze, autograph the eight-by-ten souvenir picture I'd been holding, was wish number three come true; I'd met him, I'd kissed him, and now I had his personalized autograph.

Then Eula Mae said, "Mr. Presley," and Elvis looked at her funny, "may I have your autograph for my son, darlin'?"

Elvis grinned. "Is your son's name Darlin'?"

Flustered, she said "Oh...no...his name is Bobby."

Elvis signed her picture, then she asked him, "Don't I get a kiss, too?"

Elvis kissed her, but it wasn't like the one he'd given me. Theirs was more what I'd call a respectfully affectionate smooch.

Elvis asked me how long I was going to be in Vegas. He teased me about some of the looks I'd sent him from my center stage-side seat, and asked me with an honest-to-God interest, how I got it. I told him I had begged.

He laughed.

When our visit was over, Elvis hugged us good-bye and said he'd be looking for us again at the midnight show.

And yes, Cliff did kiss like Elvis, but Elvis had his very own special, breath stealing, mentally romancing powers.

Eula Mae and I walked back to the showroom on clouds and I thought, *Next time, we talk one on one, Elvis. Somehow...some way....*

We'd entered the casino and were watching a little old lady dance a jig over winning a big jackpot, when we ran into Bobby and Sandra. I was surprised to see them together, then Sandra explained that she'd just arrived from the airport and when she went up to the room, Bobby was there with Lauren and Lynn.

"Have you seen Elvis, yet?" She was grinning from ear to ear.

"Did we ever!" I shouted.

I told them about our trip backstage where we'd met and received kisses from Elvis, and about the show and our ringside seats Mr. Shoofey had given us.

"Do we have a good table for the next one?" Sandra wanted to know.

"Sure do!" I said, then flashed my autographed picture at her and watched her turn green with envy.

Bobby was blown away when Eula Mae gave him the picture Elvis had signed to him.

We went to the casino bar for a drink and some catch-up conversation while we waited for the showroom to start seating again.

Later, we encountered no problems as we went through the guest line. We were led straight down ringside and seated next to the table we'd had for the dinner show. Sandra and Bobby were quite impressed with our seats.

Before the waiter arrived we voted for champagne all around. Sandra wanted to know if I'd learned any wine etiquette. "Don't go telling the server to just fill 'er on up like you did before, or I'll kick you harder this time."

I loved Sandra, but sometimes she pissed me off when she played mama, or aristocratic bitch, and I usually felt inclined to pump up the harassment.

"I'm gettin' real cultured, Sandra, don't worry 'bout me."

"Yeah, you sound real cultured." Then she gave me one of her famous dirty looks. It was a look that said, *Where's your brains and just who do you think you're fooling?* It was a look that usually set me off, and it was famous because everyone who knows Sandra knows that look.

Eula Mae had been around us long enough by this time to recognize our personality differences. "Now, girls, we're here to have a good time and enjoy Elvis."

Bobby started laughing. "Oh, Mom, let 'em be. They're funny." Bobby was a good-looking seventeen year old who could and often did, pass for nineteen. He said he looked forward to Sandra and me coming out to Vegas because we made everything more exciting. "I never know what to expect out of you two! You remind me of Lucy and Ethel."

When the waiter arrived with our champagne, I listened for the pop of the cork. As he was pouring for the rest of the group, I decided to light up a Marlboro. He whipped out a lighter and raised it to my cigarette.

"A lady never lights her own."

"Well, my mama told me a lady doesn't smoke....Ouch!" Sandra had kicked me under the table, again! "Stop it, Sandra," I yelled, "my legs are gonna be black and blue!"

Eula Mae started to laugh. "I don't know what to do about you two. Don't you ever get along?"

"We've been this way since we were kids," Sandra piped up, "and I doubt we'll ever change. It's the Minton blood in us, that's what it is. We clash."

The opening acts commenced, and there was this spot in Sammy's skit when he sang "Bringing in the Sheaves," where he held out a tambourine like he was taking up an offering, and we tossed our change onto the stage. Then it was time for Elvis! The moment we'd been waiting for. Also Sprach Zarathustra again introduced Elvis, and Sandra lost all her well-bred dignity.

"Damn, Frances, look at me. I've got goose bumps on top of my goose bumps!"

My heart was dancing jitterbug-to-a-waltz when Elvis entered the darkened stage in a spotlight, wearing another white jumpsuit, this one trimmed with beaded fringe. He reached for his guitar and struck that wide-legged pose of his and shook them long fast legs, the fringe hanging from his belt, slapping against his thighs.

Well you can knock me down, step in my face, slander my name all over the place...but, uh-uh, honey, lay off'a my Blue Suede Shoes...."

Our view was incredible. Sandra came unglued and was reduced to a caterwauling female like the rest of us. She screamed and jounced in her seat. "Oh, my...he's good-lookin', Frances. Look at him! Look at him! He's so close, we could just snatch him and take him upstairs with us."

"Oh, yes. Wouldn't I love that."

His music filled the room and made the world go away. And I floated on a feeling, so rapt, I just knew I'd touched the place where angels played. Then Elvis took a break from his singing, and I quickly tuned in to his humor when he walked over to the piano, poured himself a glass of Gatorade, then drank it while joking about what its golden color reminded him of. Suddenly, he spotted the money we'd thrown to Sammy, lying on the floor. He bent over and picked up a quarter.

"Well, I'll be damned. Look here Charlie, now they're throwing money. Hey, Charlie, get over here and help pick this up." The crowd laughed as Charlie walked over and assisted Elvis. "You know, Charlie, this could be profitable."

He joked around a little more, then brought up a subject the whole town was buzzing about. A paternity suit had been filed against him by Patricia Parker. Elvis made a categorical denial of the rumors that he was the one responsible for her predicament. He explained that she was just a fan who had asked him to pose with her for a picture outside his dressing room door. Then he went on to say that had been the only time he had seen her. Tempering the mood, he added, "That chick got knocked up by a Polaroid camera."

The audience enjoyed Elvis' humor concerning the situation, and roared with laughter at his explanation. He laughed too, then walked over to the piano and picked up a tiny little guitar, and grinned.

"When I was a little bitty boy, I had a little bitty guitar." The audience clapped and he just stood, holding the guitar, while noticeably savoring our response. Funny, when Elvis appreciated something, you could read it all over his face. I watched adoringly as he laid the guitar down and approached the edge of the stage and started singing "Love Me Tender." Then suddenly, he stopped.

"Oh, my boy...it gets hot under these lights." He squatted down near our table and with a flirt on his face and fun in his eyes, he said to me, "Can you help me cool down, honey?"

Trembling, I dipped my linen napkin into the ice bucket where the ice was partially melted, then handed him the cool damp cloth. He wiped his face, slow and seductively. "Oh, my boy." He glanced out at the audience, then looking back to me said, "Thank you, dear. That feels better."

Elvis returned the napkin to me and started into "Love Me Tender" again. I knew this was his kissing song and looked into his eyes with longing. My expectation must have been obvious to him because he reached over and kissed me first, then left me to crumple back into my seat, and moved on to Sandra's eager lips.

Bobby stood up and said, "Mr. Presley, thank you for the autograph."

Elvis glanced at Eula Mae then back to Bobby. "You're welcome, Bobby."

Eula Mae couldn't believe he'd remembered her son's name. "I'm glad you remembered your manners, Bobby, and called him Mr. Presley."

I could tell my hero was having fun kissing the unending line of females, while he handed out scarves. Then he stopped and looked up toward the balcony. "I'll be up there later, girls."

I studied him closely, observing everything, and that's when it hit me, full force. *He draws his life from this,* I thought. *It looks like it's heaven for him, too. He really loves his fans and there's no put-on about it. He's for real!*

All my fantasies about him were confirmed. I'd never thought it possible to love him more, but in that moment, I found it was possible. I don't believe there's ever been an entertainer, before or since, who has had Elvis' kind of love for the people who put them at the top. Elvis was one of a kind.

"Love Me Tender" had set an atmosphere of awe that continued throughout the show. Elvis held us in the palm of his hand and he knew it. He serenaded us with "I Just Can't Help Believing," he bounced us with "Poke Salad Annie," and he loved us with "Can't Help Falling in Love." When the show was over and the curtains came down, we floated out of the room, babbling endlessly. I'd been to heaven and would count the hours till I could return.

The next day Lauren and Lynn took a sight-seeing trip to Boulder Dam. I'd had my fill of that damn Dam when Sandra and I had made our trek across country. As far as I was concerned, Las Vegas existed within the confines of the International Hotel. Everything I needed and wanted was right here where Elvis was and nothing could entice me away. I was glad Lauren understood my feelings for Elvis and gave me a loose rein.

Sandra and I went down to the casino and played the slots till we lost all our quarters. Then, while we were strolling around people-watching, we saw the Sweet Inspirations. We approached them, introduced ourselves, and learned their names were Sylvia Shemwell, Myrna Smith, Estelle Brown, and Ann Williams. Sylvia asked us if we had enjoyed the show.

"You have to ask?"

"You looked like you was havin' fun out there." We talked for a while, then Sylvia said she was gonna go hit the blackjack tables and asked if we wanted to come along. We followed her, while the rest of the girls left for other interests.

"Sylvia, you like playing blackjack?" I asked.

"Yeah. I like it too much and there's nothing else to do. That's why I send my money home soon as I get paid. Except for a little bit to play with."

We watched her play a few hands, then, excusing ourselves,

Sandra and I headed back up to the room to take a nap before getting ready for the upcoming evening. We always made a royal treatment of it and pampered ourselves with the works every day. The works included everything from a bubble bath, shaved legs, and a facial, to sweet breath, a perfect coiffure, and clothes that said who we were. All of this topped off, of course, with a walk through our favorite mist of perfume.

While on the elevator, we decided to check out the thirtieth floor where Elvis was housed. As the elevator climbed higher, so did my expectations, and fear.

"Sandra, what if we get into trouble?"

"So...they can't kill us, and if they do they can't eat us, 'cause if they eat us...then they'll have more brains in their bellies than they do in their heads. Come on, Frances. We might be crackers, but we don't crumble."

When we reached the top floor the doors opened revealing a roped off room with two security guards standing near the door. One of them approached us and said, "You girls will have to leave. This is a private suite. And don't let me catch you back on this floor again." He scared the adventure out of us and we hurriedly pushed the elevator button in a rush to get out of there. They might not kill us or eat us but they could sure kick us out of the hotel.

A LOT HAPPENED during our three week stay, and after twenty-six years, it's almost impossible to unravel everything. But certain events stand out in my mind. They are the stories I've told again and again throughout the years. I saw two shows a night, every night, during the three weeks we stayed in Las Vegas.

I recall the first time I saw Priscilla. Sandra brought her to my attention. She was being escorted from backstage to the center booth where, I would soon learn, she always sat. She was accompanied by a female friend and a security guard. Wearing a long black dress with a full skirt, Priscilla was beautiful, and as we sat there admiring and envying her, I remember thinking, *It must be hard to walk in her shoes.* After all, what woman wants to share her husband with so many other women?

Another event I'll never forget happened one night at the midnight seating before Elvis' show started. Sammy Davis, Jr. was seated close to us. I'd always admired Sammy and wanted to let him know, so I struck up a conversation with him. Soon, we were all talking and he invited us to come see his act, compliments of him. I told him I'd love to see him tap dance, but that I just couldn't stand missing one of Elvis' shows, and hoped he understood. He said he did and noted that it was almost impossible to entice the beautiful girls away from Elvis.

Then he did the most unpredictable thing. He stood up next to the table and cut a few shuffles with his feet. "Now you can say Sammy Davis did a command performance for you." His spontaneity and sense of humor were captivating. Sammy was an incredible person and I was touched by the personal memory he'd given me.

Lauren and Lynn made it to another one of Elvis' performances. I'll never forget when Elvis was kissing the girls and he gave me a kiss, and Lauren stood up from his stageside seat opposite me, looked Elvis directly in the eyes, and reached out his hand. Then, as Elvis shook it, Lauren decided to be Lauren.

With his jealousy shining green as a gourd, he said to Elvis, "You know what I'd like to do?" Then he put the squeeze on Elvis' hand.

Elvis just smiled and sang at him, "You ain't nothin' but a houndog." Lauren busted out laughing and sat back down in his seat.

"Lauren! How could you? You embarrassed the crap outta me, squeezing Elvis' hand that way."

"Love, I was just jokin' with him. He's a man. He understands how it is."

"Lauren! Get that smug look off your face."

Everything about those three weeks was wonderful. The hardest part was the daily ritual of sweating out those good seats. After the royal treatment I'd received in the beginning, it was hard to accept when on several occasions we were placed farther away from the stage. I complained about it and was told other fans wanted a chance at ringside. I understood how they felt and instantly checked my grumbling, and was thankful for being center stage, even if my chair was at the farthest end of the table.

Sylvia Shemwell and I often ran into each other around the casino and in the coffee shop. We always talked and eventually developed a rapport. She told me they had a show coming up in Tampa, soon. I promised Sylvia a new hairpiece that I'd style into curls and bring to the show and give her when she came to town.

All good things must come to an end and I was feeling the sadness of those words on our last night in Vegas. I was down in the dumps so bad, Lauren wanted to cheer me up. "Precious, it's not the end of the world. You can come back out here to see him again. When's his next engagement here?"

I was ecstatic! "Do you mean it, Lauren? You would really let me come again!"

"You can bank on it, love. You can have anything you want, you know that. And I'm the only man who can give you everything you need."

Except children, I sadly thought.

FRANCES IN THE 70's.

10

Am I Ready ?

1970

Take the time to do a thing right. Otherwise, why do it?
— Elvis Presley

My head was buzzing with memories when I got back home from Vegas. **Movie TV Photo Stars** was running a contest in their magazine that called for personal stories or experiences with Elvis Presley. *How fitting,* I thought, and entered a cute little story that told of my backstage introduction to Elvis. Lo and behold, I was one of the ten winners. I remember the day I pulled the envelope out of the mailbox and opened it to read:

Congratulations! Your entry in *Movie TV Photo Stars'* Elvis Presley contest has been judged a runner-up winner. Enclosed is your check for ten dollars and your letter is reprinted in our current issue. Sincerely, Diana Lurvey, Editor.

What a thrill! I couldn't wait for the magazine to hit the stands. My story appeared in the March 1971 issue. I bought three copies for myself, then when I told my customers at the beauty shop, they all went out and purchased themselves one and had me autograph them.

One day a customer of mine was looking through a magazine while under the dryer. She'd found a picture of Priscilla wearing the prettiest creation. "Hey, Frances, look at this. You know what you should do?"

"What's that?"

"Copy this design. You're good at sewing and you'd look cute wearing this outfit in Vegas "

What a clever idea, I thought. What better way to get Elvis' attention than to be wearing a copy of his wife's original design? The white miniskirt and fringed top would be easy to duplicate, but what would I do about the sandals that buckled up to the knees? I'd never seen anything like them—they were one of those Hollywood fashion items you didn't find in regular stores. But I just had to have them. They completed the outfit.

I forged ahead and made the skirt and top, then, still unable to find the sandals in any of the Tampa shoe stores, I went to see the man at the repair shop. I always took my shoes to him when they needed resoling, or a new strap, and since I was never above asking for anything, I showed him the picture and he said he would help me.

He cut the leather to make the sandals then, instructed me how to attach the rings and rivets. We painted them white and when they were finished, you couldn't tell the difference between my creation and the one in the magazine.

Elvis' upcoming concert at Tampa's Curtis Hixon Hall on September 13 seemed to be the perfect occasion for me to debut my new ensemble.

When the big day arrived, Alice, one of the girls I worked with, styled my hair down and real big like Priscilla's. Then she went to the first show with Jolynn and me. Our seats were pretty close, about the third row from the stage, but I was spoiled by the intimate seating of Las Vegas.

I wore the white design and sandals and felt like I was Priscilla Presley. I carried in a hat box the hairpiece I'd styled for Sylvia. Jolynn was three years old at the time, and was excited about seeing Elvis, the singer her mama was so crazy about.

The concert sold out and Elvis put on a great performance. He looked drop-dead gorgeous in his white jumpsuit. I got a few good pictures, but even though our seats were close, the range of my camera didn't capture him as well as I'd hoped.

There's a cute incident that stands out in my mind from this show. It happened while Elvis was singing "In the Ghetto." He got the words mixed up and sang, "A runny little boy with a hungry nose," then started laughing. The more he laughed, the funnier it was to him. He couldn't even sing. His giggle box had been turned over and when he tried to get serious, he'd just burst into another fit of laughter, which infected the audience, and pretty soon it looked like he'd started an epidemic. It made a precious memory just to watch him get so tickled.

I have this thing about collecting memories. Some people collect stamps or coins, I collect memories. Later on, when Elvis introduced his grandmother, who was in the audience, I thought, *Another one for my collection.*

When the show was over, Jolynn and I met Sylvia and the rest of the girls in their room at the Hilton Hotel. We had a nice visit and Sylvia loved her new hairpiece. We laughed again at what had happened during the show. Estelle couldn't believe how tickled Elvis had gotten on stage. She said she'd seen him get tickled during other shows, but never like today's incident, and she had wondered for a while if he would ever get it together. The girls played with Jolynn and she took to Estelle's teasing right from the moment they met.

My brother Tommy is very gifted when it comes to music and he'd written a song called "The Piper." Sylvia was interested in it and talked to Tommy over the phone about recording it.

I wanted to take some photos of the girls, but I only had one shot left on my roll of film. I'd used the rest on Elvis. So, I took one picture. We didn't get to visit for long before we had to go back to the Convention Center for the next performance. But before leaving, I told them I'd be coming back out to Vegas in January and would see them there.

The second show outdid the first and, as usual, left me wanting more. Elvis sang a medley of songs, some made famous by other artists. But no matter what the song, he had the ability to make it his own. Such was the confidence with which he performed. I could see his gift of being able to reach another person's heart. He was loved and appreciated by a great number of people he never met, but they felt they knew him by the kindred spirit.

I recognized body talk. It was a language Elvis spoke fluently from the tips of his white boots to the top of his dark hair. Characterizing the incredible uniqueness of the man was a million-dollar smile, accented by a lip and a look, a leg, a stance, a way of holding his hands—sometimes limp wrist. He had a loose-limbed swagger when he moved, a natural rhythm to the beat, a pace that slithered in balance with his faraway eyes, and an overall realness when he teased.

INSPIRED BY ANOTHER remarkable performance, I made up my mind to call Bob Ross before my next trip to Las Vegas. I didn't think it held much promise, but I was ready to give it my best shot.

When I called Bob a few days later, again he asked me to meet him for a drink. I suggested a restaurant for coffee.

We met at the International House of Pancakes on Busch Boulevard and talked about Elvis. Then I plugged some of my brother's songs. Bob strung me along, pretending interest in my conversation while he flirted. I remember thinking, *Does this guy think I just came in on a turnip truck?* But I decided to play along.

We talked about his stepfather, Colonel Tom Parker. Bob filled me in on a few things that were not public knowledge at the time. Col. Tom Parker, Elvis' manager and Tampa's dogcatcher, met Marie Mott Ross in 1935, while she was doing some work for Have a Tampa Cigar Company. Bob (Robert Burl Ross, Jr.) was Marie's ten-year-old son.

As he filled me in on the forties, I already knew Parker had been Tampa's dogcatcher. The Colonel's dogcatcher office had been located on Armenia Avenue, the same street as Oak Grove Jr. High where I'd attended school, and the same street as Protane Bottled Gas Company where my mother had been employed.

Paul Wilder was an editor for the *Tampa Tribune*. He did stories on the Colonel's animals in the early forties and was rewarded with the first exclusive interview with Elvis after he became a superstar. Clyde Rinaldi was a Tampa printer who helped the Colonel during his poorer days. He too was rewarded with large orders for Elvis Presley printing.

Bob told me the Colonel enjoyed playing Santa Claus and called himself the Snowman. This title had nothing to do with the role he played in a red suit, but referred more to his old carny way of snowing people. He promoted country and western concerts at the National Guard Armory in Tampa (Fort Hesterly Armory) in the early forties. Parker was not a real colonel. The title was just an honorary one, given to him by Governor Jimmy Davis. But after acquiring the title, he insisted everyone call him Colonel.

The Colonel became the Grand Ole Opry's advance man for traveling tent shows. Later, he managed Eddy Arnold's singing career. Known for being a one man promoter, Colonel gave his all to his artist. But Eddy hadn't bargained for as much of Colonel's *all* as *all* seemed to entail. When the Colonel moved from Tampa, he moved in with Eddy and his wife in Madison, Tennessee. In 1948, Eddy moved the Colonel into another house he owned in order to get him out from underfoot. Eddy Arnold fired Colonel in 1953.

Colonel Parker had a knack for recognizing talent, so he and Hank Snow created Jamboree Attractions, which became one of the biggest independent booking agencies in the South. It was Oscar Davis who brought the name Elvis Presley to the attention of the Colonel. Oscar had been Hank Williams' manager till Hank died in 1953.

In 1955, Jamboree Attractions booked Elvis in Tampa. This was the concert where I first saw Elvis. It was only a couple weeks after this show that the Colonel signed Elvis Presley to contract.

Bob and I talked a little more, then decided to go to my house and listen to the tapes Tommy had left with me. Bob was hesitant at first about going to my house. He asked questions about my husband. He wanted to know if Lauren would be at home. I told him that Lauren was at work, but that I hid nothing from my husband.

"Lauren sees our meeting as an opportunity for my brother," I told him.

When Bob and I left the restaurant we got into our separate

cars, then he followed me home. Tommy had brought over his reel to reel tape player and had left everything set up and ready to go. But Bob had other ideas. It was obvious from the start that he had no interest in my brother's music, nor in helping me to meet Elvis. He tried to fake it but his blatant advances told the truth of where his interest lay. I finally had to put him in his place. Then I suggested we end the whole thing before my husband became involved.

In the following weeks I found Bob Ross to be a persistent individual, and when it got him nowhere, he dangled idle promises before me. I finally told him I had a single cousin who might be interested, but I was a married lady, and planned on staying that way for a while.

Sandra had separated from her husband and was back living in Tampa. We stayed on the phone a lot, making our Vegas plans. I told her about Bob. "But I don't think his name will do us much good. All he seems interested in is flirting. Why don't you take him off my hands before Lauren thinks something more than Tommy's music is going on between us?"

"What's wrong with him?" she asked.

"What do you mean, what's wrong with him?"

"All men have something wrong with them. So, what's wrong with him?"

"Nothing, except he's married."

"That's all? Well...bring him on over for coffee."

I took Bob over to meet Sandra, and as she put it, "It was love at first sight. Then it was coffee in the morning, coffee and lunch, then dinner, and then he never went home."

I talked about Elvis and my upcoming trip to Vegas with my patrons. I was making a new wardrobe for the trip, but my time was so limited I didn't know how many outfits I would be able to complete before it was time to leave. This was solved by the generosity of my customers, who were more than happy to loan me some of their nicer selections.

"Just bring us back some exciting stories about Elvis."

Sandra and I kept in close touch while planning for our Vegas trip. Bob was showing up at her house every day now. According to Sandra, his marriage was in trouble and Bob spent a lot of time away from home.

Our departure day finally arrived. Hot to trot and ready to fly, Sandra and I boarded the plane, while Lauren and Jolynn waved us good-bye.

ELVIS IN THE SERVICE. CIRCA 1959.

11

I'm Left, You're Right, She's Gone

1971

*I never believed that anything was a coincidence. There's a
reason for everything that happens.*

—*Elvis Presley*

S andra and I flew out to Las Vegas together in January of
1971 for the Elvis Festival. We had big plans and, aspir-
ing to meet Elvis Presley again, we carried our artillery.
This was war! Sandra was banking on her relationship with
Bob Ross to further our advance and I carried Priscilla's dress design, my brother's music, and most of all my positive attitude.

The flight from Tampa to Las Vegas was a blast of merriment
fueled with a Vegas atmosphere. The partying had already begun
for some of the card-carrying, poker-playing, cocktail-swigging
passengers—several revealing their alcohol content to the point of
being cut off by the stewardess.

When we reached Las Vegas and disembarked from the plane,
we were greeted again by signs and banners everywhere, announc-
ing the Elvis Festival. I must say, if you were an Elvis fan, those
signs really got your blood flowing. And so did the obvious competition. We saw so many pretty girls coming to Las Vegas to see

Elvis, Sandra and I looked at each other as if to say, *Reckon we stand a chance? Reckon our weapons are enough?* But, we aimed on giving it a Rebel try.

We took a taxi from the airport to the hotel. The driver pulled up in front of the Las Vegas International and stopped the cab, opened his door, then walked around to help us out and assist with our luggage.

I pushed through the revolving glass doors and missed the opening twice, before finally making it through to the other side. Then I just stood there reeling for a second, and as everything started to come into focus, my ears picked up the casino magic, and the spinning chandelier suddenly turned into a roulette wheel.

"Wow! We're here again, Sandra. Elvis is gonna be sleepin' right above our heads for two glorious weeks. It's just too much to believe!"

"Well, believe it. 'Cause if it's not real, what are you doing in my dream?"

We appreciated our early flight when we saw the long check-in lines. Even so, I still had my doubts whether we'd be settled in before the first show began. It was around noon by the time we finally reached our room, which was just like the one Lauren and I had shared: same blue color scheme and all.

I wondered if all the rooms were the same as I fell across one of the soft double beds. The beige headboards looked like tufted velvet, and a soft, powder blue coverlet that matched the carpet felt luscious. I wallowed all over it feeling rich and beautiful and able to do anything.

I got up and walked over to the huge window. The view was magnificent—a contradicting combination of peaceful mountains and exciting lights. Beyond the landscaped parking area was a city of glamour, surrounded by mountains. Dry, sandy mountains that turned soft magenta in the evenings and early mornings.

In the middle of the desert, Vegas was a world alone and anything could happen here. This would be my home for the next two weeks. I would again actually be living under the same roof as Elvis! You might have even said we were neighbors. I danced a little jig at the thought.

Once we settled in, I called Eula Mae. She said she and Bobby would meet us in the casino lounge between the first and second shows, then they'd go to the midnight performance with us.

We headed downstairs to make our reservations and begin the quest for ringside seats. As we walked down the hall to the elevator, the maids were cleaning the rooms and I glanced inside one. It was pink and red.

So, I thought, *they do have other colors.* I wondered why I always got the same blue one?

Sandra likes to take credit for those first seats, so I'll let her, being as the matter was surrounded by confusion. They were not the easiest ones we ever got, but we got 'em! Actually, what we got was a sort of promise to be relayed to the maitre'd'. We figured they would be ringside, just not exactly where. But we also knew a tip could make them better if they didn't suit us.

Feeling at ease about our viewing arrangements for that evening, we went to lunch, and on our way to the restaurant I looked around the casino and couldn't help noticing the electric atmosphere. Everybody was excited about Elvis and his name was flowing like nickels in the slot machines.

We ate at one of the restaurants in the hotel. I think it was Oriental. Anyhow, after lunch Sandra wanted to explore Vegas, but I wouldn't leave the hotel.

I met some nice people and talked, strolled through the shops, then tried my luck on the pass line at the crap table and won twenty dollars. You'd have thought it was a million the way I carried on.

Sandra got back from her taxi tour of hotels and was pie-eyed, stink-faced drunk, and happier than a fat pig in the sunshine when she located me in the casino and we finally went up to our room.

"Come on, have a drink, Frances. Hell, we're in Las Vegas! Time to party!"

She fixed us a drink, then drew a tub of bath water and filled it with bubbles. "Go ahead and take yours first. I'm gonna give myself a facial. Here...take your cocktail with you and indulge, dear cousin."

"What do you want?" I asked.

"I don't want anything," she said.

"Then why are you being so nice to me?" I laughed.

"Cause I'm drunk on my ass and in the mood for a party. So hurry up in there, and let's party. Gonna get a kiss from Elvis tonight. Yes, I am!"

We finished our beauty treatments and selected our glamour-garb for the evening. I chose the Priscilla design and wore my long mane down, with a hairpiece styled in curls piled high on top. I thought I was lookin' good in my sexy outfit. Sandra, not to be outdone, was a model of petite sophistication in her exquisite yellow silk suit by Lillie Rubin.

We were primped, primed, prompt, and slightly inebriated when we strutted our stuff through the hall and onto the elevator singing, "We've come to see our man." But the second we stepped into the casino, Sandra said, "Okay, Frances! We gotta cut the shit now. We're in public, so act like a lady whether you are one or not!"

We made it through the casino and to the showroom without giving into temptation at the slots. Once we were seated center ringside, I relaxed. It was always a breath-holding experience until these coveted seats were secured. We never really knew we had 'em till we had 'em.

Maurice was still waiting this section and remembered us when we addressed him as Hadji. He'd told us to call him by the nickname during our last trip out.

Looking over the menu, I decided to try something new. When I'd been here before, I'd eaten prime rib every night. I noticed an offering I'd never had before and ordered the roast kappin. My choice brought a look of puzzlement to Hadji's face. Then I felt a kick from under the table, followed by Sandra's informative remark. "Frances, that's roast capon." She spelled it out like a dissected dictionary word, "c-a-p-o-n."

Sandra may have been embarrassed by my mispronunciation, but I was darn right redneck pissed off, at her insinuation that I was a dumb hick. But that was alright. I'd fix her...after all, us rednecks didn't just get mad, we got even. I'd make it my business to research what a *capon* was. Then, I'd find some way to make Miss Sandra rue the day she'd corrected me. I'd fix her vocabulary.

After dinner, we ordered more drinks and got into the spirit of the evening ahead. When the waiter poured my champagne, I did everything right and even allowed him to light my cigarette with no remarks. Sandra conceded to my improved manners with a smile of approval.

The show started, and again we enjoyed the opening acts before Elvis made his quick entrance, wearing another white jumpsuit. *Shoot,* I thought, *I always get blue rooms and white jumpsuits.* Then it struck me that maybe it was a good sign. Perhaps it had a special meaning.

Anyhow, this suit had tie strings across the front, leaving peek-a-boo spaces that revealed the hair on his chest, and I remembered when he was younger and didn't have any. He'd lost the baby fat of his youth, too. But he was the same Elvis—a spoiled little boy the world loved for his charm, his generosity, and his talent.

We loved to humor him, because he was loyal and accessible. I know you're probably saying, *She's already called him unaccessible and now she's contradicting herself.* But Elvis was both. He shied away from the media but never his fans. All they had to do was hang out in front of his residence long enough and they would eventually meet him and maybe, if they were lucky, they'd be invited in for a visit. Everybody knew this. Elvis didn't cut himself off from his fans. He held us to his heart.

Just before reaching for his guitar he kind of froze for a minute, like he was giving us a chance to take in all of his perfection. Then he broke into song and "That's All Right, Mama" had us bouncing in our seats.

"Oh, Sandra, was there ever a prettier man?"

I was beside myself, as usual. Elvis had this never ending effect on me and I lost all couth and caring in the delight of my observations. People seated around us were moved in much the same way, although some were more dignified about it. Not me, I was here to have fun.

Elvis went through several numbers before reaching "Love Me Tender," my favorite part of the show. Does it get any better than kissing Elvis? My mind began to sort through my ammunition bag. What cute thing could I pull out that would make him remember me. But, before I could plunder very far, he approached the edge of the stage, and as I looked up into his face, I just blurted out what came from my heart.

"I'm back, Elvis, and you make me quiver!"

He smiled as he reached down and rewarded me with a kiss. "Glad you could make it again, honey." Then he moved on to Sandra's waiting arms while I wondered if he remembered me.

When he'd satisfied all the girls the length of the song allowed, he moved farther back on stage and began to sing "Something in the Way She Moves." There's a place in this song when Kathy Westmoreland, one of his backup singers in addition to the Sweet Inspirations, hits a high note and Elvis' admiration for her talent couldn't be mistaken.

He licked his lips, exhibiting his appreciation, and squeezed his eyes shut and shook his head. Then projecting his satisfaction to his viewers, he smiled a smile that said *I'm sexy,* and curled his upper lip on one side. Elvis' emotions were regularly displayed by his facial expressions and body movements.

He had a way of puckerin' and poutin' his lips to emphasize hold beats, and he'd whip his hand in circles to the fast ones. And when he conversed with us, teasing between songs, I noticed how he'd run his tongue up under his top lip and across his teeth. Sometimes he'd shake his head and lick his lips, keeping a closed-mouth smile, and that meant he'd hit a good note and knew it. I especially loved his double takes at our audacious actions and, of course, the freezes that were classic moments photographed in my mind.

A great performance ended all too soon and Elvis closed the show with "Can't Help Falling in Love" and the curtains came down.

As we stood up to make our exit I told Sandra, "I'm gonna get to that man again before we go back home. I mean it, Sandra, this is it! It's time. 'Cause who knows if I'll ever get another chance?"

"And how are you going to do that? He's got more bodyguards than the president of the United States."

"I don't know how I'm gonna do it. I'm just gonna do it."

We left the showroom and went to the casino bar and rehashed Elvis' performance while waiting for Eula Mae and Bobby to show up. It wasn't long till they arrived.

Sandra and I were bubbling over, about to pop our corks, while we told them about the show. Bobby was hyped and couldn't wait for the next one to start. We began to contemplate a strategy for good seats. Then Eula Mae grabbed us by the arms.

"Let's go see if Mr. Shoofey is in his office."

But Mr. Shoofey was not to be found.

It seemed our only option was money talk. Big tips spoke loud. So we took our place in the front of the line that eventually grew through the casino. A tip to Emelio got us down close to the stage, then another to the waiter moved us up ringside, two tables away from center. We smiled, smugly, at each other as we took our seats and then relaxed. Another battle won.

We ordered champagne and then took turns at flattery, gushing over each other's clothes and just catching up on everything, while we waited for the show to start. Eula Mae commented on how well Sandra and I seemed to be getting along and said she was proud of us. Bobby, on the other hand, liked it better when we were wild. He wanted to know all the little details from the performance we'd just seen and what pranks we had pulled.

Show time! Another great one that included special little tidbits of a new variety. Elvis opened with "Blue Suede Shoes" then went straight into his next song. When he finished, the applause thundered. Finally, it quieted down enough for him to address the audience.

"Thank you very much. Good evening ladies and gentleman. Welcome to the International Hotel. What's that, honey?" Someone in the audience was saying something to him. "Nah," he laughed, "that comes later." He joked around about the Cupids that decorated the showroom, then he went into a medley of songs from his early days; "Heartbreak Hotel," "Jailhouse Rock," "Don't Be Cruel," and others.

Elvis stopped occasionally to play around with us, and we ate it up. It was this kind of teasing that made Elvis so special. That, plus the way he made others feel extraordinary. When he went into his karate demonstrations, we hollered our approval and he smiled his appreciation.

Elvis was in total command of the room. His voice was incredible, his presentation warm and alive, and it was obvious how much he loved sharing with us. Sandra and I were beside ourselves, flying higher than angels on a windy day, from the kisses we'd received during "Love Me Tender."

As the show came near to a close, Elvis received a standing ovation after singing "Suspicious Minds." Shouts of "More, Elvis, give us more!" encouraged him on for a little longer, then he closed the show with his special love song to us—"Can't Help Falling in Love."

We all went back up to the room for a nightcap, so we could unwind from the high Elvis had left us with. It was a high not easy to sleep on. Like coffee.

The next day I shopped for souvenirs. While I was browsing through some books, I came across a dictionary and looked up the word *capon*. I smiled to myself when I read the definition, and thought, *Do I dare?*

That evening we were not so lucky with our seats. They weren't ringside. But they were still pretty close, so we decided to save our money and war plans for the midnight concert. The cocktail shows were usually the best anyway. Elvis always seemed to be more relaxed and we never knew what he might say or do.

Hadji wasn't waiting this section so when the new waiter came to take our orders, I put my revenge into action. Carefully looking over the menu, I allowed Sandra to go first.

When the waiter was ready for me, I innocently, without batting an eyelash, said, "I'll have the castrated rooster, please."

Sandra looked straight at me through wide, shocked eyes, along with the frustrated waiter who said, "Par'don?"

Then to my amazement, Sandra busted out laughing and continued doing so till she could hardly catch her breath. I thought for a minute she was going to snort, but she didn't, even though I wished it on her.

Our moods were running pretty close to even, by the time the show got going, and again we were blasted away by Elvis as he performed without restraint, his playful mood evident from the start. I'd come to notice the kind of audience he responded to the most, and on a scale of one to ten, tonight's was a definite ten. I wished we'd tried for closer seats, but maybe his mood would carry over to the late performance.

When he sang "Love Me Tender," Sandra and I ran up to the stage and got our kisses. A kiss from Elvis left me ecstatic for the rest of the evening. I thought, *This is wonderful. All I have to do is spend my money for a show and I get to kiss Elvis every time. Colonel, I'm gonna make you richer!*

The waiter came to remove the rest of our dishes. "You didn't like the food?" he asked.

"Oh, it was good, I'm just too excited to eat."

Who needs dinner, I thought? Elvis was a meal unto himself. Watching a live performance by Elvis, and receiving a kiss, was like an affair of taste buds savoring a new and delightful food. I rolled it around in my mouth, smacked, allowed the juices to flow and mingle—slowly experiencing the taste, the flavor, and the rich lingering aftertaste that turned sensation into memory.

I'd pigged out on Elvis and was ready to lick the plate when a standing ovation ended the first show and sent us quickly in pursuit of ringside seats for the next performance. Luckily, we scored.

After a brief intermission spent in the casino, we were back in the showroom, being led down front and center to our favorite spot. We ordered champagne and made a toast.

"To...harmony on this enchanted evening with Mr. Elvis Don Juan Casanova, lover of women, Presley."

We were silly-high and expecting almost anything to happen. But no matter what transpired, I knew it would be another exciting experience, because Elvis was in the room.

As the midnight show got under way, his intro music sent the champagne spiraling to my head as if on a mission to cloak me in an Elvisy billow. Then he made his entrance and my eyes were fixed on him more securely than the buttons on his jumpsuit. Still sipping champagne, I slipped into that world where only Elvis could send me.

He opened with *That's All Right,* then went straight into *I Got a Woman.* Finishing the number, he sniffed. "Thank you. Good evening ladies and gentlemen. Welcome to the International." Elvis sniffed again. "Just have those sudden attacks every once in a while...nothing to worry about."

His side glances, and occasional teases, bolstered my courage and I responded to them, boldly flirting my tail off.

"My first movie song", "went like this. Yeah, that's how it went. Just down the drain, boy, you know." Then he sang *Love me Tender,* and he kissed all the girls, lucky enough to reach him, while he sang.

When I got my kiss, I told Elvis, "Oooh, that was so good."

He smiled at me, and said, "I could do better" and nodding his head toward all the women waiting their turn "if I had time."

He moved on and I lowered myself back into the chair, my eyes feasting on the impossible dream before me. I followed every move Elvis made, absorbing detail, fixing it in my mind. I watched him love his audience with kisses, teases, hugs, scarfs, conversation, and accentuated words in his songs. I stared and I listened.

*"Love me tender...*Just a minute, I'll come over there so you'll get a chance to see me. *Love me sweet...*I was only three years old...*never let me go...*hold it...hey! I always look at the guy...see if it's okay, you know." Elvis was letting the crowd know he checked it out with the husbands before kissing their wives.

Continuing along the edge of the stage, Elvis stretched the microphone cord as far as it would go. "Let go my cord." He reached for lips for as long as he dared, then said "Hang loose" and quickly sent the loud message to his back-up. "Can you end it?" He raised his arms and brought them back down on a heavy finale.

"Whoa! Thank you very much. Thank you." He squinted to look out at us for a long, slow, time, then smiling, said, "I'd like to tell all of ya'll that got kissed, I got the flu."

Someone yelled back, "I'll suffer your flu any time, Elvis."

"See...now that's what I call true devotion. Anyhow, the ones who didn't get kissed, I'll get you later on in the show. I usually make the rounds."

I looked around the room in a brief moment of awareness, and noticed people dancing in their seats, unable to contain the contagious rhythm of Elvis. Screams, sighs, tears, and hair pulling were symptoms of ecstasy displayed by fans who, wearing their passion like the ancient tribesman, gave in to their emotions.

He finished the fast-paced song with more thanks. "Thank you very much."

Then the lights dimmed and Elvis poured emotion into *You've*

Lost That Loving Feeling, sending it directly to my heart, in a spot-light that put me in his trance till he concluded the song.

A little instrumental solo led him into *Poke Salad Annie,* and he entertained us during the song, by exercising Karate. Finishing his exerting song on a heavy breath, Elvis said, "Thank you. Whew! You work your dinner off that way, boy."

It was quiet in the huge room and Elvis coughed. "I'll never finish the show. I'd like to introduce the members of my group to you. First of all, the young gentlemen...back here...they're the number-one gospel quartet in the nation...the Imperials. The ladies that opened our show tonight...the Sweet Inspirations. On lead guitar is James Burton. Now, let's play it James...we are goin' down to Louisiana." And he belted out, *Johnny Be Good.* The song came to an end with Elvis extending a hand toward the guitar play-er, James Burton.

"On the drums is Ronnie Tutt, ladies and gentlemen. Our thunder bass is Jerry Scheff. So he's Tutt, and he's Scheff. Comes out Tutt Scheff any way you cut it." The audience laughed along with Elvis at his joke.

"On the piano is Glen Hardin." Elvis turned toward the band. "Something?" Then he sang *Something in the Way She Moves.*

I saw a cloud of faces wearing a look of rapture and knew this was their moment—a celebration of golden memories being lived out right now, that they would later press into remembrance books like leaves of autumn, preserving them for enjoyment in other seasons.

The song concluded on a thunder of applause. "Thank you. Thank you, Kathy. Young lady doing that high voice, ladies and gentlemen, her name is Kathy Westmoreland. Kathy...." Elvis mo-tioned for her to back him in a brief encore to display her talent. *"Something in the way she moves",* Kathy's beautiful high voice rose behind his, *"I don't need...."* Elvis stopped, smiled, and continued with his introductions.

"On rhythm guitar, ladies and gentlemen, is Mr. John Wilkin-son. John." The microphone squeaked. "Damn you, John, cut out that noise...noise making fool." Looking over at Kathy, he teased, "Kathy, don't warm up, you know, on stage." Then he turned his attention back to his audience. "Our orchestra conductor is Mr.

Joe Guercio, ladies and gentlemen. We'll get this show right, yet, Joe. Might take us two or three months, but we'll get it straight. Joe Guercio orchestra, ladies and gentlemen. They're fantastic. And the guy that hands me my pick and everything...his name is Charlie Hodge. Gimme some Gatorade, Charlie.

Elvis stepped over near the piano to quench his thirst, then fumbled the glass as he went to set it on top of the piano. "Thought I'd knock it over, didn't you?" He glanced at Charlie while directing his words at us. "I don't know about him. Ya'll...watch him when I got my back to him, would ya? You know how word spreads in this town, Charlie."

Everybody laughed.

"I had a record last year that did pretty good. It went like this. *When no one else can understand me.*" Elvis got tickled while singing *The Wonder of You.* And when it ended, I noticed a man full of thanks. It was amazing how many times Elvis said thank you.

"Thank you. Gimme a G, I mean a E. *Well, since my baby left me....*it's higher." Finding the right key, he crooned *Heartbreak Hotel,* then with another thank you, he broke into song. "*Well, you can knock me down, and step in my face....*" Blue Suede Shoes was great.

"Thank you. I did that song a long time ago."

Elvis tested his voice range. "You gotta stand like this to sing it because it's very high." Positioning himself in a daring bent-knee stance, he explained, "If you stand straight up you'll strip all your gears, man." He held the mike hard and blared "Youuuu, you ain't...he cleared his throat. "God-O-Mighty." Then he sang out, "*You ain't nothin' but a hounddog...crying all the time.*"

"Thank you." Elvis laughed at a song request for *One Night.* He finished with still another thank you to his fans. "Anymore requests?"

Someone shouted, *"Teddy Bear!"*

Elvis aroused us to the core of our natural instinct and we were convinced, he was the answer to every woman's need.

My hero turned to his back-up. "Do we know *Teddy Bear?*" Elvis smiled a sneer and hummed around in search of the song, suddenly, brandishing forth the cherished relic. He wrapped up the song on a note of laughter.

"See, we just learn 'em up here when you tell us—we don't know." He grinned and shook his head. "Nah, it's funny, but all kidding aside, we've done so many until...unless somebody reminds us sometimes, we really forget a lot of 'em."

"*Suspicious Mind?* Okay."

Elvis put the strength of his jumpsuit fabric to the test during this strenuously displayed song. He took his stage play seriously, sometimes to the point of splitting the seat of his pants. But not this time. He did his half splits with graceful form and expertise. This performance was definitely a ten and I knew I would never forget any of my evenings with Elvis.

One particular one I won't forget is brought to my mind with embarrassment. It happened while I was sitting at a table directly in front of the red velvet booth where Priscilla sat.

Sandra and I were seated across from each other. I was wearing a long fall over my own hair with a cluster of curls on top. I, at one point, eased back in my chair and somehow sat on the ends of the fall. Sandra said something to me and as I leaned forward to hear her better, the fall pulled loose and fell off my head. When I realized what had happened, I was humiliated, and like the Dumb Dora I was, I shouted my embarrassment loud enough to attract the attention of every ear within range of my voice.

"Oh, my gosh, Sandra, do something!"

She was trying not to laugh at me but it was proving to be impossible. Our seats were jammed together so tightly, Sandra couldn't easily get out to come to my rescue. So, the lady sitting next to me offered her assistance. She stood up beside my chair and pinned the fall back on my head, while Priscilla struggled to hide her amusement as she watched.

Sandra's face was pinched from trying not to laugh but it was a losing battle. She exploded into loud snickers and said, "Frances, I'll bet Priscilla won't forget you."

I was so embarrassed. "Please, Sandra," I hissed, "you're making a scene."

"I'm making a scene?" she softly screeched back, her face really pinched now. "I'm making a scene! If I'm making a scene then you're the whole damn production!"

And so it was that the following days were filled with fun,

fights, fits of laughter, and the ongoing conniving for good seats. I never missed one of Elvis' shows even though Sandra did. One night she opted to see *Hair*, which was playing in the hotel's legitimate theater. I called her a traitor and she told me to go to hell. But instead, I went to Heaven and saw Elvis.

During the daytime I amused myself by cruising around the casino and people watching. It was on one of these occasions when I met Elvis' father. Vernon Presley was seated on one of the blue tufted seats placed about the casino. I walked over to where he was and sat down near him.

Mr. Presley acknowledged my presence with a smile and "Howdy-do," which was all the opening I needed to strike up a conversation with him. He recognized my southern drawl and asked what part of the South I was from.

When I told him I was from Florida, he said, "Lotta pretty girls in Florida."

I laughed at his remark and discovered as we continued to talk that Elvis' daddy had a bit of the devil in him. I remember thinking, *Why, he's a flirt.* We soon discovered we shared an interest in people and made comments back and forth about clothing styles, appearances, and how people acted when they were not aware of being watched. He had a good sense of humor and told me some funny stories on Elvis.

Then he asked me, "So, do you like my son?"

"He's the greatest entertainer in the world," I told him.

His face lit up with pride and as he stood up to leave, he said, "You gonna be around long?"

"Yes, I'm here for two weeks."

"Well, maybe we'll bump into each other again sometime."
I told him it had been nice talking to him and that I'd look forward to people watching with him again.

Another time I ran into Sylvia, and while we were walking through the casino together we saw Fats Domino. Sylvia introduced us, and I told him what a fan he had in my mother. He was a friendly person and told me to tell my mama he sent her a great big hug.

Sometimes, I went to the lounge shows that didn't conflict

with Elvis'. I saw Ike and Tina Turner, and Redd Foxx. Tina was great, and so was Redd, but I thought he was a bit too raunchy for my taste.

Another experience I treasured was when Priscilla brought Lisa Marie to the dinner show for her third birthday. They were wearing long, matching white dresses. Elvis introduced his daughter to the audience with pride glowing all over his face. She was a pretty little thing. *Just like her daddy*, I thought.

WE HAD ALMOST REACHED THE END of our first week at the International Hotel, when Sandra started complaining of bursitis in her shoulder. She went to see the house doctor and was given a shot of cortisone. We thought this would solve the problem. But that evening during the dinner show, she kept grumbling about her shoulder.

I was convinced it was just one of her moods and am ashamed to say I showed little compassion for her misery. I was completely involved with Elvis and had a buzz from the champagne. But Sandra fussed through the whole show till I was as agitated as my mama's old washing machine by the time it was over.

Sandra snatched up the doggie bag she'd saved for Eula Mae's dog, then, as we walked into the casino, we got into a killer argument. Sandra said something, I don't recall now what it was, but she had her head cocked back trying to look down her nose at me, but she was so short her expression scowled up her face like she'd smelled a polecat. And wearing that look of hers that invariably set me off, she said, "I'm not going to the next show with you," and that did it.

Planting my hands on my hips, I glared back at her. "So...do as you please."

She made another sarcastic remark that hit a nerve in me and before I realized what I was doing, I'd knocked her on her know-it-all, highfalutin' ass. The doggie bag fell from her hand, spilling its contents all over her and the floor around her.

I was so bad! I couldn't hold back the hysterics that consumed me, as I stood looking in amazement at the sight she made laying there in her Lillie Rubin dress design, now trimmed in prime rib. I threw my hands over my mouth in an effort to muffle my giggles, but it was useless.

Sandra was disgraced beyond her limit, madder than a wet setting hen and ready to peck my face off. Hers was so pinched with anger, she looked like she had lockjaw from sucking a green persimmon.

She backhanded the trimmings off her dress while trying to stand up, and through gritted teeth said, "You've done it this time! I'm gone!" and she turned around and left with what dignity she still possessed.

I laughed my butt off, never thinking for a minute she meant to go back to Tampa, and went on to the second show without her.

When the midnight performance was over, I went up to the room to check on her.

What I found sobered me up, quick. Sandra wasn't in the room and all her things were gone. She'd left me! I couldn't believe it. How could she do this to me? I understood her anger but we could have worked it out. She didn't have to leave me stranded. I started to cry. I didn't have enough money to stay for the remaining week by myself and panicking, I gave no thought to check out time. All I knew was I had to pay up and get out of that room or I'd be in a real pickle.

"Ooooh...Sandra, if you were here right now I'd knock you on your butt again for leaving me."

I packed up my things, crying the entire time, then started down to the lobby. I didn't know what to do unless I called Eula Mae. But I wanted to stay in the hotel near Elvis. As I got close to the elevator, I remembered Sylvia's room was down the hall, so I walked down to her room and knocked on the door. When she opened it, I was sitting on my suitcase with red swollen eyes from crying.

"Frances, what's the matter with you, girl?"

I told her what I'd done to Sandra and how she had left me. "I don't know what I'm gonna do now, Sylvia. I'm on one of those excursion flights or whatever they call it. Anyway, if I leave early it costs more money. And if I don't leave, I gotta pay for another week here and I can only afford half and I don't know what to do. Shit!"

I was surprised when she told me to come on in, then invited me to stay with her. "But won't the hotel say something about an extra person in your room?"

"It's my room," she defended. "Besides, who's gonna know?" Her reasoning was fine with me, so I moved my things into her room and checked out of mine.

The first night I spent with Sylvia, we clowned around, had a couple of drinks, then took some silly pictures. I styled her hair up in curls and she tried to teach me to sing my favorite song from her group's opening act—"Creole Lady Marmalade." Sylvia got tickled at my attempt at the song. I couldn't catch on to the words and my cracker substitutions didn't seem to work well.

I asked her a lot of questions about Elvis and found out she called him Squirrelly.

"Sylvia, what's it like to sing backup for Elvis? It must be really good for you and your group. It should make you famous."

She said, to the contrary, it would probably be the downfall of her career. "Elvis is the star," she explained. "People come to see him. Don't get me wrong, I like working with Elvis. He's one good-looking man and he knows how to sing. I like performing before the big audiences he draws, too. It does something to you, standing up there on stage before such big crowds. That man packs 'em in. We never have to worry about if people will come, that's for sure. They love Elvis."

She told me about her earlier ambitions and how it had been when the group was starting out together. Cissy Houston (Whitney Houston's mother) used to be with them but had left for personal reasons.

We talked about my brother's music. Sylvia was still interested in recording Tommy's song "The Piper." She had talked to him on the phone when she'd been in Tampa and had explained that although the song would be done with a new arrangement and carry a different sound, it would still be his song. I showed Sylvia some other lyrics he'd written and asked if she thought Elvis might be interested in the gospels.

"Gospel! Yeah, I bet he would be."

So, I stuck them in my purse in case an opportunity presented itself, then Sylvia and I talked some more about Elvis. She showed me some of the TLC (tender loving care) and TCB (taking care of business), jewelry he'd given her.

I told her about my encounter with Tom Jones, and how I'd obtained a kiss and his necktie from him, and with wide eyes that spoke her admiration for the singer, she said, "No kiddin'! Tom Jones is my man!" Then she opened her billfold and displayed a picture of Tom with her and the rest of the Sweets. I begged her for the photo and even though she didn't want to let it go, when I promised I would make a copy and give the original back to her, she finally relinquished it to me. I did have a copy made, but it seemed like every time we got together the picture was forgotten.

Sylvia told me about the rest of the girls in the group and said that Myrna was going with Jerry Schilling, one of Elvis' guys. We were joking around and, just teasing, I told her I'd like to put my shoes under Elvis' bed.

"Hey, girl, you and everybody else." Then she laughed and said, "Who knows? You never know what might happen."

"Yeah, in my dreams."

We finally went to sleep, and in my night visions, I enjoyed what I'd wished for. I dreamed of Elvis.

FRANCES IN SUITE AT LAS VEGAS INTERNATIONAL HOTEL 1970

12

I Got Lucky

1971

The image is one thing, and the human being is another....It's very hard to live up to an image.

—*Elvis Presley*

When we awoke the next day, we dressed and went downstairs to the coffee shop for breakfast.

Around two o'clock in the afternoon, Sylvia and I were in the casino and she was hot at the blackjack table when she got a page to go to the house phone. We walked over together, and when she lifted the receiver and started talking, I could tell from Sylvia's side of the conversation that it was Elvis on the other end.

I listened closely and picked up from Sylvia's side of the discussion that he was telling her to round up the gang and come up to his suite. I mouthed to her, "Can I go, can I go?" But she'd hung up the phone before I could get her attention.

Sylvia repeated their conversation to me, and as I started to ask if I could go with her, she said, "Darn! I was gonna ask him about you." Then she shrugged her shoulders, "Oh, what the heck...come on. If he don't like it he can kick us out. I'd rather be on the tables anyway, but you don't say no to Elvis." Then she remarked that it was early for him to be awake.

"When do we go up," I asked?

"Now."

"Now!" I looked down and gave my clothes a quick assessment. I had on a melon colored, bell bottom pantsuit, and my hair was up in curls. I looked okay, I was neatly groomed, but not spectacular, like if I'd been able to prepare for this big event. If I'd known...oh, heavenly days...I'd have dressed with snazz, something really eye-catching! I knew how to put on the dog when I wanted to.

Startled back from my concerns, I heard Sylvia saying, "Come on. We have to find somebody to spread the word to the others." We looked around the casino until she spotted someone from the group. "Elvis wants everybody upstairs, now."

Priscilla had gone home and as Sylvia expressed it, sometimes Elvis was up and sometimes he was down after her visits. "You never know what to expect till you get there," she said, "but he sounded like he was in a good mood."

Before the full impact of what was happening reached my spaced brain, I found myself following Sylvia into an elevator I hadn't seen before. I thought about all the girls, staying right there in the hotel, who would have given their kids, husband, and next year's salary, just to know where this service elevator was located and where it led.

While we were on the elevator Sylvia teased me. "Well, this is your big chance, Frances." *She has a beautiful smile*, I mused, *big and warm*. Her tips on the rules of no-no's caught my ear. "Just act natural. Elvis hates it when people sit around and stare at him. Says it makes him uncomfortable." Sylvia, aware of my state of mind right then, tried to ease my tension. "Come on girl, you'll be alright. Look at you...got your hair all fixed up pretty."

The elevator came to a stop and we got off and walked past the roped off one that Sandra and I had used the time we'd checked out the thirtieth floor. When we reached Elvis' room where a security guard was standing, he recognized Sylvia and opened the door for us to go in.

I whispered under my breath to her, "I hope I don't throw up on something," then I walked in behind her. We had taken only a few steps into the foyer when I looked up and my eyes fell directly on Elvis! I felt r-e-a-l-l-y tipsy, liked I'd been whammed by a zombie and twisted with enchantment.

He was seated on a yellow sofa watching television, facing in my direction. He wore sunglasses and I thought, *Why's he got those on when he's inside? 'Cause he's Elvis, stupid!* He had on a fancy black coat over a red shirt, with black pants, and a big, extravagant, jewel-encrusted belt adorned his waist. I remember thinking how uncomfortable his clothes looked in the cozy atmosphere. But he appeared to be relaxed in his Hollywood attire.

I stood gaping at him, then remembered I was supposed to act casual. *But,* I thought, *how do I visit Elvis in his private suite for the first time and act like it's ordinary?* I quickly shifted my eyes to the surroundings of the room. Ample windows with drapes pulled open revealed an extraordinary view of Las Vegas. The decor was done in a soft, canary yellow, accented with black. I recognized Red West, a body guard, and James Burton, Elvis' lead guitarist, standing at the bar to my left, and Joe Esposito, who was walking away from the bar toward the back of the suite.

I glanced back at Elvis and he'd pulled his sunglasses down onto the bridge of his nose, and was staring over them, straight at me. Even with the normal sounds of conversation flowing around the room, the silence was deafening. We walked into the living room and Sylvia headed in Elvis' direction and I followed. Then, she stopped in front of him.

"Elvis, this is Frances." She grinned, "You know, the one in the audience?"

He looked at me, a smile tugging at his lips, and said, "Yeah, I know who you are. You're the one likes to get crazy."

I was relieved and comforted by the laughter in his voice. I hadn't really considered how I must have appeared to him during his performances, when I was caught up in the excitement. Now, facing him in his own domain, I felt awkward about my audience participation.

"I'm embarrassed."

"Don't be embarrassed for bein' yourself. That's what I noticed about you out there in the audience...I like it."

Sylvia explained that we'd been together in the casino when he sent for her. Elvis, in a good mood and wanting people around him that day, said, "It's okay." Then he patted a place next to him on the sofa and told me to sit down. In a trance, I sat beside him. Sylvia took a seat in a black stuffed chair near us and Elvis went back to watching his movie.

I can't believe this, I thought, *I'm sitting next to Elvis watching TV.*

I felt his aura—a captivating air that seemed to drift over and settle around me, drugging and pulling me into a fog. Struggling to hold onto a grip of reality, I noticed people milling around the bar area and going back to another room, which I would later learn was the dining area. Estelle and Myrna played cards at a table nearby. Suddenly, the sound of a voice caught my attention and I realized Elvis was speaking to me.

"I said...do you want something to drink?"

I jumped in my seat. "Oh...Yes...Thank you."

"What would you like? A mixed drink? Coke?"

Staring at him, I'm sure with swooning eyes, I said, "Coke, thank you."

"Coke it is."

He got up from the sofa and went to the bar to get my Coke. I was astonished that he'd gone for it himself instead of having someone else extend the courtesy.

While he was away, Sylvia leaned forward in her chair and whispered. "I'll mention you want to see the rest of the suite when I think the time's right, and if he takes you on a tour of it, then the rest is up to you, girl."

I didn't catch her meaning at first. Then I remembered telling her that I'd like to put my shoes under Elvis' bed. I found it hard to believe it could be so simple, though. Surely Elvis didn't take just anyone to bed on a whim. If that were the case, I supposed he'd have no need of ever getting out of bed. It did seem he was showing unusual interest in me and this confused me. Here was a man who commanded attention...I mean this was Elvis, staring at me when I'd entered the foyer, then patting the sofa for me to sit beside him, and personally going for my Coke. So, how did it figure?

Your imagination is working overtime, I told myself. And what if he did offer a liaison? What would I do? This question shocked me as it posed fantasy against reality. To fantasize was one thing, but to act upon that illusion was a whole new "real" thing. Metaphorically speaking, as I cast myself into the role I played in my dreams, Elvis' unlawful good looks made me feel not like Priscilla, but more like her lady in waiting.

Elvis returned with my Coke, handed it to me, then removed his glasses and his eyes penetrated mine. Suddenly, I was drowning in a sunny blue sea that sparkled reflections of light. The corner of his mouth tilted up and he sat back down beside me. I noticed he'd removed his coat and admired the puffed sleeves on his red shirt. Getting past the nervous lump in my throat, I worked up the courage to tell him, "I like your shirt. Especially the sleeves...you look real hot in red."

He threw his head back and laughed. "I look hot?"

Then he slipped his glasses back on and returned to watching the movie. Elvis puzzled me. Everything puzzled me. And why did I feel like I was on exhibition? A world of emotions battled inside me while confusion and crazy thoughts danced through my mind. It was a real challenge, keeping my nerves intact enough to hide my discomposure.

As we sat watching the movie, I realized I'd seen it before. *The Roman Spring of Mrs. Stone*, starring Warren Beatty and Vivian Leigh, held no interest for me when I was sitting next to Elvis Presley! I wanted nothing more than to just turn around on that sofa, face him, and stare hard enough to suck in everything about my pretty idol. Maybe even lick his face. I fantasized doing such a thing, while I sat there like somebody with an itchy butt yearning to scratch but, bound by rules of etiquette, couldn't. *Alas, no scratching, no gawking, and no licking faces. I must fit in*, I thought. I tried to fix everything in my mind so that I'd never forget one moment, and silently, I prayed for my insides to calm down. *My dream has come true!*

It was fun observing Elvis while he watched television. He commented on everything and it wasn't hard to figure out what he liked and didn't like. He made jokes, he laughed, he critiqued, and when he was bored with something he got up and strolled out of the room for a few minutes, then came back. The first time he did this, I wondered if he would return at all. But in just a minute or two he was back, wearing a different belt, and brought it to our attention by grasping it with both hands and looking down at the buckle. "What do you think of this one?"

After several of his trips, I finally caught on that he was doing a fashion show of belts for us. Another thing I noticed when Elvis entered the room was how everybody went stone-cold dumb until he spoke. I felt like I was in the presence of royalty. It was so blatantly obvious that Elvis set the mood of the room and the people in it. Even when he said something funny, it was like everyone laughed on cue. And I knew I had met a King—a beautiful, pampered, little boy King. And I loved him.

After each change of belts, Elvis sat back down beside me on the sofa and casually asked me questions. "What part of the South are you from?"

"Florida," I answered. "Tampa." I wanted to say something clever to let him know his conversation was appreciated. But he'd removed his glasses again and as I looked into friendly, blue eyes, contemplating what I could say, suddenly the matter was out of my hands. Joe Esposito approached him about something. When Joe left, Elvis went back to watching television.

I still wasn't interested in the movie, and glancing around the room, I noticed a tiny record player sitting on the floor to the left of me. It struck me funny that someone with Elvis' wealth would have such a dinky little record player and I couldn't help giggling to myself. Elvis glanced over at me as if to say, *What do you see funny in that scene?* I shrugged my shoulders at his expression and said, "Don't mind me, I'm just that way." Then I thought to myself, *What a dumb thing to say, Frances.* And by the look on Elvis' face, I was wondering if he was thinking the same thing.

Time for another belt change. Elvis left the room singing to himself. I loved listening to him sing that way—under his breath with no musical accompaniment, just singing for the fun of it, to himself, to anyone listening, so natural. I loved it!

Sylvia looked in my direction and asked, "How's it going?"

"I'm so nervous I can't think straight. Does it show?"

Before she could answer me Elvis walked back into the room sporting another belt. He was still singing to himself when he came to an abrupt stop in front of us. "What ya'll talking about?"

"Frances was just telling me how much she'd like to see the rest of the suite," Sylvia piped up, while looking my way and grinning.

Oh, Lord, not now, I thought. *My insides are shaking like Elvis' legs*. But I said nothing.

Elvis looked at me with a devilish grin on his face, reached for my hand, and pulled me up from the sofa. "Come on, I'll show it to you." I set my drink down on a nearby table and let him lead me on a tour of the suite.

We went into a room where a number of people were gathered and Elvis introduced me to his daddy, his stepmother, Dee, and one of his stepbrothers. (I'm not sure which one.) When Vernon and I were introduced, he was holding a toothpick in his mouth.

"How ya doin'? Been doin' anymore people watchin'."

"Yes, sir. All the time, when I ain't doin' something else. It's nice to see you again."

Elvis looked curious. "Ya'll know each other, Daddy?"

Vernon twisted the toothpick around in his mouth, then pulled it out. "Yeah, we met down in the casino. We was both watchin' people lose their money."

I met Charlie Hodge, Joe Esposito, Red West, James Burton, Ronnie Tutt, Elvis' drummer, some of the Imperials, and I'm sure there were others. It's just hard to remember, what with Elvis holding onto my hand. I was truly—and without a doubt—spaced. I do remember that some of them were getting ready to go somewhere. Vernon and Dee and her son were among the ones who were leaving. People were constantly going and coming, like at a party.

Elvis and I continued our tour of the suite, and as he pointed out each room, my attention focused instead on the smooth sensation of his hand that was holding mine, and I was lost in the power of his touch. The electricity he generated warmed my palm and my hand began to sweat. I was in his aura again and everything but Elvis was swallowed up in a mist.

When we reached his bedroom he let go of my hand and I stood frozen, just inside the entry, my eyes taking in for a moment the massive bed, set upon a raised dais. Staring at that bed, and its implications, zapped me with a dose of reality. I was in such an overwhelmed, emotional state, I only got a quick glance before I spun around and bumped into Elvis, standing right behind me. He stood his ground, looking down at me over his glasses with eyes that I knew could see right through me, and I almost lost it. My nerves were peaked to the point of nausea. And I was scared.

Then I felt his aura, pulsing like a live thing and it was so personal. I couldn't talk. I felt self-conscious and shy. *Where is all my mettle when I need it?* I thought. I wasn't morally able to handle this situation, not to mention this was Elvis Presley; so beautiful, so perfect, so married, and I was so married, too, even if I hadn't mentioned it and wasn't wearing my wedding rings. I'd been afraid Elvis, maybe, wouldn't be tempted to flirt with a married lady the same way he might with a single one. And I just knew Elvis was a flirt and doubted not that he knew what women wanted to hear.

He'd removed his glasses and was staring into my eyes while all these thoughts wrestled through my brain. I had set this man atop a pedestal for almost sixteen years. He was my hero, and in my mind, his perfection was unequaled by that of any other living human. His charisma was overpowering and I felt insignificant by comparison. Reality has a way of dumping cold water on a fantasy.

I didn't want anything to change and I knew if I went through with this it would change things. I was sure that in my state of mind, I would fail to live up to his expectations, and I wanted no failures. What I craved was to retain the mystery and keep my hero, but grab all the accessories of my fantasy and hold on to them forever. I wanted all the foreplay; the fulfillment of things I'd wished for, hoped for, and dreamed of. These revelations were unveiled in my mind in moments that seemed like eternity.

I was conscious of the uneven hammering of my pulse under the steady gaze of his blue eyes looking right into mine as if he could read my every thought. All my nerve ends tingled under the scrutiny of those eyes. *Oh, God! He can read my mind.*

Elvis bent forward and I felt his breath on my face when he lifted my chin, softly kissed me, and said, "It's all right, darlin', I understand." I felt like he really did, and it made me feel special, like he was seeing me in a different light than the one he viewed from the stage.

Elvis was singing a gospel song under his breath as we walked back to the living room and I thought of Tommy's songs. "Elvis, you like gospel music a lot, don't you?"

"It's my favorite. It relaxes me...you know."

I told him I had some gospel songs in my purse that my brother had written. Seeing by the look on his face that I'd piqued his interest, I went on to explain. "Tommy wrote 'Dark Is My Only Color' while he was in the hospital. He'd just gone through two life-threatening surgeries, within two days' time, and came close to dying."

When we reached the living room and sat down on the couch, Elvis asked me if he could see them. "Sure," I said, then opened up my purse and pulled out the songs. He looked them over and selected two that he said he really liked. "Dark Is My Only Color" was his favorite and his second choice was "He Drank a Little Wine."

He asked if he could have Tommy's phone number. He said he wanted to talk to him about recording them on a gospel album he was considering. I gladly gave him the number, and he went directly to the phone and tried calling him, but there was no answer. Elvis said he would try again later and put the phone number away. I was thinking, *Tommy, you don't know what you just missed.*

Sylvia and another girl I hadn't seen before were watching television. No one else was in the room when Elvis and I returned and sat on the sofa. We talked about Tommy's music.

"My brother looks like you, Elvis."

He laughed, "I've heard that one before."

"No, not that way. I mean...not by imitation. He doesn't try to imitate you, Elvis. He just has certain features like yours. Kinda like this guy I went to school with, Cliff...that's his name. It's almost freaky how much he reminds me of you." Suddenly, I realized I was babbling and tried to think myself into calming down. *Get hold of yourself, Frances. This is really happening!*

We talked about religion, comparing our Assemblies of God backgrounds. Then Elvis asked me about my family and seemed interested in Papa Minton, my grandpa, who I'd chosen to discuss as a diversion from my marriage. I couldn't get over how relaxed I'd become. Elvis was easy to converse with if I pretended I was talking to his picture—like when I was a teenager.

"How long you been a fan of mine?"

"Since the first time I heard you on the radio, Elvis...when I was eleven years old. I fell in love with you that day and I hadn't even seen a picture of you. But once I did, I talked to it."

"You talked to my picture?"

"Uh huh, I talked to your picture. All the time."

Elvis didn't say much after I told him he was the one I confided in. He just seemed to be psyching out the nature of my spirit by encouraging me to talk. I told him about the vow I'd made to him when I was thirteen, and thanked him for always having been there for me. His eyes took on a look I couldn't figure out. But, as complex as his expression was, my spirit identified with it and that confused me.

Suddenly he smiled his crooked smile, reached over and gave me a quick hug, then planted a kiss on my forehead and leaped up from the sofa and left the room. Sylvia looked over at me and said like an announcer, "Elvis has left the building!"

"He's gone!" I moaned, wearing my disappointment.

"That was a joke, Frances." She pointed toward the back room, "He just went back there." I breathed a sigh of relief and Sylvia laughed. "You got it bad, girl. He does it to 'em all."

I laughed with her and we were still going strong when Elvis came back into the room. "What's so funny?" he asked.

We tried to stop snickering but couldn't, so Elvis joined us, then wanted to know what the heck we were laughing about. Sylvia's eyes were squeezed almost shut when she said through her giggles, "Just being around her...is funny."

Elvis collected himself, then went over to the bar and telephoned home. I couldn't help overhearing some of his conversation, and I realized he was talking to his daughter, Lisa Marie. I heard him say good-bye, and he had barely hung up the receiver when the phone rang again. It was Lisa Marie.

They called back and forth a number of times before Elvis came back into the living room where Sylvia and I were sitting in chairs placed side by side, with a little space between them. The other girl in the room, I never did learn her name, was sitting alone in a straight-back chair against the wall directly across from us. She never said anything. She just sat and stared at us. Elvis walked over to Sylvia and me, dropped to his knees between us, and put an arm around each of our necks. Then he pulled our heads together and whispered, "She's nuts."

I thought he was teasing with Sylvia, but then Sylvia said, "Elvis! That's not nice." I glanced up toward the girl and she was still sitting there, staring at us. *I thought to myself, somebody should have told that girl it's not polite to stare.*

Elvis whispered, but loudly, "She's not all there." Then he lowered his voice. "One of the guys brought her up to my room once...but she couldn't handle it. She was so nervous...she threw up all over herself. I had to give her one of my pajama tops to wear. Man, what a turn off...puke everywhere."

I could see this was funny to him and was glad he didn't know how close I'd come to doing the same thing. Or did he?

I said softly, "You're not supposed to whisper like this in front of people."

He smiled, a twinkle of mischief sparked from his eyes. Then he looked at the girl, "You're nuts, aren't ya, honey?" The girl nodded her head up and down and Elvis cracked up. He fell on the floor and laughed.

I thought his actions were insensitive and was disappointed for a moment. Then, that old nature of forgiving Elvis for being human, and loving him unconditionally, melted my heart.

Later, when we were talking, I came to discern better the way things were when Elvis said, "You understand how it was in there, doncha? I mean, with that girl? I was only teasin'....Man, if you're stale all the time life gets borin'."

"Elvis, you can't do any wrong as far as I'm concerned. I'll always find a way to defend you."

"Us all would?"

He was teasing me and I laughed at his exaggeration of my drawl. "Us all sure would...Elvis, why do you tease me 'bout the way I talk?"

"Because you make me laugh, honey."

He walked over to the little record player that had intrigued me earlier, bent down, and put on a record. The song, "Rags to Riches," was his, but I'd never heard it before. I asked him about it and he said it was a demo that hadn't been released yet.

While we were listening to the record, Elvis asked me if I'd be coming out in August for his next engagement. "I'd love to," I told him, "But I don't know if I can afford it. And then there's my job."

"You work? What do you do?"

"I'm a hairstylist."

He touched my curls. "Did you do this?"

"Yes."

"I like it. You do good work."

"Thank you." Elvis looked at me, hard, like I was a newspaper and he was reading me.

"Frances, if you want to come here again...just do it. Everything'll work out."

"But..." I started, and before I could finish my sentence...he spoke.

He said, "You just gotta have faith, honey."

Elvis was fidgety, always drumming his fingers on the arm of the sofa, and getting up and down from his seat. "Man, I wish I could go downstairs for a while. Just get out of this room."

"Why don't you disguise yourself?"

"It doesn't work. I've tried it. Sometimes I think they can smell me." I thought about what he said and figured he was right. I was sure I could have smelled him out.

Elvis asked us if we wanted something to eat. "Do they have collard greens and black-eyed peas?" I teased.

He cast a double-take smile at me. Then, looking toward Sylvia, he said, "Now there's a girl knows how to eat." He looked back at me. "Nah, those people down in the kitchen don't know what's good." He told Sylvia to call downstairs and put in the orders. She ordered shrimp but I declined. I couldn't have held anything on my excited stomach. Besides, I'd be eating at the dinner show.

The food arrived and right behind it came a man carrying a black bag. Elvis went to his room and the man followed him. I asked Sylvia who he was and she said he was Elvis' doctor. I raised my eyebrows in question.

She smiled, "He's gonna give Elvis his vitamin B shot." I felt like something might be going over my head, but wasn't sure I wanted to know the answer.

Kathy Westmoreland arrived with some of the other band members. Sylvia introduced us, then everybody talked, told stories, and joked around while they ate.

Most everyone had finished eating when Elvis came into the dining room. Sylvia was nearly done when he stole a french fry off her plate. "Hey, get outta my food!" She looked at my funny expression. "You have to watch your plate around him."

Elvis laughed at her, made some remark about her smelly ole shrimp, then checking the time, said "Gettin' about that time." Everybody started moving and talking.

"Time to get to work."

"Where's so and so?"

"What's so and so doing?" I watched, and thought, *It's like a well-organized little ant farm, everyone taking care of business.*

Sylvia said it was time to go and I hated to leave. I had never enjoyed myself so much in the twenty-seven years I'd been living. Besides getting saved before I died, an afternoon with Elvis topped the list of things I wanted to experience in my lifetime, and it was about to end.

Sylvia must have known what I was feeling when she said, "You'll see him again, Frances." On our way back to the room she told me there was something going on between Kathy and Elvis.

"Everybody knows it. Just watch 'em when they're around each other."

*Hmmmm...*I thought.

As we readied ourselves for the evening ahead, I took my hair down from the teased curls and brushed it out. I'd planned on wearing another hairpiece I'd already styled before coming to Vegas. But my hair looked so pretty down. It was long and the back-combing had given it plenty of volume. The curls dropped into soft waves that fell down my back. I thought, *This is how I wished it had looked when I was up in Elvis' room.* So, forgetting about the static electricity that abounded in the hotel and the effect it would have on my hair, I wore it down.

We finished our grooming and headed downstairs and backstage to the Sweets' dressing room. The rest of the girls were already there when Sylvia and I arrived, and the door was open. Elvis was standing near the doorway when we walked in and the minute he saw me, he busted a gut laughing and wasn't even polite about it.

I couldn't figure out what was so funny. Elvis was doubled over holding his stomach and struggling through his laughter to speak. "You look like Baby Jane."

Puzzled, I said, "Baby Jane?"

"Yeah, you know, Betty Davis in *What Ever Happened To Baby Jane*." He was laughing so hard he could barely talk. "Your hair is sticking out all over the place!"

When I saw myself in the mirror, I started laughing, and took a brush from my purse and tried to tame my mane back down. But, my nickname had been established, and from then on I was Baby Jane.

Everyone stood around, mingling and talking in the dressing room before the show started. Of course, I hung as close to Elvis as was possible without being too obvious a pest. Anyhow, we were talking about something when suddenly, I looked up at him and without even thinking, I said, "Where did you come from, Elvis, and how did you get so pretty? There's no one like you."

His eyes loved me for what I'd said. Then he laughed, "And there's no one like you, Baby Jane. You're an original."

I didn't know why he thought that, unless it was my tenacity he was referring to. But it made me happy. Elvis always made me happy. Everything he said was another golden nugget, lovingly deposited into my memory bank.

FRANCES AT STARDUST HOTEL. LAS VEGAS 1975.

13

Too Much Monkey Business

1971

Gossip is little talk for little minds.

—*Elvis Presley*

I left the dressing room, went out into the audience, and was seated two tables away from center, but still next to the stage. There was a lady and her daughter seated directly across from me and we introduced ourselves and started talking. Her name was Jo Necessary. Her daughter, Sherry, was about eleven or twelve years old. I commented on the rhyming and uniqueness of her name.

"No one could ever forget a name like Sherry Necessary."

As we talked, I found it difficult to govern all my enthusiasm and told them I was staying with Sylvia. "She took me up to Elvis' suite today and he was wonderful to me."

They were captivated by my "to be envied" narrative. Jo told me they loved Elvis, and that they lived in Oklahoma, and how hard it had been to save up the money for their trip to Vegas. She hinted it would be nice to go backstage and meet him. I liked her at once, and I guess that's why I overstepped myself and boasted.

"Well, maybe I can get you backstage to meet him."

I knew this was a no-no, and realizing I'd just overloaded my mouth with promises I had no right to offer, I immediately regretted what I'd said. But my pride wouldn't let me back down. I was hoping Sherry Necessary's name would win Elvis over and save my hiney.

We had fun during the show. Elvis teased us a lot and when he started kissing and got to our table, I told him Sherry's name. He seemed intrigued by it and I was feeling a little bit better about the situation I'd boxed myself into. But I didn't stop worrying. I knew my hiney wasn't saved yet.

When the show was over I bravely forged ahead and led Jo and Sherry backstage. Amazingly, the security guard recognized me and allowed us to pass on through. I prayed under my breath the whole way. When we reached the dressing room Sylvia was a sweetheart about the situation. She didn't reprimand me or anything, just started talking to Sherry.

Elvis came to the dressing room carrying a glass of water in his hand. He stepped into the room while talking to a couple of the guys that were with him. He was touching his lip.

"She bit me! That girl bit my lip! Man...they get c-r-a-z-y wild out there."

I thought Jo was going to pass out when he approached us and I introduced them. Elvis flashed his charismatic smile at Sherry. "That's some name you've got." She was a child, and the adoration shining from her eyes instantly won him over.

They asked him for autographs and as he signed their pictures, he looked over at me and said, "You want one, too?"

"I already have one, Elvis, that you signed the first time I came backstage. But since you're offering, could I please have one for my girlfriend? Sign it to Janice."

He signed the picture as I'd requested, then, when he handed it to me I said, "Oh yeah, I forgot, can I have another one for Betsy? She's the daughter of a friend of mine."

Elvis smiled, a tease in his eyes. "Anything else, Baby Jane?"

"That's a dangerous question. But...it would be nice to have another scarf."

He told someone, I can't remember who, to get him one of the previous Summer Festival promotional scarfs. When it was brought to him he handed it to me. "Here ya go, darlin'."

Jo had a tiny camera concealed in her purse and asked Elvis if she could take some pictures. He said, "Yes," and she took some of all of us with him. This was a thrill because cameras were not allowed in the casino or showroom, so I never had one on me when I was around Elvis. Sadly, she wrote later, and told me something had been wrong with her camera. None of the shots turned out.

While everyone was mingling and talking, I explained to Elvis about bringing Jo and Sherry backstage. "I just couldn't help it, Elvis. "It seemed *necessary*."

"Well, I think we should hang you." My heart started pounding and it must have showed, because he busted out laughing. "That is an unusual name. I've never heard it before and I thought I'd heard 'em all." I guess he knew I was worried and waiting for a pardon for bringing someone backstage, because his eyes went soft.

"It's alright," he said.

"Thank you, thank you, thank you!"

He looked at me like I'd lost my marbles, and again, he busted out laughing. "You're crazy!"

"I know," I told him, "but I'm grateful, too."

"You're a riot, Baby Jane."

"Is that bad, Elvis?"

His laughter calmed down some, but he was still smiling. "Nah, you just make me laugh."

We continued to talk, and being curious, I asked him, "What's your secret, Elvis?" He looked at me strangely, like he was trying to decide whether or not to answer my question, then his mouth broke into a slow smile of resignation—that instantly transformed into his love-me-tender smile.

"Give 'em what they want, Baby."

"You know, I'll probably write a book about all of this one day."

Suddenly, his expression changed. "You're a writer?"

"No, but it's always been my dream."

He studied me for a second or two, then shook his head and laughed. "Well, don't write a book about me till I'm dead...then write one that'll bring me back to life." Elvis laughed again, as though it were a joke. I remember thinking, *I guess I'm too funny for him to take seriously.*

He told me he'd thought about writing a book himself, "But I don't think it will ever happen. There's too much goin' on in my head. Being Elvis Presley is a full-time thing." I was hanging on every word and I could tell he knew it.

As showtime drew near, Jo and Sherry said their good-byes and left for their room. They were leaving to go back home the next morning. But before they left, Jo thanked me. "I'll never forget you for this, Frances." She asked for my address and promised to write. "I'll send you copies of the pictures when I get them developed."

That night after the midnight show we all partied at the Stardust Hotel. My memories of that night, and who "we all" were, are foggy. Between the champagne at the last show and the drinks that followed, I somehow got separated from Sylvia. Later, when I went back up to the room and knocked on the door, I got no answer. I knocked and knocked, but to no avail. I finally went downstairs and spent the night in the ladies' lounge.

There was a pink daybed in the restroom at that time and I piled up on it and tried to go to sleep. But people were constantly coming in and out and staring at me. Finally, the lady who attended the bathroom facilities moved her chair close to where I lay and said she'd watch out for me, and I managed to get a wink or two of twilight sleep.

When daylight came, I called up to the room but Sylvia didn't answer. It was late afternoon before I finally got through. Then, she apologized for forgetting about me.

"Come on up, now," she said.

I understood how she could have forgotten. It was easy to lose track of time. Especially with those heavy blackout drapes closed. Even days were hard to keep up with. I'd woken up several times without knowing if it was day or night until I called down to the front desk and asked.

The next day went pretty much the same as the day before, except we didn't go up to Elvis' suite. We went down to the casino where Sylvia again chose to try her hand at the blackjack table. I stood watching as she fought a losing streak.

I had told Sylvia about Eula Mae's dog when I'd explained why Sandra was carrying a doggie bag when I pushed her down. So, I cracked up when she said, "Damn, the way my luck's running, girl, you better save your prime rib leftovers for me instead of that dog."

I knew she was teasing, but when I said, "Okay," I'm sure she thought I was fooling, too.

Later that evening when we were backstage, Elvis asked me, "How'd you come to be staying with Sylvia?" I explained about Sandra and how I'd knocked her down in the casino.

"Then she abandoned me, Elvis. And Sylvia took pity on me and let me stay with her. Otherwise, I'd be sleeping in the parking lot."

Elvis thought this was funny. "You knocked her down in the casino?"

"Yeah. I know it was bad, but she shouldn't have left me. She's my cousin and I don't think family should abandon family."

"Well...what did you expect after you knocked her down?"

"I know. Oh, well, if it hadn't been for her leaving me I probably wouldn't be standing here talkin' to you. So, I'm grateful to her. Oh, I forgot to tell you, she's going with Bob Ross, Col. Parker's stepson. Do you know him?"

"She's going with Bob? Yeah, I know him. Isn't he married?"

I looked at Elvis and raised an eyebrow, "Since when would that matter to Bob?"

Elvis smiled and nodded his head, indicating he understood, then asked me how it was going with Sylvia and me. I told him about the night before. "But, other than having no sleep, everything is going great."

I went to the dinner show by myself that evening. My seat was ringside, not center but more to the right, placing me nearer where The Sweet Inspirations were positioned for backup. When I finished eating, I remembered what Sylvia had said in the casino that day and was provoked, by the capricious mood I was in, to ask for a doggie bag.

Sylvia was in a playful mood herself that evening, and during the opening of the show she got tickled at my shenanigans. I kept teasing her with silly faces, making her laugh while she was trying to sing. Our humor carried over into Elvis' performance. I don't remember all that happened, but everybody seemed to be a little nonsensical that night. Then, while Elvis was singing, I lifted up the doggie bag where Sylvia could see it. That's all it took. She completely lost it right in the middle of the song.

The incident did not get past Elvis. He looked back and forth between us, a question on his face, as he continued to sing. Sylvia got the message and tried to straighten up.

Later, after the show was over and we were in the dressing room, Elvis came in. He walked up to Sylvia and me, then stood in front of us holding a glass of water in his hand, looking at us with a curious stare. "What was all that stuff going on between you two tonight?"

Glancing back and forth at each other, Sylvia and I snickered, then she turned to Elvis. "What stuff?"

"Don't give me that. You know what stuff I'm talkin' about. That stuff, with the doggie bag?"

We started to laugh again but stopped when we saw Elvis give us the eyebrows. "I don't know what you're talkin' about," Sylvia said.

He looked at me as though he expected an answer and I melted under blue eyes and started to fess up. I guess Sylvia decided she'd rather he hear her version and butted in.

"Today when we were in the casino I was teasing Frances and told her the way my luck was running she should save her leftover prime rib for me."

"You're kiddin'?" Elvis laughed.

"No," Sylvia answered. "And then when she held up that bag, I couldn't help myself from laughin'."

Lucky for us Elvis' mood was running in the same direction as ours that night. He thought it was funny and we were off the hook. I was starting to get the feeling that Elvis loved a good joke and didn't want to be left out of the know of anything.

Sylvia had a date after the midnight show so we agreed to meet back at the room by a certain time. I didn't want a repeat of what had happened the night before. But unfortunately, she didn't make it back, and I faced another night in the ladies' lounge.

I was walking through the casino when I ran into Glen Hardin, Elvis' piano player. Sylvia had introduced us at breakfast one morning and we always spoke when we saw each other backstage or around the casino. We got to talking and I explained my situation to him.

"Why don't you come up and stay in my room," he offered. "I'm gonna' be working with Elvis tonight and you can get some sleep. Don't worry, you'll be safe."

I thanked him and took him up on his offer. It would surely beat sleeping in the ladies' room again. I was tired, slightly inebriated, and hadn't had any real sleep in about thirty-six hours.

When we got to his room I wanted to take a shower but my clothes were locked in Sylvia's room. So Glen loaned me his thick, red, cotton robe. It was plush and had his initials monogrammed in white. I took a shower, put on the robe, then sat on the bed and watched as Glen toiled over the music arrangements. He had sheets of music scattered all over the room.

The telephone rang. It was Elvis wanting to know if Glen had the arrangements ready and for him to bring them upstairs where they were working. Glen told me to go on to bed, that he would be working through the night and I needed the sleep, then he left.

I don't know how long I'd been asleep, I'd literally passed out from exhaustion, when I was awakened by a noise in the room. I thought it was Glen and reached over to flip on the light. I was shocked wide awake when I saw this guy I'm going to call Johnny, (not his real name) standing beside the bed, naked! I recognized him and knew who he was.

"What the hell are you doing? How did you get in this room? Get out!" I yelled.

"Ah, come on now," he said, "you know what I'm doing here." Then leaning over the bed he pinned my arms down with his hands while I tried to fight him off.

"Get off me right now or I'll scream this hotel down on you!" Johnny released me, bent over and picked his clothes up off the floor, and put his pants back on. He cussed and called me names while he dressed, then abruptly left the room.

A few minutes later Glen walked in. "What are you doing awake?" he asked. "I thought you'd be sound asleep."

"How did he get in here?" I was angry, hurt, and confused.

"He who? What are you talking about, it's just me."

I told Glen what had happened and he said he didn't know how he'd gotten in. I believed Glen. He'd given me no reason to doubt him. But I was concerned about the incident and afraid it would get back to Elvis. I didn't want Elvis to think I was the kind of person who would be party to such goings-on. I had learned by now that certain people were the eyes and ears for Elvis. He was aware of everything that went on. I didn't understand what was happening, but this was nothing new since stuff was always going over my head. I guess I was pretty naive at the time.

Glen had come back to the room for some sheets of music he'd forgotten. After he left to go back upstairs, I checked to make sure the door was locked, then went back to bed.

That afternoon when I awoke, no one was in the room but me. I went back to Sylvia's suite, changed clothes, then went with her down for breakfast in the coffee shop, where we met Ann and Estelle. We were sitting in a booth eating breakfast when some of Elvis' group came in and took the booth across from ours. We were talking back and forth, when this guy I'll call Brad (not his real name) brought up what had happened to me the night before.

I turned to Sylvia, "How did he know about last night?"

"Frances, ain't nothin' a secret around here."

Again, Brad said something. I don't remember exactly what he said, but the truth about the night before had a very warped twist when he told it. It hurt my feelings and I started to cry.

When the guys finally left the coffee shop, I asked Sylvia if she thought Elvis had heard about the night before. "He probably has," she said, "but I wouldn't worry about it."

But I did worry. I worried about the twisted version he had probably heard. I told Glenn about my disconcertment. He was sympathetic and said he'd straighten the mess out.

Glen must have said something, because the next time we were backstage and I was talking with Elvis, he said something very strange. "Stay loyal, Baby Jane." Then he lowered his voice. "I've stayed loyal to you."

Elvis stayed loyal to me? I thought. *I don't get it.* "What do you mean, Elvis?"

"Just be careful around the guys, especially Johnny." He

looked like he was thinking about something. "Stay away from Johnny and the rest of 'em, honey. Those guys are animals. They'll eat you alive. I'm only telling you this for your own protection."

I was so glad the problem was behind me and that I hadn't been banished from Elvis' kingdom. "Thank you, Elvis. Thank you for believing in me."

That night, Sylvia and I went up to her room together and while we were talking the phone rang. It was Elvis. He talked to Sylvia, then asked to speak to me. He said he had tried to contact my brother several times. Then he laughed, "Doesn't he ever stay home? See if you can get the copyrights and lead sheets and bring them with you the next time you come out."

He asked me how everything was going with Sylvia and me and I told him, "Great." He said he'd just wanted to make sure I'd got in the room alright.

The next night in the dressing room Elvis cornered me alone and asked me how much longer I was going to be in Vegas. I told him, "Two nights and three more days, after tonight."

"Baby Jane, I want you to move out of Sylvia's room and into this one." He reached for my hand, placed a key in my palm, then closed my fist around it. "It worries me when you get locked out of Sylvia's room and have to sleep in the bathroom."

I couldn't believe my ears. "You got me a room, Elvis?"

He smiled and nodded his head while shushing me. Then, almost in a whisper, "I'll feel better knowin' you have a room of your own. But I don't want you to mention it to anybody. When you check out from Sylvia's, just tell her you called home and got some money or somethin'. Don't tell her I had anything to do with it."

"I don't understand. Why are you doing it?"

"I told you, I worry about you." The corners of his mouth lifted into a smile. "Besides, you make me laugh. Do you need any money?"

"No...thank you, Elvis. I have enough since I haven't had to pay for a room this week."

"If you need anything just let me know."

"What if Sylvia wants to know why I didn't think of this solution sooner?"

"She won't."

"How can you be so sure?"

The look he gave me made me feel like where did I get the nerve to doubt him, and he repeated, "She won't."

One thing I knew was when Elvis said don't tell, you didn't tell. I noticed how observant he was. He watched people like a hawk, what they did and what they said. I was coming to think that nothing went on that he wasn't aware of. It reminded me of what he'd said during an interview after his return from Germany, when he was asked if he might go back to school for acting. He said, "Going to school wouldn't hurt me any, but I never did well in school. I learn best by experience."

I was starting to understand what he meant when he gave that answer. He paid close attention to everything and everyone around him. From the way things had been going over my head lately, I figured I'd better get it out of the clouds and start paying some heed, too. Of course, when Elvis was anywhere near me, all I could see was him.

Sometimes I felt like a bimbo, like the outsider to an inside joke. Not that anybody was purposely trying to make me feel that way. I simply couldn't make sense of what was going on half the time. After all, I was just a fan. I was not one of the inner group. I kind of felt like Elvis knew where I was coming from though.

When it was time to leave the dressing room I went to the dinner show by myself. My seat was wonderful. I didn't even have to prompt anyone for the ringside table, I was just led straight to it. I didn't know why, but was glad for it.

After the show I went into the casino and while I was playing the slot machines a tired, sad-looking young man approached me and asked if he could talk with me. I saw no harm in it since we were surrounded by people and security was everywhere. We walked over to a bench and sat down. He introduced himself, then said he'd noticed me with some of the members of Elvis' group. He had some music he'd arranged for Elvis, but was finding it impossible to reach him with it and wanted to know if I'd try and get the music to him. I was surprised by his request and told him it was impossible. He pleaded with me and my tender heart sympathized with him, but as I explained to him, I had no clout in that area.

"I'm just a fan and I don't have access to Elvis on demand. Every time I've seen him it's been through sheer luck and circumstances."

"Well, if you get a chance, will you try to bring it up? It would mean so much to me." I gave him no hope, apologized, then excused myself and went back to playing slots until it was time for the next show. But his face haunted me, and I thought, *Elvis, I'll bet you've felt this, many times, the pain for things that are out of your power to change or do anything about.*

I sat at a table full of hard-core Elvis fans at the late show and their zealousness was refreshing. I was able to let my hair down, shake the face of that desperate musician, and really enjoy myself. There was a guy with a tape recorder sitting at the table, and we all helped him keep it hidden, and protected it when girls tromped us trying to reach Elvis.

There's absolutely no power outage on that body, I thought, as Elvis shook his stuff. His moves were definitely 210 volts tonight. His natural rhythm sparked the audience, setting us ablaze. He teased, and propelled his body, simulating karate moves. The more he moved the more we were moved and the more he played it up. He romanced, seduced, then made love to his vulnerable audience.

Our receptiveness was greatly rewarded during "Love Me Tender," when I again received a kiss from the King, along with a grin and a warning. This gorgeous man had offered me a room. Some things are just hard to believe, even when you're standing in the middle of them. This was one of those things. I checked my purse for the key, then clutched it in my hand and smiled.

After the last show, Elvis came up to me in the dressing room. "Baby Jane." He stared straight into my eyes. "I'm trustin' you to keep this to yourself. It's nobody's business."

"I promise, Elvis." For some reason, I knew that he knew I would keep my promise.

He clenched his jaw, grinned, and said, "Good girl."

PAPA MINTON (FRANCES' GRANDFATHER) AT 100 YEARS. CIRCA 1964.

14

Don't Ask Me Why

1971

Friends are people you can talk to...without words, when you have to.

—Elvis Presley

That night when Sylvia and I went back up to her room together, I was uneasy, and not quite sure about how to bring up the subject of moving into my own room. Would she buy my story, or would she question why I hadn't thought of the solution earlier?

I decided to wait for the right moment. In the meantime we talked and I was reminded during our conversation of the stranger who'd solicited me with his musical arrangements. I told Sylvia about the incident and she told me to forget it.

"Things like that happen all the time. Don't worry about it."

I told her I'd come to the same conclusion.

Finally, not being able to put it off any longer, I told her I'd called home and gotten some money. "Now I won't have to be a burden on you, anymore. I really appreciate everything you've done for me; giving me a place to stay and taking me up to Elvis' suite with you...I'll never forget any of it."

"Hey, girl, I'm sorry about lockin' you outta the room. I just got to playin' and forgot."

"Well, you still saved my tuchas and I won't forget it. You'll always be special to me, Sylvia." I told her I'd like to keep in touch and she gave me her telephone number and home address in East Orange, New Jersey. "But," I added, "I'm not leaving Vegas, yet. I've got a few more days before I go home, so I'll still see you at the shows...and in the casino!" We laughed. "I'm gonna miss our talks, though."

"Me, too. You're okay, Frances....Hey, we've had some laughs, right?"

"I know." I must have looked like I was going to cry.

"You'll make it...yes you will. You're gonna do alright, girl."

The next day I moved from Sylvia's room into the one Elvis had arranged for me. It was on the twenty-eighth floor and again, identical to the room Lauren and I had shared, and the one Sandra had left me in. *It has got to be a sign*, I thought. I would have liked to have had one of the pink and red rooms, but fate has its way. Anyhow, this one was special because it was from Elvis.

I missed Sylvia in the time it took to move my things. Moreover, I questioned my foresight in changing rooms. Las Vegas is a town for people. It is not a place you go to be alone, for the loneliness is profound. Sylvia's company had provided me with a sense of belonging.

The blue room matched my blue and lonely mood. I stood looking out the window at the lights of Las Vegas and the darkness of the desert that stretched beyond the neons. The quiet room was getting to me. I needed to be around people, to hear laughter, slot machines, anything that would shake this bleak feeling. *How does Elvis do it*, I wondered? Always shut away like this. Of course *he* could have people around him at the snap of a finger if he wanted them. *But it would still feel confining if you couldn't leave, I thought*. I dressed to go down to the casino with Sylvia on my mind.

THE SWEET INSPIRATIONS were a singing group with a string of hit singles that had sold in the hundreds of thousands. They could sing anything from pop, to rhythm and blues, to gospel, and their music was filled with feeling and soul. They appeared many times at New York's Apollo Theater.

The Sweets had performed as members of the Gospelaires and the Drinkard Singers, and this experience as gospel singers helped them develop their own style. After they started working as a vocal group on recording sessions, it wasn't long before they were doing two and three sessions a day. They also backed up Aretha Franklin, appearing with her in concerts, besides performing and recording on their own prior to employing their talents as backup for Elvis.

The Sweets were a success in their own right, and I thought, *How lucky for me to have been befriended by someone with such great talent.* Had it not been for Sylvia, I doubted I'd have made it up to the penthouse. Elvis would never have seen Tommy's music. And for sure, I would not be staying in this room provided by Elvis-himself-in-the-flesh Presley.

Pinching myself was no attestation for what was happening here. *So what's next.* Had I traded companionship for this lonesome, melancholy feeling? *What's wrong with me,* I thought. *I'm in Las Vegas and by gosh I don't have to stay in the room. There's a whole casino full of people right downstairs.*

Entering the casino was like an injection of life. My spirits were lifted into optimism and confidence in the opportunities ahead. I ate lunch, played the slots and won twenty-five dollars, went to a lounge show, then, maintaining the energy I'd absorbed from the crowd, I went up to my room and dressed for Elvis.

I had a good seat again, not center, but only two tables down and next to the stage. A girl I'm going to call Grace (not her real name) sat across from me. She'd driven in from Los Angeles for the one show. She said she tipped the waiter fifty dollars for her seat. Grace was okay, I guess, but she seemed a bit stuck-up, and I got the feeling, too, that she thought she was better than me and everybody else at our table. I didn't tell her anything about my friendship with Sylvia or Elvis.

Later, when I really let loose, getting into the show, Grace looked at me like I was something less than a cockroach, with no couth at all. Elvis started singing "Love Me Tender," and I reached out for him in the crazy way I usually did, and he dropped down on his knee and started teasing me.

"Want a kiss, Baby Jane?"

I nodded my head.

He leaned forward like he was going to kiss me, then drew back and smiled. "You want a kiss?"

"Yes, Elvis, I want a kiss!"

He leaned back down and pulled away again, getting real tickled this time. "Do you want a kiss, Baby Jane?"

"I sure do, Elvis!" When he leaned down the third time, I threw my arms around his neck and tried to kiss him while we laughed into each other's mouths.

He continued kissing girls along the stage. Grace got a quick kiss herself. But you should have seen the look on her face when she asked me what all the Baby Jane business was about and I told her that was Elvis' nickname for me.

"He knows you?"

"Yep," I said, "and he's 'bout crazy as I am." *Let her put them gems in her Suzy Creamcheese shopping bag,* I thought, while grinning like a Cheshire cat.

After the last show I played at some more slots. I wished I'd gone backstage, but I wasn't sure enough of myself to parade back there without Sylvia. Elvis had been nice to me. I figured it was best to play it cool. I dreaded going upstairs but a long soak in a hot tub sounded mighty enticing. So I had one more cocktail for the road, then caught the elevator home.

I was tired and a bit tipsy from the champagne when I reached the room. But my heart was set on a relaxing bubble bath. I turned the faucet on, tested the temperature, and poured a triple measure of French perfume bubble bath into the rushing stream of hot water. The privacy Elvis had afforded me with this room would allow me a long, slow soak.

I pulled my hair up into a ponytail and removed my makeup. The tub was full. I turned the water off, dropped my clothes on the floor, then stepped into my bath and slowly eased down into the steaming froth. I sat still, waiting for my skin to accept the heat, and let my mind drift. The scent of French perfume rode on clouds of steam, filling the room with its seducing essence. I leaned back in the tub, rested my head against the tiles, and closed my eyes. The water felt good, and I thought of Elvis.

What was he doing right now, I wondered? I envisioned his beautiful blue eyes—knowing eyes that could read my mind. Eyes that had seen firsthand the want in poverty, and the soft, rich prison of fame. His life boggled my mind and I was unable to comprehend how he'd made the transition—from nothing to everything. An extraordinary man, that's who Elvis Presley was. A beautiful, extraordinary man...I fell asleep in the bed of hot water, blanketed with bubbles, and pillowed by billows of French steam.

A knock at the door half-awakened me. But I was still in the twilight zone, that place between sleep and reality. Then, I heard a second knock and came fully awake. The water had cooled, but not enough for me to have slept very long. "Who's there?" I called out. No answer. I knew they could hear me. The bathroom was close enough to the door that opened to the hall.

Stepping from the tub I reached for a towel, "Just a minute." I hurriedly slipped into my long white, terry-cloth robe, wondering who it could be. No one knew I was in this room except Elvis. It was too late for a maid and I hadn't called for room service. *Must be somebody lost*, I thought. When I reached the door, I opened it to a crack and peeked out. I was stupefied!

"Hi, can I come in?" It was Elvis!

I opened the door wider and stood dumbstruck, staring at him.

"You gonna invite me in or make me stand out here in the hall?"

I was paralyzed, bumfuzzled, and my mouth wouldn't work. *I'm dreaming*, I thought. Then suddenly, my adrenaline was pumping and I shouted, "Come in!"

This was the first time I'd seen him totally alone. *Alone*, I thought, *alone with Elvis.* Just the thought of that word in the same sentence with Elvis set me to trembling. I stepped aside to allow his entrance, then closed the door behind him.

"Where are your bodyguards?"

Elvis didn't answer. He simply walked ahead of me until he reached the small table and chairs that sat next to the window. I followed him, stopping about halfway into the room to collect myself. It was always the same. Every time I saw him was like the first.

He took a seat in one of the chairs, removed his sunglasses, and laid them on the table, then cast me a long, slow look, with blue eyes that spoke pure mischief. I was still in shock, my adrenaline was up and down, and I couldn't seem to come out of the cloud I was in as I stood gaping at him. I wondered if he was a figment of my imagination, or if I was still asleep in the bathtub having a wonderful dream. He wore a blue shirt under his coat and I thought, *He looks so pretty sitting there, blending with the blue room.* His blue eyes and blue shirt in the blue room just blew me away.

"Cat got your tongue?" Elvis' gaze fixed on my gape. I shook my head while searching for the misplaced organ, then finding it, I told him I couldn't believe he was alone.

"How did you get here without being seen?"

"You ask too many questions. Sit down, honey, and let's talk." *Is he teasing me about being speechless,* I thought, as I sat on the edge of the bed. Then, suddenly aware of my appearance, I dropped my eyes to the floor.

"What's the matter?"

I looked back up and our eyes met. "I look terrible without makeup, Elvis. I was in the bathtub when you knocked."

My hair was damp and loose strands that had escaped the ponytail now clung to the sides of my face. I brushed them back with trembling fingers, then tilted my head away from the scrutiny of his eyes. I glanced back up and tried to articulate in my mind what I'd seen on his face. Was it curiosity or did I look that bad without makeup?

"Come over here." Elvis reached out for my hand. I saw his picture in my mind. The one that had been in my brother's frame. My special one with the smeared mouth...and I moved toward him. He took my hand and pulled me onto his knee. I felt like a cone of ice cream in an oven, and thought, *I'm alone with Elvis Presley. ALONE, and I'm sitting on his lap. I don't believe this.*

"Isn't this better? Don't tell me you're bashful now that we're alone."

I thought, *Bashful has little to do with what I'm feeling.* "I just don't get it, Elvis. I can't believe you're here...and I can't help wondering why." My voice trembled as I talked.

He tilted my chin up, "Isn't this what you wanted?" I nodded my head. "What happened to the girl who makes me laugh, huh? Where's Baby Jane?"

"She's on the bathroom vanity in the makeup jars."

Elvis laughed. "Oh, I don't think so. I think she's right here sitting on my lap...you're blushin'!" He nuzzled his nose up close to my neck and sniffed. "Mmmm...You smell good, what is that?"

"French perfume bubble bath."

"Mmmm, I like French." Then, putting on a beguiling face while assuming an undeserved innocence, he said, "French perfume, french fries, French kisses, French connection...you know... all that French stuff."

He struggled now to remove his coat, and as it slid from his shoulders, my eyes were drawn to the gun strapped underneath it. Elvis must have seen the question in my eyes.

"It's for protection, honey. There're a lot of freaks runnin' around this place. You can't be too careful."

I watched as he stepped over and laid the coat and gun across the back of another chair. He sat back down and indicated with a motion of his hand where he wanted me to sit. I'd been busy taking inventory of his pretty blue shirt, fancy belt, and cute buns.

"Come here." he said. I pulled my robe tighter around me and was slowly drawn back to his lap by a force beyond my resistance. My heart did flip-flops...and as for my head, I didn't know where my head was—lost somewhere.

"I just wanted to be with someone I could talk to, you know. His face was close, melting me with a sweet, teasing smile. "Tell me some more about your grandpa."

"What!" You could have knocked me over with a broom straw. "You wanna know about Papa?"

"Yeah...You know, what did he eat? What were his habits? You said he lived to be, what was it, a hundred and three or four?"

My mouth hung open for a moment while my mind struggled to grasp what he'd just said. Elvis remembered Papa! *From our conversation,* I thought.

"Almost a hundred and four," I said. "He died in November of 1967, and would have turned a hundred and four in February of 1968."

Even though I loved being there, I got up from Elvis' lap and moved to the chair on the other side of the table. I just couldn't think while I was sitting on his lap, and my nerves were so bad, I sure didn't want to puke on him.

"Elvis, would you like something to drink?" I pointed to a half-bottle of mineral water and two Cokes, sitting next to the ice bucket on the table.

"Maybe later. Why'd you move?"

"It makes me nervous, sitting there."

I'd like to take off this belt...that's if you're not gonna have a nervous break-down?"

My heart was beating so fast and loud I wondered if Elvis could hear it. "Of course. Sure, Elvis...make yourself comfortable." And he did.

He told me to get up and pulled my chair around to face his. "Sit here. I wanna be able to look at you when we talk." I sat down while he walked over to the foot of the bed and laid his belt on the bench, then came back and took the seat across from me. He had moved the chairs so close together our knees were almost touching and there was nowhere for me to look but at him.

"So...tell me, you know, about your papa. I want to know all about him."

His eyes were only a couple of feet from mine. Nervous, I clutched at the edges of my robe and cleared my throat. "His name was David Michael Minton. But everybody called him Dave."

He smiled at the vaguely puzzled look I must have had on my face and I was sure he knew the impact his presence had on me.

"Relax, Baby, it's just me...Elvis."

Doesn't he know the power of his name, I thought? Just hearing it spoken by the true, live, and loving lips that owned it, was enough to send my blood rushing in a thousand different directions.

"You were saying...his name was Dave.... "

"Oh...yes...ah, Elvis I can't believe you came here to talk about papa!"

"Why not? Is it so hard for you to believe I might be interested in your family? Ever since you told me about him, up in my room, you know, I've thought about it...and I'm curious. I wanna know why he lived so long. What was his secret? And I think you should know this wasn't any simple damn task gettin' away by myself. Sometimes I just get sick of everybody breathing down my neck. So consider that...and quit acting so damn nervous. I'm not gonna jump you. I just wanna talk."

I was crushed by the impatience in his voice. "Elvis, I'm sorry." A lump, forming in my throat, made it hard to speak. "I didn't mean to get you upset, it's just that I'm shocked by this visit. You've been my hero since I was eleven years old. I talked to your picture, Elvis, every day, and told you stuff I've never told another living soul."

Suddenly his expression changed and tenderness filled his eyes. "It's okay, Baby." He reached across the short distance that separated us and wrapped his hands around mine. "Is um gonna be ah... wite now?" He had the cutest expression on his face, like a little boy. It made me smile and to my surprise, relaxed me.

I nodded my head and asked what it was that he wanted to know about Papa? He got up and walked over to the door and back, paced for a minute, then sat back down. He seemed hyper and I remember thinking, *Wow, he's loaded with energy.*

"You okay now?"

"Yes."

"Your papa...like I told you, I'm curious about his health, you know." He leaned back in the chair, rested one foot on his knee, and didn't say anything, just looked at me like he was expecting to hear something. Then I realized he was waiting for me to speak.

"Well...he drank at least three large cans of Golden Key evaporated milk every day. He bought it by the case."

"That sounds fattening."

"Yeah, but he was a tall, skinny man, Elvis. He looked just like Abraham Lincoln. Oh yeah, I forgot to tell you. Mr. Lincoln was the president when Papa was born. I remember him saying that his father used to tell him about hearing Abe give a speech once."

"That's amazing! This was your grandfather, or your great-grandfather?"

"My grandfather. His daddy lived over a hundred years, too. I don't know why they lived so long. Papa chain-smoked Lucky Strike cigarettes till the day he died. I remember, on his hundredth birthday the newspaper did a story on him. When they asked what he accredited his long life to, he told 'em, 'Good whiskey, good lovin', and Lucky Strikes.'"

Elvis laughed when I told him what a smart aleck Papa was and seemed to be totally engrossed in my story, so I continued. "Another funny thing Papa used to say, whenever anybody asked about his eyesight, 'I can see three things real good; the face on a dollar bill, the sights on a gun, and a pretty girl in shorts.'" This really cracked Elvis up. I watched him laugh and thought, *This is how I'll always remember him.* His laughter came from his soul; genuine, heartfelt, and like he loved living. When he recovered from his side-splitting bout, he asked me to continue.

"Papa loved to tell his stories. I don't know how many times I heard him tell the one about the Dalton gang and how he rode out west with them to California once."

"Man, no kiddin'!" Now he had a look of amazement on his face.

"I don't know how much of what he said was true, Elvis, but Papa was an incredible person. He named my brother Sam Dalton, and he got a kick out of showing us his hand where a bullet had worked its way down over the years, lodging itself in the skin between his thumb and forefinger."

Elvis didn't say anything; he just stared at me with a cat-ate-the-canary grin on his beautiful face like he knew something I didn't, while his fingers tapped on the table, and his foot moved a mile a minute. I couldn't get past the feeling someone was hanging around in the hall waiting for him. Then I thought, *Well, maybe he gets a kick out of pulling the wool over their eyes.* Then again, maybe he *was* pulling the wool over my eyes. Whatever, I knew like so many other things that went over my head, this was probably another puzzle I'd never have an answer for. I couldn't help but wonder how many others had shared similar experiences. Elvis was a mystery and I think he liked it that way.

"Was he in good health when he died?"

"Huh...who...Oh, Papa? Yeah...he was in good health. He'd just finished eating a big meal and was on his way outside to sit under an oak tree, and he stopped and sat down on the steps and called out to his daughter-in-law. When she reached him, he said, 'Well, Maxine, tell everybody good-bye,' and then he died."

Evidently, Elvis had heard enough because he suddenly got up and walked around the room, then came back and sat down. Man, he was fidgety. Then he suddenly froze and stared at me with unreadable eyes. "What do you like about me?"

My mouth dropped open and a heady sense of excitement swept through me. "What's not to like about you, Elvis? I don't just like you, I love you."

"But you don't know me."

"Oh, yes, I do. I've known you since I was eleven years old."

"No, Baby, you know an image...you don't know me."

"Well, I feel like I do."

"Why? Why do you feel like you know me? Everybody thinks they know me when *I* don't even know who I am. Now tell me... how's that *possible?* Do you have some special power or somethin'?"

"You're serious, aren't you?"

"Quite serious. So tell me, who am I?"

Nervous as I was, I wanted to answer his question, so I took a deep breath and began to talk. "You're Elvis Presley. You're gorgeous to look at, and you're rich but with a poor man's heart. You're sexy like no other, you're talented, and you love God and you're not ashamed to show it. You have a chemistry, Elvis, that I think many people can relate to. You represent their own personal dreams and give them hope. I think they feel sincerity in your love for them and just naturally love you back. They look at you and feel like they can do anything. Well, at least I do," I giggled. "And you're the greatest entertainer in the world. Just a big hunk of love ...and soooo pretty."

Elvis furrowed his eyebrows in a grimace of distaste, then asked, "Why do you refer to me as pretty? It sounds so feminine."

"No, that's not true. Pretty is pretty, and you're the prettiest thing I've ever seen." It struck me funny, what I'd just said, and I laughed. "This is a weird conversation. And funny, too."

He looked at me strangely, and trying to hide his amusement, he said, "Why do you say that?"

"I don't know."

"That's who you think I am? All those things you just said...you really think that?"

"Absolutely."

He reached over to the table, picked up one of the hotel glasses, removed the wrapper, and filled it with water. "Want some?" he offered. I shook my head and watched him take a drink. "What's weird about us just talkin'?"

"I don't know. It just seems weird for me to be sitting here, with you, and talking about my family...and what I like about you. I've talked to you all my life like this. But this is real, Elvis. You're really sitting there and this is so weird. I guess I never really thought it would happen."

"That's not what you said up in my room when you told me about your vow. You gave me the impression that you wanted to have this conversation with me."

"I did, I mean I do. But I just can't believe it's happening and no one else will believe it either."

"That's good, because I don't want you to tell anyone."

"Why not?"

"Because I want it to be our secret." He leaned forward so his face was only inches away from mine and whispered in a soft voice, "Don't you like secrets, Baby Jane?"

I was hot and cold at once and felt my face flush with color. "Well, sure I like secrets, but..."

"Secrets are what make things special." He took another drink of water, then set the glass down on the table and leaned back in his chair again. He watched me as I sat in my hypnotized state. I was overwhelmed by what he'd said and my eyes lost themselves in the blue depths of his.

Elvis could connect with those eyes of his. Funny, his eyes are what I remember most. I recall how they used to just mesmerize me. I think I was always staring into them every time I came face to face with him. It was like he just locked me down with them, then held me spellbound. I don't know why Elvis tolerated my staring. But he did.

"You're wondering what I'm doing here?"

"Yes, I am wondering. I just can't believe..."

He leaned forward in his chair and placed his finger over my lips, silencing me. "Baby Jane, this is a special time and it's our secret." He reached for my hand, cupped it between his and continued to talk. "Call it a test of trust." Something in his eyes was sending me a message. I could feel it.

We talked about secrets and trust and he told me how to keep a secret Elvis style. "You gotta keep 'em confused, then they never know what to believe. Keep 'em interested, you know, by throwing 'em off the track every once in a while. Always look 'em in the eyes, honey. And never, never, ever, admit anything. Not even if you're caught on camera. And this is very important. Never... WRITE... what you don't want read."

His emphasis on *"write"* concerned me when I saw that far-away look enter his eyes. Then in a soft and distant voice, he said, "It's funny...the more you make 'em believe you can't keep a secret...the easier it is to keep one."

He'd been holding my hand while he talked. Now he let it go, leaned back in the chair, raised his arms above his head, and clasped his hands together. "What do you think of me now?"

If it was shock he was after, he surely got it. I was dumbfounded. Not so much by what he'd said, but by the fact that he'd shared it with me. Now he sat looking steadily at me, while receiving no verbal answer to his question, just the stupefied expression on my face. He dropped his hands back to his knees.

"What if I wasn't what you think I am? What then?"

"But you are what I think. Everybody has secrets, Elvis, but that doesn't take away from who they are. I believe it's part of what makes them that person."

He looked at me with an inquisitive interest, then leaned forward and asked, "What secrets do you have, Baby Jane?"

I hesitated. This was an area I didn't like getting into. "You wouldn't wanna know."

Wrong answer. Now he persisted with an Elvis determination to extract my secret from me. I had perfected hiding the hurt, even from myself, for many years. But as he coaxed me, I felt a warm sense of connection pulsing powerfully between us, and it wasn't hard for him to persuade me to reveal my secret. Elvis had that effect. Tears collected in my eyes as suppressed memories flashed through my mind. I hesitated to speak them aloud. Then his voice softly encouraged me.

"What is it, Baby? You know you can trust me."

With those magic words, Elvis had tapped into the secret I kept locked so deep inside, and I spilled it all out; the nightmares, the suicidal feelings, and the dark memories. Elvis' firm warm fingers held onto my arms. "Talk, Baby. Get it all out."

When I finished talking, he leaned closer and touched my face and I saw sympathy in his eyes. "You've had a rough road, darlin'. I admire your strength. Some people could never overcome what you have." His eyes were flooded with compassion, and I cried. He brushed my tears away with his thumbs, then stood up, bringing me with him. He pulled my head to his chest and wrapped me in his arms.

We stood that way for endless moments, saying nothing. Then I raised my face to look at him and was astonished. Elvis was crying. I hesitated to speak, but only for a moment. "This is so strange. It's like we've been through this before. Sort of deja-vu. You know what I mean?"

"I know." His eyes strayed again to that far away place. "But it wasn't your fault, honey." He stopped talking and seemed to be in deep thought for a moment. "You understand that now, don't you?"

Even though I wasn't sure what he was talking about, I nodded my head.

Still holding me close, he said, "Kids get weird ideas about things they don't understand. I think it's only natural."

"Elvis..."

"Talk, honey. I'm listenin'."

"I always talked to your picture...about everything." He stroked my hair. "You're the only one I could tell. When I held your picture and poured it all out, I felt like you could hear me, you know. Like you were right there with me."

I sniffed, trying to stop crying while Elvis stroked my hair and patted my back. He held me and crooned in baby talk as though I were a child, and at that moment, I felt like a child. Then I heard him say more to himself than to me. "Some people should be shot."

I remember thinking that Elvis sounded like he knew something I didn't. Then I thought of his gun, *No, it's probably just more words to comfort me.* But now, when I think back and recall again the way he said it, I'm not so sure what he was thinking. I know one thing; whatever Elvis felt for someone, be it love, anger, passion, or compassion, you could believe it was real and from his heart.

"It was a long time ago, Elvis."

"And?..." He was waiting for me to say something but I couldn't understand what he was about. Suddenly, his face froze in a bewildered expression. "You don't know, do you?"

"What? What, Elvis?"

He shook his head and I tried to figure out the expression on his face. Then he just kind of looked at me and said, "You know, Baby Jane..." He held his hand to his forehead, "Whew...Man, it's like I sensed something about you from the beginning and the fact that... man...you know how I say you make me laugh?" I nodded. "Well, it just amazes me that with all you've been through...you still make me laugh. I mean that really moves me...you're special, Baby Jane, very special." His eyes looked soft when he smiled and whispered, "You're my special Baby Jane."

He hugged me up to him tightly, then pulled back and placed his hand over my heart. "Baby...do you ever feel like there's more than one person in here?"

"There is," I told him, "Jesus lives in there. And Angela. She lives in there, too."

"Who's Angela?"

"You know who Angela is. You introduced me to her."

Elvis looked like he was concerned about my sanity. "When, honey? When did I introduce you to Angela?"

I laughed at his serious look. "When I was about thirteen. You know, I told you I used to talk to your picture. Well, when I thought I was an ugly earthling, you turned me into an angel. And when I saw the angel in the mirror, you named her Angela. You told me that I was the angel in Angela."

He smiled. It was quiet.

"Anybody else?"

"What?"

"Are there any others inside here?" Now he was holding his hands on each side of my head.

"I don't know?"

"Well, do you think maybe, no? Or do you think maybe, yes?" It's important that you remember, honey."

Scared out of my wits for voicing it, I said, "I think maybe, yes."

"Frances?"

I looked at Elvis, sort of stunned. "You don't usually call me Frances. Are you mad at me?"

He patted my back. "No, I'm not mad at you. Listen, you believe in the power of prayer, don't you?" Elvis was nodding his head for me to say yes.

"Yes."

"Okay, honey, I'm gonna pray for you." He held my hands and prayed. And as he prayed, I thought, *I don't believe this. Elvis is praying for me.* When he finished, he asked me if I felt free.

"Free?"

He dropped his head...and slowly shook it.

FRANCES IN THE SHOWROOM OF THE LAS VEGAS HILTON. 1975

15

My Wish Came True

1971

All of this is but for a day.

—*Elvis Presley*

lvis flashed me an I'll-win-your-heart, love-me-tender
smile, while humming softly a familiar tune. Then he
sang, "Hush, little baby don't you cry, Elvis's gonna
sing you a lullaby, and if this lullaby don't work, Elvis's
gonna cry like a big ole...ole...ole what?" I laughed and he continued, "gonna cry like a big ole...!"

I looked up at him and, smiling, said "Jerk." Then quickly, explained that it rhymed. He chuckled and I told him, "Elvis, I'll always love you for this."

"Always?" Holding my face between his hands and still grinning, he rubbed his nose against mine like when it's cold—like an
Eskimo kiss.

"Always!"

He started to sit back down, then didn't. "Ah...'scuse me, honey, I need to find the bathroom." I must have had a funny look on
my face because he started to laugh. "What's the matter...you
didn't think I used the toilet?"

He laughed all the way to the john, then I remembered my clothes were still lying on the floor where I'd left them in my haste to answer the door. "Elvis!..." Too late. Half way there I heard my hero peeing and walked back to my chair and sat down. *Imagine that. Elvis pees!* Then I thought, *I gotta pee, too.* All that champagne I'd drunk was catching up with me. But I was too embarrassed to go.

A few minutes later he came out of the bathroom holding my panties up in the air and grinnin' like a poop-eatin' mule.

"And what have we got here, hummm?"

I leaped from the chair. "Elvis! Gimme those!" He held my panties out to me then snatched his hand back before I could grab them.

"Gimme my panties," I giggled.

He gave me a quick up and down sweep with his eyes. "Hum-mm...since I'm the one holdin' your panties..." He cocked his head downward and smiled a sneaky smile. "I wonder...what've you got on under that robe?"

"I have more than one pair, you know."

"So that means these are mine?" He tilted his head toward his shoulder and curled his lip, then nodded his head in answer for me.

"What would you need my panties for?"

"Oh...I'll think of something." Then he walked back over to the chair where his coat was hanging, rolled up my panties, and stuck them in the pocket. I didn't say anything, but in all honesty, my guts were playing the Superbowl.

"Come over here," he patted the chair, "and sit back down." I did as he asked, then he sat across from me.

"Tell me some more about when you were thirteen...and what you liked most about me...you know, when I'm performing.

Mercy, I couldn't get enough of looking at him, and catching me staring, he teased me.

"Let me guess. My looks?"

I felt like all this playfulness was his way of distancing my mind from the hurtful secrets I'd bared to him. *Well, if that's his motive,* I thought, *it's working.* I sure didn't want to be bogged down with nasty old memories. Not when I had Elvis all to myself.

"Are you interviewing me, Elvis?"

He laughed, "Maybe I am."

"You!"

"You? What does that mean? You! That's no answer!"

"YOU were my teen years. And, YOU, my pretty Prince, are what I enjoyed most about your performances. Oh...and I absolutely lo...ve it when you tease."

"How's that?" He was doing an Elvis-tease as the words came out of his mouth.

"I don't know. I guess it's because I feel like I'm seeing a part of the real Elvis." Now we both laughed.

"Tell me something funny. I like it when you make me laugh."

Caught off guard, I couldn't think of anything funny to say at that moment. "Like what?"

"Anything. Just whatever pops into your head."

I thought for a minute, then started to laugh. "This is funny Elvis! This, right now. I mean...here I sit, the court jester, and I ain't got a joke in my bag."

Elvis laughed. Then everything got really quiet and we just sat there looking at each other.

"Man, Baby...you sure can make some eye contact. But that's good. You can tell a lot about a person by their eyes. The eyes are the windows to the soul," and that led into a conversation on religion.

We had already discussed our mutual denominational fostering to a small degree when I'd been up in his suite. But digging a little deeper into our Pentecostal backgrounds, we found we shared some viewpoints, and Elvis tried to explain a few scriptures I didn't understand, but it was all so foreign to me at the time that most of what he said just seemed to float right over my head. I pretended to comprehend it all, but I'm sure he knew he'd spaced me.

"Man, those preachers made you feel it. I know they're good people. But I'm not so sure they interpret the scriptures right. The thing is, it works for them. But I'm lookin' at a bigger picture and I'm askin' myself, where do I fit into all of this? What does God want me to do? Me," he pointed to himself, "Elvis Presley?"

Although I couldn't grasp everything he was telling me, I felt the hunger of his search. All my life I'd wanted to be close to God, understand His purpose for me, and know what He was all about. I wanted to be a better person and rise above myself. I told Elvis this. "It all boils down to 'spiritual self,' doesn't it?"

He looked at me like he was amazed by what I'd just said. "Man, Baby, that's exactly what I've been tryin' to tell everybody, but the fools act like they don't even wanna know what I'm talkin' about."

I only wish I'd known then what I know now. In the light of my present Christian beliefs, I feel like Elvis was ahead of his time. I believe he had hold of some major truths the religious world was not yet ready to accept.

We talked about other things, then he said, "You remind me of somebody. I can't place her right now, but...have we met before? I mean before you came out here...to Las Vegas."

"Well, I was out here in August and I met you backstage. I'd given you a scrapbook and..."

"And you put your picture in the front. I remember."

I was hoping Elvis wouldn't remember Lauren and ask if I was married. "I've seen you on other occasions, but I doubt you'd recall them. I was just a face in the crowd, Elvis."

"I remember faces in a crowd better than you think. You see, Baby, I have these powers. They're special, you know. I know things before they happen." He shrugged his shoulders and twisted a ring on his finger, his eyes so distanced I wondered what planet he was on. Then suddenly he was back, the aloof, far away look gone, replaced by the strange playing gleam that now danced in his eyes.

His pirating scrutiny sent a thrill up my spine that tickled when he flipped me a heartbreaker grin. "I wanna give you somethin', honey."

"Give me something? But you've already given me enough."

"What have I given you?"

"You gave me this room, and you came to see me! That's more than I ever dreamed, Elvis."

"I still wanna give you something special." His face beamed when he said "special" and the twinkle in his eyes told me he enjoyed giving. "If you could have anything you wanted...what would it be?"

I knew what I wanted from Elvis! I'd always known what I wanted from him. *This is just too good to be true!* I thought. But, dare I ask?

"What is it? What's that look in your eyes?"

"What look?"

"That look, that makes me feel like you're gonna get crazy on me."

I could tell by the inquisitive expression on his face that I had his curiosity going. Maybe he'd be willing to play my game. It was worth a chance. After all, I was in Las Vegas.

"Elvis, if you really meant it...I mean...about wantin' to give me something special..."

"I mean it," he interrupted. "What is it you want? He chuckled. "By that look you're wearin', I hope I can afford it."

"Elvis..." I cleared my throat, then dove in. "Well, during the years after I made that vow to meet you, there were a few fantasies I...what's the matter?" He looked to me like he was stifling on something, then he tried to straighten up his face.

"This sounds serious. Is this fantasy of yours gonna get us into trouble?"

"I don't think so. I mean, that's...sorta like part of it, you know, not going too far. You know what I mean?"

The expression that grabbed his face, just before he busted out laughing, made me stare while he tried to talk through his hysterics.

"Yeah...I know what you mean, but go for it...I'll take the bait."

"I want you to give me a kiss like the one you gave Peggy in *Jailhouse Rock*, you know, when you told her, 'That ain't tactics, honey. That's just the beast in me.'"

Elvis did a double take. "That's your fantasy!" Then his look of surprise exploded into laughter, and he howled so hard his eyes teared.

I'm sure I must have had the saddest ole-houndog-look on my face when I asked him, "What's so funny about my fantasy?"

"Just a minute," he gasped, "let me get my breath." Then he laughed some more. Finally, his eyes still misty from laughing, he stopped and stared at me. "I...tell...you...I wanna give you somethin', anything, and all you want is a kiss? I'm sorry, honey...but that's funny." Then he cracked up again.

Feeling I was on a roll, I played an ace that I hoped would ensure me the best kiss possible. "Not just any kiss, Elvis. I want an *energy* kiss."

"Ah what?" He was still snickering. "I'm scared to ask, but...what in the hell is an energy kiss?"

"It's when Elvis Presley puts the same energy into a kiss that he puts into his music."

He really flipped out laughing now, and I started to think he was never coming back. But he did. Then he stared at me. *I wonder if he's thinkin' 'bout playin' the role for me,* I thought. My lips twitched. It was difficult to keep from laughing because I was, absolutely, out of control under his scrutiny and just barely hanging on. But I didn't want to get him started again.

Elvis got up and turned out the lights while he talked. "What does your fantasy feel like?" He left the bathroom light on and it provided just enough visibility to be romantic.

"It makes me feel good," I told him while trying to keep my knees from knocking. *What's he gonna do?*

"No," he said, as he walked back over and sat down across from me. "That's not what I mean. I wanna know where your head's at in the fantasy." He reached over and took both my hands in his. I could tell he was enjoying this too, so I closed my eyes and took a deep breath...and went for it.

"I want you to romance my mouth...like I'm the only girl in the world and like you really mean it." Instantly, I regretted my words and quickly added, "Just pretend, really mean it." *He's going to think I'm nuts.* I was sure I'd said too much. "Elvis, it's just a game of pretend." Still concerned over the silent stare in his eyes, I humbled mine to him. "I know...it's a dumb idea, huh?"

He'd been sitting so still, letting me stutter through my embarrassment, that it startled me when he suddenly reached over and touched my face.

"Don't look so uptight, Baby. I understand. You just wanna play, doncha?"

I nodded my head.

"You're so damn honest about your feelings. I like that about you. Romance your mouth. That sounds sexy. I think I could handle givin' you a special fantasy. Live and in color, how's zat sound?" He hiked an eyebrow. "I dig on fantasies. Hell! My whole life's a fantasy." He lowered his hand from my face, and reaching for mine, he pressed my palm to his lips.

I stared at him, preserving everything about him. He was so handsome I feared he could stop my heart. He leaned forward, moving his face to my neck, then nuzzled up close to my ear and whispered.

"I know what you want. I know exactly what you want."

Goose bumps popped out all over me as he nibbled along my neck, softly moaning and kissing. Then, in a soft, breathy voice, he said, "You want some tease lovin'."

Leaning back now, so he could look at me, his sexy sneer made me go all soft and crazy inside. Then he stood up and held out his hand to me. He pulled me up to my feet and close to him, his eyes locked on mine the entire time. I looked at his mouth, and his lips were a soft, full promise of pleasure. When he pulled me even closer, I let my heart and soul bask in the wonder of him, while his hands slid down my back and up again. With my nose buried in his shoulder, I inhaled the personal smell of him; clean, rich, and masculine.

Grasping my arms he stared right into my eyes, then quickly lowered his head to mine. When his soft, wet, mouth covered my parted lips, I melted into him and his kiss consumed me, making me dizzy, and I responded with every measure of feeling I possessed for the handsome man who was kissing me.

He was a romantic kisser and our long, deep kiss was eager and demanding, yet soft and heady, gratifying all my fantasies. The more we got into it, the more of my mouth he explored. I swayed and my loss of balance forced me to hold onto him or fall. Elvis felt me slump and tightened the embrace.

Feeling secure in his arms now, I completely lost myself in his kiss. My feet sank into the cloud I floated on as I stood a little above the earth, thinking, *This moment belongs to me.*

This part of Elvis' life was mine. Here, now, for this twinkling instant, he was mine and I made it count. They were precious moments and if it were possible, I'd have frozen them. But, since that was not feasible, I settled on remembering the tangibleness of it all. If I had to live in a dream for the rest of my life, this was real. Not a wish, not a dream, but Elvis in the flesh and me in his arms— Elvis, a song come to life and a dream lived. His magic had made it possible.

I feel like he put his best into that kiss. Like he was making sure he lived up to my fantasy. When it ended and our lips parted, I felt the loss acutely. I wanted to kiss him again and sample him more thoroughly. My eyes were still closed and when I opened them, he was smiling down at me like he knew he was good.

"Say it, Elvis."

He grinned, real saucy-like, and cocked his eyebrow. "That ain't tactics, honey. That's just the beast in me."

He did it better than in the movie and I faked an elaborate swoon, then asked, "May I have seconds?" And Elvis broke out laughing again, so hard, I could feel his chest jerking against me.

"Baby Jane...are you greedy?"

Lowering my lashes in a Scarlet O'Hara fashion, I said, "Yes." Elvis dropped his arms from around me, backed up, and doubled over laughing. I felt his amusement like one feels sunshine as I sat back down and laughed along with him.

"I guess I don't get seconds, huh?"

He glanced up at me from his bent-over position, then fell to the floor where he continued to laugh, while I sat mollified and watched. Finally overcoming his spell, he rose up onto his knees and crawled over to where I was sitting.

My robe had fallen open below my crossed knees, and he gently, bit me on the ankle. "You have pretty legs."

Ooo-eee, I thought, then thanked him. "Does that mean I get seconds?"

He looked up at me for a moment, a little-boy twinkle in his eyes, then he arose from his knees, reached for both my hands, and pulled me up and over to the bed. We sat down on the edge and I was nervous and I guess it showed.

"Trust me," he said. But it wasn't Elvis I didn't trust. It was me. I was messing around with fire and might set the woods ablaze. Maybe I'd only be singed, but even if I went up in flames, I knew I was powerless to stop myself. The physical attraction I felt for him was something I'd thought I could handle. Now I was feeling that maybe some things might be better left alone. But I wasn't ready to relinquish this gift of favor.

And so I trusted him.

Elvis gently pushed me back until we were lying across the bed, and then he kissed me. His soft lips moving over mine again had a dizzying effect on me. He moved us up farther onto the bed, then suddenly rolled over on top of me, pinning my hands above my head, and gazed down into my eyes.

"How do you want it, honey?"

"Elvis...that's a very dangerous question."

He grinned like a fox. "It's your fantasy, Baby." And then he kissed me again. "Damn...you kiss good." His eyes traveled over my face.

"I had a good teacher."

"And who was that?"

"You."

"Me?"

I laughed at the puzzled look on his face. "Yes, you. When I was thirteen and talked to your picture, you told me to kiss the mirror and pretend it was you."

"Really?" His face was beaming. "Did you really, sweetheart?"

I nodded my head, "Really. And when I listened to you sing 'I Was the One,'...oh, Elvis...that's my favorite song, 'cause I've always known you were the one. You were my first love, you know. You were the one who taught me to kiss when I was kissing someone else."

"Damn...honey, do you know how that turns me on? Tell me again." I told him again and he wanted to know what I'd been wearing when I kissed the mirror.

"Lots of different things at different times," I said, "from babydoll pajamas to prom dresses."

This time he kissed me with an excited, passionate, almost out of control urgency. I opened my eyes to peek at him.

His eyes were rolled back and half shuttered by his eyelids. I felt exactly as I'd known I would, and sky-rocketing sensations blasted through my entire body, lifting me, higher and higher. But, somewhere, way down deep inside, there was a sadness for all the times I'd never feel this again. And the realness of it was a tangible thing.

Compulsively, before I even thought of it, I pulled back from his kiss, then reached up and gently touched the sensual curve of his bottom lip with one finger. I stared at him with a fierce longing, loving him, wanting him, and yet determined not to let my body rule my mind.

A smile lifted the corner of his mouth and he crushed me to him. Elvis knew what I was feeling. Don't ask me how I knew. I just knew that he knew. My heart knocked joyfully against my ribs and a fluttering sensation took over in the pit of my stomach.

Shifting me slightly on the bed, he dropped a kiss on my forehead. I started to speak and he laid a silencing finger against my lips. Suddenly, his mouth was everywhere; on my lips, my face, my neck. He pulled me even closer to him. Elvis knew what he was doing and I completely trusted that he had the situation in hand. A safe feeling cocooned me, heightening the pleasure, and I thought, *Miracles from Heaven. Just what I wanted—a heavy kissin' session with Elvis.* When our kiss ended, his face lit with a grin.

"Is this as good as your fantasy?"

I flirted back, "The...real...Elvis...is much more than a fantasy. The real Elvis knows, exactly, what I want."

"Tell me again...what were you wearing when you kissed the mirror?"

"Elvis...why?"

A tease twinkled in his eyes. "It's just...I just like to think of you kissin' the mirror in your panties, honey, that's all."

"Elvis, you like fantasies too, don't you?"

"Uh huh...the kind with pretty girls who kiss the mirror," he tickled me, "in their panties before going to bed at night."

We were just lying together across the bed, when Elvis reached up to the head and snatched the pillows from under the covers, fluffed them, then placed one under my head and one under his.

"Isn't that better?" He sat up and started to unbutton his shirt. He must have thought from the look on my face that I was going to have a heart attack or faint. "You're not afraid of me, are you? I would never hurt you."

"I know you...wouldn't hurt me. I'm just nervous."

"Still? You're still nervous with me? Why?"

"'Cause. El...vis, you're Elvis Press...leee."

"Yeah...I am," he laughed. "How about that! I hadn't noticed." He continued laughing while he buttoned his shirt back up.

"Oh...you...make me laugh," I stuttered.

He reached over and tickled me in the ribs, then fell on the bed beside me. Soon our laughter quieted down and we lay there gazing into each other's eyes.

"Baby? When you talked to my picture, you know, when you were thirteen and kissin' the mirror and all that stuff...damn that turns me on...oh, I got sidetracked there. That mirror, it does things to me...makes me lose my train of thought." He smiled and became quiet.

"Elvis?"

"Oh...yeah...where was I? Oh yeah...ah, ah, ah...oh, yeah..."

"Elvis...you were talking about when I used to talk to your picture."

"That's right! I oughta put you on the payroll. You could remember my lines for me."

"Elvis, what were you gonna say, I mean about me talking to your picture?"

"What? Oh, that. What was I gonna say?"

"Yeah, what were you gonna say?"

"Well...I was just gonna ask if I ever talked back." Elvis wasn't smiling—exactly. Actually, I didn't know what might be going on in his head, but I sensed there was some humor hidden in his question, somewhere.

"Yes, as a matter of fact, you did."

Now, in a supposedly serious voice, he told me, "That's because I reach into my soul when I sing those songs. So you can hear me, you know? And it takes a lot of concentration. You know?"

"You're teasing me now, aren't you?"

"What do you think? You said you heard me." He leaned over and gave me a quick kiss.

I touched his face and just lay there, looking at him. "You are so pretty, Elvis Presley."

Looking back at me, he smiled.

"Elvis Presley, Elvis Presley. I love saying your name. Elvis Presley. Mmmm...it even tastes good."

"How does this taste?" Quickly, he brought his face up close to mine and stuck his tongue in my mouth.

Mmmm...I moaned my pleasure and Elvis moaned his back. When our mouths parted, I brushed my fingers across his soft lips. "I love kissing your lips, Elvis."

"Humm?"

"I said, I love kissing you."

"Mmmm...then do it again."

He didn't have to invite me twice.

After I'd kissed him, I said, "Elvis?"

"Humm?"

"Can I call you Baby? I mean just once." Elvis wasn't saying anything, he just lay there looking at me. "I know it sounds dumb but I wanna taste how it feels in my mouth...I mean...to call you Baby to your face."

Now he laughed, "You are crazy." He paused, looking I guess at the yearning in my eyes, then said, "You can call me anything right now."

Using the sexiest voice I could muster up, I said, "Anything, will you kiss me, huh, Baby?" He laughed at my joke, then kissed me again, and while he was kissing me I thought about my favorite song. Funny, I remember trying to think of all the things I'd fantasized as a teenager. I wanted to make every moment matter.

"Elvis, would you sing 'I Was the One' for me?"

"Your favorite song?"

"Un hunh."

"For you?...Here?...Now...Sure."

There's that little boy grin, again, I thought.

"Why not?...I was the one, who taught you to...what...whad-di-di say..." then still singing he went into Ray Charles' "What Did I Say." "Tell me wha-di say..."

"Elvis, sing it seriously. Pleeease."

"Oh, seriously. She wants it serious." Then tickling me again, he said, "You want serious? Serious, hummm...gotta get serious for Baby Jane...I was the one, who taught you to...wha-di teach you? Somebody needs to teach *me* the words to this song." I gave him a serious look. "You gotta help me out here. It's been a long time since I sang that song."

I attempted to sing part of it through for him but was giggling so bad I messed it up.

"Okay...I think I can do that good...I got it now. Here goes. I was the one, who taught you to kiss, when that you're...kissing me now" He leaned down and kissed me, and I thought, *He's into the scene. He's really into it with me.*

"You know, I'll never sing this song again without thinkin' about you." Then he continued with the song and I really thought for a minute that I'd died and gone to heaven. There aren't enough words to describe what I was feeling at that moment, as we lay on the bed, Elvis looking straight into my eyes, and singing my favorite song to only me.

His voice raptured me to a dreamlike place, and when he finished singing, I asked him, "Are you aware of the aura that's always around you?"

"You mean my special powers?" His lips quirked as he fought to restrain his laughter.

"I'm serious. You have...like this aura that just seems to hang around you all the time. And right now, I mean, you being here with me, like this, you know..."

"Yeah..."

"Well, it's like I've stepped into your aura with you." I ran my hands up and down my arms and shivered. "You know I won't forget this, don't you?" Elvis was still as a rock, just watching me. "You're unforgettable, Elvis."

He shrugged his shoulders and shook his head. "Nah, that's Nat King Cole you're thinkin' about."

"No, that's you! Unforgettable Elvis."

"We...ll, if you say so." Then he seemed to get serious and in a manner of statement, he said, "Baby, we share secrets now."

"What's your secret?" I asked.

"Being here with you is my secret!" The tone of his voice made me feel stupid for not realizing. "You understand what that means? Neither of us can tell the other's secret." He chuckled, then smiling a mischievous smile, added, "Besides, if you tell, I'll use my special powers on you." And then he kissed me.

We ended our embrace in silence. Elvis wasn't saying anything. "What does it feel like? I mean, being where you are now, and having so many people adore you. What's it like, Elvis? What's it *really* like?"

"Baby...you're too deep. I think maybe you should become a writer." Looking at me skeptically, he cocked an eyebrow. "If you're not one already."

"I'm just curious, Elvis. I'm not a writer, but thanks for thinking so. I'd sure like to be one." It was hard to read his expression, but it didn't make me feel like he believed me. Was it possible he actually thought I was a writer?

He appeared to be in deep meditation now, almost as though his life were passing before him. He was lying on his back, and I lay on my stomach next to him, elbows pressed into the pillow and my head propped on fisted knuckles. I gazed down into fathomless, blue eyes. "Hard to describe what it feels like?"

"What?...Oh, you mean what it's like to be me? I thought you were talkin' about being a writer."

"Yeah, about you, Elvis."

"It's like a fantasy, honey. A fantasy that could all be over in the blink of an eye, you know. Just that quick." He snapped his fingers in front of my face.

"I know what you mean. It's like *this*, right now, you, me, here together...like a fantasy."

"Yes, like a fantasy. When I was a kid I had these dreams. You know, like most kids have dreams about what they wanna do with their life. Only in my dreams...I was able to move around." I watched as he closed his eyes.

"Does it bother you, not having the freedom?" Slowly opening his baby blues, he looked up at me.

"That's a hard question to answer. Probably because in real life...you have to take the bad with the good. Baby, you should know that."

He reached up and touched my face, studying my eyes for a moment. "I'll tell you one thing, I'd never give up the love of fans like you just so I could have my freedom. I'd miss it too much. And that's what scares me, you know. People can be fickle."

"Not your fans, Elvis."

"I hope you're right, honey." We gazed silently into each other's eyes.

"Did you mean what you said...you know, about becoming a writer?"

"That would be my next dream-come-true. But I don't really know if I could do it."

"You could do it. You just have to want it bad enough. But don't write about me, okay Baby. Not while I'm alive. Promise me?"

"I promise, Elvis. But don't talk that way, you're gonna live forever."

His eyes quietly gentled as they swallowed mine, "Everybody's gotta go sometime, honey." And I came spiraling back to earth with a jolt when in the next breath he said, "And I've gotta go, now." He wrapped his arms around me, and cocooned in the sweet, safe, heaven, I felt like nothing bad could ever touch me. I knew this was from his heart and was meant to make me feel special—a gift, and what a wonderful gift it was.

He leaned his head back a little, his face a mere inch away, and analyzed my eyes. He deliberated for a moment, then settled his mouth on mine and I melted against him. He pulled back, teasing my lips, sweeping his tongue across them and finally between them. Deepening the kiss, he made me feel like I didn't have a muscle in my body, and I fell right into it, relishing every moment, wanting it to last forever, until he broke away, smiled, and said, "Sweet dreams, Baby Jane."

I wanted to pull him back into my arms. But I didn't. "And remember, darlin', this is *our* secret. It's my special gift to you, so keep it special, you know, personal between us and don't tell anyone." He smiled, "Now we share secrets. Do you like that, honey?"

I nodded my head. "Yes, Elvis. I love sharing secrets with you. I always have."

"Good girl. You know if you tell secrets they can turn against you." His intimate eyes nailed me to the wall.

"Then I'll never tell." And looking straight back into his piercing probe, I promised, "Elvis, you can trust me."

Firmly, and without a flinch, he replied, "I know I can."

We stood up from the bed. He straightened his clothes, put his belt back on, then hugged me. He gave me a sweet innocent kiss on the forehead then walked over to the chair where he'd hung his coat and gun.

"I need to use the phone."

He didn't ask me to leave the room, but I had a feeling he wanted to talk in private.

"Sure, Elvis...could you excuse me for a minute, I need to visit the ladies room. My champagne is bubbling."

He laughed and walked over to the phone as I headed for the bathroom.

When I came back into the room he was hanging up the receiver. "That was Red...they'll be down in a minute." We sat at the table and talked till someone knocked at the door. I started to get up but Elvis was faster.

"Honey, nobody knows it's you in this room. It's better this way. I don't want Johnny or any of the others findin' out you're alone here. So it's best you stand over there by the bed till I'm gone."

Then, as though my lips had a mind of their own, I said it.

"Elvis, I love you."

He watched me, silently smiling so sweetly. Then he said, "I know. And I love you too, honey." The love-me-tender smile in his eyes painted the moment in my mind. "Dream about me tonight."

He put his glasses on, then turned toward the door and left the room.

"LOVING YOU" CAST PARTY. CIRCA 1957.
(FROM THE COLLECTION OF SANDRA ROSS)

16

Memories

1971

---

*They cut both ways. There's no way to forget the worst pain,
but nothin' gives you the same kind of pleasure as remem-
berin' your greatest happiness.*

—*Elvis Presley*

After Elvis left, I stood looking at the closed door and thought how strange it had all been—like a poetic fruition. And knowing we'd held back, the mystery lived inside me—a breathing thing. Elvis was magic. And magic is an illusion. It's never what it appears to be. But the awesome marvel of it is very real. I would always wonder and that was the best part.

The room seemed empty now, his voice a spark of sound that followed me like an echo. I thought about our conversation and was blown away by the whole scene as it played out in my mind again and again. There was so much I didn't understand. Why had Elvis come to my room? Perhaps he'd plucked me out in boredom as a way of reflecting on his fans. Or maybe he was testing me. Or could it have had something to do with writing? He sure seemed to get uptight over that word. *Imagine that*, I thought, *Elvis actually thinking I might be a writer.*

I didn't know the answer, but I knew that revealing my secret to him had been a turning point. I decided to accept it for what it meant to me: a special gift to a special fan. Even now, when I look at the experience in retrospect, Elvis remains an enigma.

I slept late the next day then went down to the coffee shop, and while I ate breakfast, I thought about the night before. *What had brought Elvis to my room?* It just didn't make sense, none of it. I don't know how long he was with me, I hadn't looked at the time. Thinking about it now I found it odd he'd showed so much interest in my family background, yet never once asked me if I was married or had children. I wondered if he knew? I wondered if he remembered Lauren.

I thought about all the things I wished I'd asked him. Funny, when I was around Elvis my brain was like an exclusive sponge, designed to absorb only him.

Then I remembered the gentle, caring way he'd comforted me when I revealed my secrets to him. Warm feelings pulsed through me at the memory and I knew I would cherish his compassion for as long as I lived. I would treasure it all; the tenderness, the craziness, the humor, and the kisses.

I pinched myself on the arm, discerned I was still in Las Vegas, and knew it was not a dream.

When I started back to my room I ran into Estelle and we talked for a few minutes, then I went on upstairs. I was running a tub of bath water when the phone rang. I turned the water off and went to answer it.

"Hello?"

"Baby Jane?"

"Elvis?"

"Who were you expecting?"

"Are you sick? You sound funny."

"It's my throat. I think I might be coming down with the flu or somethin'. I got some medicine from the doctor, so I'll be okay... what were you doin'?"

"Funny you should ask. I was running bath water. Seems you either catch me coming out or gettin' in."

He laughed, "I just wanted to talk. You didn't tell anybody about me comin' to your room last night?"

"No. You told me not to."

"Good girl. Know what that makes you?"

"What does that make me?"

"My special Baby Jane." My heart was flopping over like an omelet in my chest and I couldn't talk. We both remained silent for a moment. "You're different. You make me laugh and you don't expect anything from me. 'Cept a few fantasies," he laughed. "Man, sometimes I just wanna feel like a regular person, you know?"

"You mean I make you feel like a regular person?"

"I think in a way you do. I feel like I can trust you. And believe me when I say I don't give my trust away easily. Don't ever let me down, Baby. Keep me laughing and stay special."

"Always, Elvis. You're my angel of inspiration."

"Hey, I like that! Angel of inspiration. Man, that'd make a good song! Which reminds me, don't forget to get those gospel songs worked out with your brother. I really like 'em."

"I will. Oh, Elvis! I forgot to thank you for the room. Thank you. It was so nice of you to do this for me. I really appreciate it. I'll never forget it either. You've made this trip so special for me. I won't forget any of it...especially my fantasy gift."

"Did you dream about me last night?"

"You know I did."

"What were you wearing?"

"Elvis! What are you thinking?"

He chuckled. "Well, that's just it, you know. I can't very well think anything unless you fill me in on the details." I noticed he sounded better than when he'd first spoken.

"Your throat sounds better. You must've had a frog in it."

"Ah frog! Nah...you must just be good medicine."

"Elvis, what really made you think of calling me?"

"You make me laugh...and I like hearin' you talk about your family. They sound like real people, you know...fascinating."

"Yeah, they are...fascinating, that is. I wish you could meet my mama, Elvis. She's the love of my life."

His voice suddenly dropped to a melancholy tone. "I can relate. My mama was my life." His brief pause made me feel like it was time to switch the subject.

"Elvis, the funniest thing just crossed my mind."

"Funny? Well, let's hear it. I need somethin' funny."

"I was just imagining you at one of our family reunions. We have them all the time, but my family's so big we have to wear name tags." I heard him chuckle. "Anyway, I was thinking of what it would be like if you were there. I can just see it. What a hoot! They'd be all over you. Lordy, they'd be askin' questions, you know, about everything. We're all talkers."

By this time I was laughing and he started to laugh, too. "You come up with the damndest things. Is everybody else in your family as crazy as you?"

I wondered if I'd made a mistake. "I'm sorry, Elvis."

Now he busted out laughing. "Don't be sorry, Baby Jane. I think that's what's so funny about you. You have this habit of just sayin' whatever pops into your head and it makes me laugh and wonder where your head is."

"Are you saying I'm weird or crazy?"

"No. I'm saying you're so damn real it's refreshing," he chuckled. "But you are crazy. Hell, we're all crazy...it's a crazy world." We both got tickled this time. "You're leaving tomorrow?"

"Yeah, but I'll be at both shows tonight."

"I'd be disappointed if you weren't. Hey, why don't you wear that red thing with the lace. You know which one I'm talkin' about?"

"You remember my red outfit?"

"Sure I remember it. You look sexy in it. And wear your hair down. I like it that way...when it's not sticking out all over your head, that is." His reminder made us both laugh.

"Okay, I'd feel honored to wear it for you."

Still laughing, he said, "You're a woman after my heart, Baby Jane. Easy to influence."

His inference to my devotion cracked me up.

"Baby, I'm gonna have to hang up now. I got a show to get ready for, you know, givin' pretty girls like you fantasies." I heard his soft, low laugh. "But I'll see you later. Stay sweet. And remember our special secret and don't tell anybody." He sent me a kiss over the phone, then hung up.

I wondered what he meant by 'I'll see you later.' *Probably at the show,* I thought. I stood there for a moment, holding the receiver in my hand, thinking, *This is like a movie sequence.* Only it wasn't a movie and I wondered what would happen next.

I took my bath, singing "Love Me Tender" the entire time. I floated on a cloud as I donned my red silk pants outfit with a midriff top, the one Elvis had requested. While I was brushing out my hair, I thought about the night it had stood up from the static and smiled at my reflection as I carefully applied my makeup, and thought victoriously, *I did it*! I had actually made it happen! If only those girls back in junior high could see me now. But it was enough that I knew. Elvis had given me something from the heart and that's where it would stay. In my heart.

The dinner show was fabulous. Elvis outdid himself, even though it sometimes looked like his nose was running. *How does he do it*, I wondered? Even when he feels bad, he still gives his fans what they want. Like when he was singing "Poke Salad Annie." He humorously looked toward me and sang, "Polk Salad Frannie."

I was sitting center ringside, one seat away from the stage, and as I sat there knowing I'd only see one more show after this one, I observed Elvis very carefully.

I noticed his song selections were often intimate and revealing. It seemed as though he'd attached himself to the audience with a bond that was forever. I saw adoration on faces around me and knew this was the arena in which he thrived. It was like medicine to him and food for his soul. His audience had become the very cornerstone of his identity.

After the dinner show I went back up to my room. I'd wanted to go backstage but was afraid of seeming pushy. Elvis had said one of the things he liked about me was that I didn't expect anything and I didn't want him to change his mind.

I fixed myself a cold drink and turned on the television, more for company than anything else. My mind was on Elvis and I was in a down mood about having to leave for home the next day. I hoped I'd get a good seat for this last show. The one at dinner had cost me a sizable tip, considering the bite it took out of my flat purse.

I sat staring at the television, feeling lonely, and the secrets I'd told Elvis invaded my mind. I cringed at the emotions I experienced any time it was necessary for me to stand in front line battle against those demons. I preferred they stay buried. So it was my alter ego, Angela, that dealt with them.

I was screaming, "Daddy! Daddy! Daddy!" And Daddy came running into the kitchen where I stood, holding my arms out and away from my scalded skin, wailing my pain.

Daddy dropped to his knees and started checking me over. "Holy shit! What have you done to yourself?"

"I'm burned, Daddy, I'm burned," I sobbed, while the intense burning pain seared my fair, tender skin.

He scooped me up in his arms. "I can't even ask you to do one simple damn thing." He's mad at me, I thought. "All you had to do was turn on the pot of water sittin' on the stove. Ain't no damn body told you to pour that g...d... coffee. I just said turn the stove on. That's why kids get in trouble, 'cause they don't listen, damn it to hell!"

Daddy acted like it was my fault I'd got burned. But if he hadn't sent me into the kitchen in the first place...if he hadn't needed the coffee to sober up before Mama got home from work, if...

Daddy had carried me into the bedroom and was now laying me down on the bed. He inspected my burns more closely. "Lay right there, I'm gonna get some salve."

"Hurry," I cried out, *"it hurts sooo baaaad!"*

Suddenly, I heard the telephone ringing and I was back staring at the television. Then it rang again and my heart thumped with optimistic jubilation. Maybe it was Elvis. I picked up the receiver in anticipation.

"Hello."

"Baby Jane?"

"Elvis! I was hoping it was you."

"Why didn't you come to the dressin' room?"

"I didn't know I could. I mean...now that I'm not staying with Sylvia."

"Well...maybe it's better you didn't. Man, there's so many people down here it's crazy. You looked real sexy tonight."

"Thank you. So did you. And so pretty."

"I'm gonna have to teach you that men are not pretty. Chicks are pretty. How'd you like the song I did for you?"

"You mean 'Polk Salad Frannie'? Elvis, were you poking fun at my home state?" I teased. "After all, we do have a lot of gators in Florida."

"Yeah, I know, but did'ja catch what I was gettin' at?"

"What?"

"You know, your cousin, the one named Polk who's going with Bob. I thought about that song when you told me her name. Man, she sure did put you in the salad after you knocked her down." I could hear laughter in his voice, while in the background someone was calling him.

"Listen honey, I gotta go, but I'll see you at the next show."

"I'll be there. I hope I get a good seat."

"Why, has there been a problem?"

"Yes," I laughed, "but I'll manage somehow. I always do."

"You're incredible...but I gotta go now. I'll see you later."

He hung up the phone leaving me to absorb the abrupt silence. Our conversation had been cut so short, I was left with a feeling of desertion. *What did you expect*, I asked myself? He didn't have to call you. But he did.

Then I felt a stillness...and with it came a feeling of bliss and loneliness—a lifting sensation tinged with abandonment. I needed to get out of the room and go downstairs where I'd be around people. Being in a crowd was the best way to fight the memories.

I went to the casino lounge and ordered a drink. I wished it was time for the grand-room seating. I didn't like being alone right then. So many memories had been aroused in my mind. Mud?...no. Shit? That's what it was, all stirred up in my head, and it was inevitable that the stinking waste should begin to click through my brain like an old silent porno film.

My earliest memories go back to Seattle, Washington. That's where we lived when I started school. I went to Georgetown Elementary from the first grade until I was halfway through third. We were living in the house down on Maynard Street when I'd entered first grade. But I remembered things from the house on Maynard that went back to before I started school. Things that were fuzzy in part. Things like Mr. So-and-So.

Mr. So-and-So gave me pink marshmallow bunnies, then held me on his lap. That was all nice until...no one was looking. Then, Mr. So-and-So rubbed my fanny and said it was cute. It didn't feel right and the feelings I had made me uncomfortable. I tried to scramble down from his lap, but he held on to me and said it felt good when I wiggled that way. I could feel something beneath where I sat and the more I squirmed to get down, the larger it seemed to grow. Mr. So-and-So forced my hand down between my legs and onto the bulge in his lap. I couldn't free myself from his grip, no matter how hard I tried. Then I heard a soft, whiny sound. I thought Mr. So-and-So was crying because his eyes were closed. Then he opened his eyes and finally let me down. I remember thinking that I didn't want his ole bunnies anymore.

I shook the memories, brushed away a tear, and set my mind on happier thoughts. It was time to go see Elvis. I swallowed the last of my drink, then headed for the showroom. I was pleasantly surprised when I was led down front and center and seated in my favorite spot. I suspected Elvis had a hand in the effortless occurrence. Whoever, whatever, it was a grand gesture that greatly enhanced my last night in Vegas.

THERE'S A MAGIC that envelops the crowds of people who comprise an Elvis audience, indescribable in words. It's a feeling that permeates the air, the fiber of everything... an energy so dynamic, its force can be seen in the way it transforms normal people into fanatics. The transition is quick, overtaking an audience suddenly—like magic.

I glanced around and saw an impatient crowd, hungry for the show to begin. Then the orchestra sounded and the atmosphere sizzled with increased loudness, exciting, and priming the beast for the feast. A fast switch to a get-ready beat brought Elvis from behind the side curtain, his eminence as an entertainer undisputed. He stood like the "Super-Star" he was, shining forth the only light in the vast room. He curled his lip, reached for his guitar, then faced his insatiable audience and stirred the embers. And the fire exploded.

"That's All Right, Mama" held me spellbound. I slipped into a state of rapture, induced by the burning passion in his voice and my recollections from the previous night. Elvis' unusual insight into his fans emotions, and their reactions to his sensitivity, was a stimulus to the man. A performer led by instinct, Elvis embraced his audience and they were bound to be entranced.

He was the epitome of a cavalier that evening and the charming smile he directed my way thawed my misplaced feelings of abandonment. *Or was it perhaps the other way around*, I debated. Maybe my undisguised enthusiasm had somehow won him over. Anyway, I relaxed in the warmth and familiarity of the vibes transpiring between us now.

I was lifted higher when, during "Love Me Tender," Elvis did something I'll never forget. He bent down to give me the first kiss and when his soft lips touched mine, he made the world spin. His lips clung, with a leisurely sweetness that held still the very moments of time. He lifted his head, only slightly, his half-shuttered eyes gazing into mine, smiled, then licked my lips with his tongue and moved away. Needless to say, I did an instant meltdown. It was an intimate gesture, conveyed before a crowd in such a way that it was ours alone, and went undetected by onlookers.

It's strange how sometimes a little thing in one moment, between two people, can be so monumental that a million words could not express the emotions transferred. Elvis knew he had reached my heart and given me exactly what I wanted one more time—one more moment to remember.

When the show was over the waiter brought my check and again it was stamped complimentary. "Who's comping this time," I asked? He shrugged his shoulders and waited for me to sign the check. I considered going backstage after the last show, but since Elvis hadn't offered me an invitation, I was still reluctant to set myself up for disappointment or embarrassment. Surely, if he had wanted me backstage he would have made it known to me. I realized he was just one person and everybody wanted their chance at him and I couldn't blame them.

My better judgment told me to be cool and sent me straight upstairs on the chance that he might call. I turned on the television and tried to get interested in a movie, but it was impossible. What was he doing now? Would he call me? Should I just take a chance and go to the dressing room? Maybe he'd gone up to his room by now. I waited, but the phone didn't ring.

I encouraged my ego by musing over the past week. The events that had taken place, as mind-boggling as they were, comforted me. The memories Elvis had given me, perfect and pure, were worth more than gold, diamonds, homes, or Cadillacs. They represented the culmination of years of dreams.

Fate had brought me a fulfillment far beyond any well-laid plans, and tomorrow I would pack up my treasured memories along with my clothes, and carry them back to Tampa. Some would be recounted to friends and customers, while others would stay hidden in my heart, shared only with the man who had put them there.

BILLY IN 1972.

17

Jailhouse Rock

1971-1975

---

*There's no escapin' it. I don't care who you are or what
you're worth: there's trouble at every level of life.*

—*Elvis Presley*

Not long after I returned home from Vegas my marriage was in trouble. I can't blame Lauren; he far exceeded being merely a good husband. The problem was with me. I was having the nightmares again, brought on I suppose by the things I'd told Elvis. My dreams were always similar, involving guns and knives. Maybe a little something new here, or something new there, but basically the same dread.

Daddy is going to kill us all and Aunt Inez is trying to get the gun away from him and save us. Mama's head is rolling down the hill from the house we live in on Coalfax Place. It ends at the brink of discovery—something terrible, something awful. Suddenly, I sit straight up in bed, soaked in sweat and trembling like I'd met the devil himself.

The nightmares subsided after a few weeks, and I jumped back into the swing of things. But it didn't help my marriage. Las Vegas had redefined my outlook on life and I now found my day-to-day existence lacking excitement and challenge.

I filed for a divorce, still living in the house with Lauren in a platonic relationship. He wanted to be close to me and was agreeable to the conditions of the arrangement that was convenient for both of us. He didn't have to look for another place to live and I felt safer with him in the house. Lauren was still my best friend and bouncer.

Soon after our divorce was final my girlfriend and her brother, Billy, came by the house to visit. Billy had just been released from Florida State Prison the day before, where he'd served seven years for breaking and entering, grand larceny, and escape.

This particular evening I'd planned to go dancing for the first time since my divorce. Sammy Smith had a hit record, "Take the Ribbons From My Hair," and was appearing at the Imperial Lounge. I wanted to see her but dreaded making the nightclub scene by myself.

Lauren, Jolynn, and I were finishing supper when my friend and her brother arrived. I cleared off the table while we talked, then my girlfriend and I went into the bathroom to continue our conversation while I put on my makeup. I asked her if she'd like to go out with me.

"No, I'm too tired. I just wanna go home, Frances. I really don't feel up to going out tonight."

"Ah...I don't want to go by myself." Then I thought of her brother. "Maybe Billy would like to go. I mean, after being locked up for seven years, I'd imagine he'd be ready for some fun."

"I doubt he'll wanna go, he's kinda shy. But I'll ask him."

She went into the family room to speak with Billy. A few minutes later she came back wearing a surprised look on her face.

"He said he'd go."

I finished getting ready, then Billy and I left for the club, leaving Jolynn in the care of Lauren. As soon as we got in the car he asked me who Lauren was. When I told him he was my ex-husband, he got the strangest look on his face.

"Man, things sure have changed in this world while I been locked up."

"Like what?" I asked.

"Hell, everything. Mini skirts, hippies, ex-husbands who live with their ex-wives and baby-sit the kid for her to go out with another man."

"Well...it's not like we're on a date, you know. You're my friend's little brother. Besides, Lauren and I are divorced and he has no say-so over what I do."

Billy shook his head like he couldn't believe my situation, then turned on the radio and sang along with the song that was playing.

"Sweeten my coffee with a morning kiss."

"Hey, you sound good! You've got a great voice." He had those far away eyes like Elvis, only Billy's were brown and deep set and that seemed to make him look more dark and dangerous. He winked at me and clicked his tongue twice.

"I just like singing." Then he laughed and bumped the palm of his hand against the top of the window opening. "Little brother? Is that what you think I am?"

We'd reached the lounge. I parked the car and we went inside and took a seat in a back booth. Billy had waited for me to slide in first, then he sat beside me. We ordered drinks and listened to Sammy Smith's one hit, while I kept wondering why he hadn't sat across from me.

When the dancing started I asked him, "Do you dance?"

"Well, it's been awhile, but I'm ready to give it a try if you're brave enough to risk it." He looked happy. I mean he really looked happy. Like it might have been the happiest moment in his life kind of happy.

We went out onto the floor and I noticed him glancing around at the other couples, as if taking note of their steps. We started dancing and suddenly, he really got down. I mean he was tearing the floor up. I'd met my soul mate when it come to dancing.

"Hey, did you do a lot of this in that place you just came from?"

"You mean the joint?"

"Yeah, I guess, if that's what you call it."

"This is the boxer's step. You just bounce around, kinda watch everybody, then kick in a few new steps. Anyway, it works."

He was smiling as he hotfooted and shuffled all over the dance floor, which we stayed on for about five consecutive numbers before taking a rest and ordering another round of drinks.

Still huffing and puffing, I told him, "Hey...you were good out there."

"You think so?" He winked and I was starting to wonder if he was flirting with me.

I glanced sideways, trying to sneak a peek at him while taking a sip of my drink, and couldn't miss the hungry-wolf eyes staring back at me. He knew he'd caught me trying to cop a look at him.

I blushed and before I could even stammer something out, he said, "I ain't kissed a chick in seven years, can I kiss you?"

I was stunned, caught off guard again, and had only had an inkling that he might be flirting. I tilted my head to study him for a moment and that was the first time I really looked at Billy, not like my friend's little brother, but as a man. He seemed to be nervous and I presumed his intensity stemmed from a slight fear of rejection. I sensed his feelings of displacement and found this rare innocence intriguing. I was taken aback for a moment, but I must admit that the thought of kissing a good-looking, younger man, who hadn't kissed a girl in seven years, was a real turn-on.

"Really, you ain't kissed a girl in seven years?"

"Well they sure as hell don't have women in Raiford."

"Oh, that's right, I forgot."

His expression displayed his impatience and I thought it would be cruel to deny him a little ole kiss.

"Yeah, I'll let you kiss me."

The words hardly left my mouth before he lunged forward, throwing me backward onto the seat, and kissed me like he was starving to death and there was no tomorrow.

It wasn't tender and it wasn't soft. He ravished my mouth, raping it with a sexual passion so fierce, so powerful, so wild, so free. And like the Fourth of July, fireworks exploded into brilliant colors all around us.

I fell in love that very moment; passionately, obsessively, and blindly in love. It was a kind of devotion unfamiliar to me; overpowering, consuming, frightening, and I could feel my control slipping away. Somewhere deep down inside, I knew from the beginning it would be an elusive relationship. But I wanted the memory, even if that was all that came of it.

My relationship and eventual marriage to Billy took me down a path I'd never walked before. It was an explosive learning experience charged with good and bad—a rough road and one I wouldn't want to travel again.

Billy was twenty-four when we met, almost twenty five, and I was twenty-seven. He had lived the last seven of his years behind prison bars and had become a master of manipulation, as I would soon find out. But, he had a refreshing vitality for life unlike anything I'd ever seen. Watching Billy discover his new world of freedom reduced me to a teenager. His energy was like a magnet, pulling me into his excitement and distancing me from the responsibilities of daily life—like going to bed at a decent enough hour to be able to work the next day and remembering that house payments and utilities had to be paid.

Billy compared himself to the boy from the wrong side of the tracks and viewed me as the American dream. But I certainly didn't see it that way. Still, my head was easily turned by his good looks, teasing ways, fun-loving spirit, and beautiful singing voice. I was captured by the songs that flowed from his lips. Songs with words that spoke to my romantic heart. Billy's personality and attitudes reminded me of Elvis, so very much.

Lauren moved out of the house after Billy and I started dating. Then Billy moved in with me and we lived together for a little over a year before we were married. This went against everything I believed in and the only reason I agreed to the unsanctioned life-style was because of his parole officer. He wouldn't give us permission to marry. He felt that Billy needed time to adjust to living outside prison before taking on the responsibility of a ready-made family.

We applied for a license five times during the first year. But each time we went to pick it up we were turned down. The parole man read the marriage applications that appeared in the newspaper, then attached his card of refusal to ours every time.

Living with the many oddities of a newly released convict took some getting used to. Billy continuously paced in an effort to work off his pent-up energy. He took five to six showers a day, relishing in the freedom of being able to bathe at his own inclination. He slept with his eyes open for over a year. And he loved to stand in front of the kitchen cabinets, after we had gone shopping, and stare at the groceries that filled them.

Waking up in the mornings lying beside him, I'd scrutinize the blank stare in his big brown, deep-set eyes, as he lay sleeping. I remember brushing his hair back from his forehead and studying his handsome face.

Billy was one quarter Cherokee and his strong Indian features demanded respect. I wondered about all he'd lived through. *What horrific things he must have witnessed in that place!* And as I studied intensely this creation of the penal system, it just broke my heart that even in sleep he couldn't escape.

Mornings were magic for Billy and me. Like Heaven reached down and touched us and that's when we saw the best in each other. Tenderness swelled within me every time I woke up first. I'd watch the man I loved in slumber and my protective instincts were overwhelming. I was sure my love would change him, and I was going to love him with an immeasurable devotion, and he'd be distanced forever from the thrashing nightmares of prison—free to know a life of prosperity and contentment.

Sometimes Billy woke up first, and I'd ascend to the morning cuddled in wispy emotions, arms embracing me, and his face so close to mine our noses lay side by side, our lips barely touching. I remember the feelings...always the feelings, of his lashes softly brushing my brows, and his lips moving ever so slightly against mine, and he'd sing:

"Sweeten my coffee with a morning kiss, soften my dreams with your sighs, tell me you love me for a million years, then if it don't work out, then you can tell me good-bye."

The words of his song inspired deeply intense, prophetic intuitions within me. Alas, I had no idea where our road together would lead nor how long it would endure. It seemed most of the time like a dead-end highway, so wild and unpredictable that my sound mind said it couldn't last. But my feelings during the ride were sensational, erupting to match the volatile, romantic lover who lifted me to touch Heaven, grasp a piece, and bring it back to earth where we were isolated by its magic.

These were the tender times. Intervals that carried us through the turmoil periods that come as part of the package when you love a rogue. A handsome rogue. That's the way I thought of Billy and it was no wonder I loved him so desperately.

Billy's playful nature enlivened everything and covered a multitude of sins. I am reminded of one particular demonstration of this. I'd come home from work and rushed through cooking supper. It was the weekend and we were going out that evening to our favorite dance club, the Holiday House. Billy was terminally impatient, so I left the kitchen and dining room in a mess and made my exit for the shower.

That evening things between us went smoothly and we got down on every number they played. Billy's natural rhythm had developed till he was now a master on the floor and our mutual love for dancing was a strong bond between us. We danced till the band stopped playing, then left for home. It was late and I was exhausted and Billy was busy telling me jokes while he drove, and forgot to stop for breakfast, which was our usual habit.

When we reached home, I dragged my tired body straight to the bedroom and fell across the king-size bed onto my stomach. I was so bushed, I dreaded the effort it would take to get out of my clothes. Billy came into the bedroom and flipped on the light.

"Baby, we forgot to stop and eat breakfast."

He was in a good mood and tried to tease me into cooking for him. But I was sleepy and the last thing I wanted to do was make breakfast.

"Ah, come on, baby, feed your man."

"No, Billy! I'm wore out. Leave me alone and let me sleep."

He pleaded, begged, and teased me, and when none of it roused me from the bed, he pulled off his belt and whacked me across my bottom.

"Fix me somethin' to eat, woman!"

I flipped onto my side and stared at him through squinted eyes. "Don't you dare hit me with that belt again. And you can fix your own breakfast!"

He wouldn't give up and continued to pester me. Finally, I jumped up from the bed and stomped into the kitchen while he followed. Everything was still in a mess from dinner. Dirty dishes were scattered everywhere. I yanked the refrigerator door open and took out a carton of eggs. The frying pan was sitting on the stove, crusty from the green peas that had dried up and hardened to it. Billy stood in the kitchen doorway watching me.

"You want breakfast? I'll fix you breakfast!"

I took two eggs from the carton, placed them in the filthy frying pan, then using my open palm I smashed the eggs and turned on the burner. Billy never said a word, just stood watching the incredible scene I made. His expression was one of disbelief when I stirred the eggs and shells around in the pan with a dirty fork, then dumped the inedible concoction onto a nasty plate and shoved it at him.

"There! You've got breakfast!"

He stood for a second, staring at the plate he held. "What's this...?" Then he shouted, "You expect me to eat this crap?" and threw it upside the wall.

I looked at the mess he'd made, and madder than a piss-ant, I grabbed a saucer and sailed it at him. He in turn threw one at me. Before we stopped, every dish in the house was broken and we were laughing. Our anger had spawned passion and breakfast was forgotten as we made our way back to the bedroom to make love. This was the way we settled our differences.

The next morning Billy was up early, sweeping our madness into the garbage can. He used a garden hose to wash down the battlefield and warped all my cabinets in the process. When I saw what his handiwork had done to my kitchen, I asked him, "Who do you think you are, Elvis Presley?"

DANCING EVENTUALLY TURNED into an every night event and life was one big party. But parties cost money and somewhere down the line the bills have to be paid. Billy worked when he felt like it and left the responsibilities of being a parent and home owner to me. He was not a person I could depend on and I soon found myself knee-deep in debt and heartache. Working all day and partying all night was expensive and took its toll on my mental and physical being as well as my finances.

When the newness of being a free man had worn off, Billy

started cheating on me with other women and that's when the fighting really heated up. However, by this time he was in my blood like an addiction. It seemed I couldn't live with him and I couldn't live without him.

I asked him why he cheated on me and he said, "Baby, you know you're the best. But I haven't tried 'em all yet."

I guess he thought it was all a big joke. But it wouldn't have been a bit funny if I'd done the same. He said it was different for the woman. A man could cheat, but a woman was supposed to stay home and wait for her mate to return, then ask no questions. Of course, I didn't buy this line of bullshit, but as Mama would say, I wallowed in it.

As I sank deeper into a life foreign to me, my mother cried and worried over her daughter, who had seemingly taken leave of her senses. Abandoning my faculties was precisely what I did when along with the drinking and partying, I allowed marijuana to enter the picture. And even though I never went beyond pot to stronger drugs, it still played havoc with my life.

My world crashed down around me one morning while I was at work. I was teasing a customer's hair when two men in suits came through the shop door. They stood in front of the reception desk till Reynaldo went over and spoke to them. Then, Reynaldo walked anxiously over to my station and whispered, with his Cuban accent, "Fron'cess, the two gentlemen that just came into the shop are narcotic agents and they want to speak to you. What have you got yourself into this time, my darling?"

Fear choked me and I was strangling on it as I walked toward the men. I remember thinking, *What has Billy done now?* I knew I hadn't done anything wrong. What had Billy done that could get me in trouble? He was so secretive.

Anyway, they read me my rights then charged me with conspiracy to commit a felony. "Conspiracy to commit a what?" I stammered out. I hadn't conspired to do a damn thing but work my butt off. So not understanding the charge, I asked them to please explain what it meant I'd done.

They repeated, "Conspiracy to commit a felony," and that was all the explanation I received before I was handcuffed and led outside to their car.

I was surprised, but not shocked, to see they had Billy in the car, too. As I climbed into the back seat beside him, seething from fear and frustration, I asked what all of this was about.

"Billy, what does conspiracy mean? What felony have you done?"

"Me! Why's it always me?"

I was crying hard, near hysterics. Nothing like this had ever happened to me before and I wanted to know why it was happening now. "You're the card-toting cell mate, not me. I'm scared shitless."

Billy told me to keep quiet. "Don't say anything, Frances, until we've talked with a lawyer."

Jolynn was foremost in my mind, and it was imperative that I find an answer for this frightening dilemma before 5:00 p.m., when I had to pick her up from the nursery. I wanted no one to know of my incarceration, especially my family. So after I was booked and put into a cell, I hounded the jail matron until I was allowed my one phone call. I used it to contact the real estate agent who had been after me to sell my house.

My situation demanded a radical solution. I needed $10,000 for our bond and I needed it fast. So I came to an agreement with the realtor; my house and all its contents for the bail bond. He would in turn allow me the use of my home for three months.

Upon our release, Billy asked me how I'd gotten us out of jail so fast. "I gave up my house, furniture, everything, and now I want an explanation of the charges against us!"

He told me it had to do with a telephone conversation between him and a girl who was involved with a big-time drug dealer. "All I said was, can I get a joint from you. How was I to know her connections? But her line was tapped and because I'm on parole they thought they could drag me into it for information...but I don't know anything, man. Every time I make a move they're on my ass, blaming me for crap I don't know anything about!"

"Well, that still doesn't explain why they arrested me!" I shouted.

"It was your phone, baby," Billy gritted back at me, "and they don't care who they take down."

"What's gonna happen to us now?"

"We have to get a good lawyer. I can't make any deals. I'm on parole and that means it's gotta be a clear case of innocence on my part."

"How long will it take before we're off bond?"

"Could be a year."

My heart sank, then swam around in my stomach till it digested into a ten-ton weight on my shoulders. How was I going to explain losing my home to Mama? How, in the name of sanity, had I made such a mess of everything? It was just too much to think about. So I didn't. Throwing all my burdens and doubts to the wind, I followed whatever Billy said to do, and wherever it led, I kept giving haircuts and perms. After all, I reasoned, I loved him. And like my granny used to quote from the Bible, "Whether thou goest, I will go." At least till the bumps in the road knocked some sense into me.

Billy's estimate was close. It was seven months before the charges against us were dropped. During that time we moved from place to place, trying to get our life back on track. When we were finally cleared, I tightened my emotional armor, got a grip on our situation, and agreed to follow Billy's suggestion. With money I'd been awarded from injuries sustained in an automobile accident, plus a loan from Mama and Pap, we located an old drive-in restaurant in Plant City. It had been closed down for a long time, but Billy saw great promise in the location, so we leased it.

That same day, we found out Elvis had been booked for two concerts in Jacksonville on April 16, 1972. Billy was almost as anxious as I was when it came to seeing Elvis, so we ordered tickets and made plans to go for both shows.

The trip was a long drive that provided plenty of time for my Elvis stories. Billy had heard them all before, but his interest was piqued because he was on his way to a live performance for the first time. As I repeated my tales of adventure with Sylvia, he hesitated to believe them. He'd looked at my pictures many times, and read the story in **Movie TV Photo Stars** magazine, but he still found it hard to believe I'd be remembered.

"Just you wait and see," I told him.

The coliseum was crowded when we got there and Elvis' fans were clamoring to purchase souvenirs from hawkers at the entrance. Programs, T-shirts, pictures, the Colonel hadn't missed a trick of the carnival man he was and the atmosphere it created was a definite hype for Elvis' fans.

Our seats were at the top of the coliseum steps, about as far away as one could be placed and still be considered within the perimeter of the coliseum. The only saving grace was the second show tickets tucked safely in my purse. Although they weren't ringside, they were for far better seats than the ones we now occupied.

We sat through the usual opening format and Billy loved the Sweet Inspirations and looked forward to meeting them. "But, Frances, what if they don't remember you and you make a fool of us?"

"Stop worrying, Billy. You act like you don't believe me."

"Yeah, I believe you, but I don't think you realize how it is with busy important people like them. They meet thousands of fans all the time. They can't remember all of them."

"But they'll remember me!" I assured him.

Eventually, Sprach Zarathustra began the introduction. Expectations sizzled and snapped when Elvis came on stage wearing a blue, jeweled jumpsuit and cape. *Wow!* I thought, *a blue jumpsuit!* I watched Billy's face and his expressions tickled me.

"Wow! Man, he is the King! I never thought I'd ever see him in person."

I was floating on a happy cloud. I loved Elvis and I loved Billy and watching them both enjoying themselves made me happy as a double-dip ice cream cone.

Billy watched the screaming girls and couldn't hide his envy of Elvis' place. He loved pretty girls and thought Elvis was the luckiest guy alive.

"You know...man, Elvis has got the cool every guy envies."

Billy really dug Elvis' physical presentation and, of course, so did I. His music was full of energy and again left the audience wanting more. And I was more than happy to know we had tickets ensuring more.

When the performance ended we stood up and started to work our way out of the concrete bleachers. It was push and shove all the way. Billy finally suggested we sit down and wait for the crowd to thin out.

"But I want to get to the phone and call Sylvia before it's too late," I reminded him.

"What'cha gonna do, Frances? Walk over all these people?"

"No," I'll just fly over 'em."

When the upper seats had cleared and we finally stood up and started our descent, I slipped on some ice somebody had spilled. I fell and landed on my rear end, then slid down the flight of concrete steps. Billy rushed to my side, found I was still breathing, and started to laugh as he helped me to my feet.

I was in horrible pain, and yelled at his insensitivity. "It's not funny!" He still didn't realize I'd been hurt and couldn't stop laughing.

"Baby, I didn't really think you meant it when you said you'd fly."

"Stop laughing! I think I broke my tail bone." But he couldn't stop and continued to laugh as I struggled to walk in a bent-over position. The pain was excruciating.

"Well, baby, if you're hurtin' that bad, ha, ha, ha, maybe we'd better not try to make it over to the hotel."

I could tell by his blatant humor that he still didn't believe I was hurt very bad. I struggled to straighten up but found it impossible. I knew I'd seriously injured something, but I wasn't going to let it stop me from making the journey to see Sylvia and maybe Elvis.

We found a pay phone and I dialed the hotel where I knew they were staying. Sylvia answered the phone. She sounded happy to hear from me and said for us to come on over. Billy was in shock.

"She knew you!"

"Of course she knew me. I told you she would. Now come on, honey, let's go. She said for us to come right over."

Looking at the strain on my face and the awkward way I was standing, he asked me if I was sure I could make it. I told him yes, then had to reassure myself several times before we got to the car.

When we reached the hotel, I called upstairs and Sylvia told us to come on up. We went to her room and had barely knocked on the door when it flew open.

"Hey, girl...what's wrong with you?"

Bent over, still unable to stand upright, I told her. "I fell down the steps at the coliseum and I think I broke my tail bone."

"Come on in," Sylvia invited, frowning like she could feel my pain.

I hobbled into the room with Billy right behind me.

"Sylvia, this is Billy. Billy this is Sylvia."

"Hi, Sylvia. Frances told me a lot about you. Man, I liked your group. Ya'll gotta good sound."

"Watch him, Sylvia, he's a flirt."

"Girl, you look like you're in awful pain," she winced. "Sit down."

Billy sat in a chair and I tried to sit around my pain, on the bed next to Sylvia. Then Billy told her I'd jumped from the top of the coliseum trying to reach Elvis.

Sylvia laughed. "I believe it. This girl was always crazy."

"Don't buy his con, Sylvia. I slipped on some ice somebody spilled...talk about pain. So, what have you been up to, besides touring?"

She said she was still living in New Jersey, putting away money. "You know, nothin' lasts forever, Frances."

Just for a fleeting moment, I felt a tinge of sadness at her words and then it was gone. I told her Billy was a singer and tried to coax him into singing for her. But that was like trying to move a mule when it didn't want to move. Billy was more interested in quizzing Sylvia about all my Vegas stories, like he needed confirmation to believe them.

"It's all true, all of it. Less she left some of it out." She was smiling and Billy looked at me skeptically.

"You mean there's more?"

"I guess so..." She looked at me. "You didn't tell him everything, did you?" I smiled and quickly changed the subject.

Sylvia had ordered a steak for dinner, "But the staff down in the kitchen's been so busy gettin' Elvis' dinner, they ain't had no time to get around to my little ole steak. I ordered it over an hour ago and Elvis ordered his dinner twenty minutes ago and he's already eaten it! I think they're out to starve me to death."

I asked her if there was any chance of us seeing Elvis. "I doubt it. Doc's up in his room right now giving him his shot and no-body's allowed in when he's with the doctor. Make sure you come to the last show though, 'cause it's gonna be the best. Elvis is al-ways best after he's had his B12."

"We'll be there. We got tickets for both shows."

We sat around talking till Sylvia had to start getting dressed for the next concert. Her dinner still hadn't arrived.

"I don't guess I'm gonna get to eat my steak." She walked us to the door then gave me a hug. "Take care of yourself, girl, and go see a doctor when you get home. And take care of this good-lookin' man here, too."

"Nice meetin' you, Sylvia," Billy said as he hugged her good-bye.

"Call me at home, Frances, after the tour's over and we can talk."

Our seats for the next show were much better, at least the view was. The concrete bleachers were sheer hell on my tail bone. The Sweet Inspirations were superb, and true to Sylvia's prediction, Elvis was at his best. The whole concert was just fantastic. Billy lik-ened it to the twilight zone...that place between sleep and awaken-ing.

The coliseum was dark, all but a spotlight that roamed the are-na. An obscure shadow lurked to the left of the stage and fans got excited thinking it might be Elvis. Then, heavy beats sounded from the kettledrums, followed by a crescendo of horns blaring out the theme from *2001*, building anticipation to a climax.

Then a fast tempo overtook the introduction, and the crowd roared as Elvis made his entrance from the right, wearing another blue jumpsuit and cape.

Cameras flashed and the sight looked like a World War II bombing. Thousands of flashbulbs, popping everywhere, ignited off the jeweled cape Elvis was now holding spread eagle as he made his grandiose bows. Reaching for his guitar, he quickly led the band into "See See Rider."

Billy said the audience's reaction reminded him of a Superbowl game, when it comes down to one field goal kick that decides the winner. You don't know what the outcome is going to be, then all of a sudden, your team scores!

The first song ended and the audience froze in a trance for just a few seconds before the applause burst forth into an ear- shattering thunder. Elvis quickly went into a medley of songs, pumping out his energy and mesmerizing the audience with his charisma. And we were caught in the maelstrom, transformed into screaming, crying, shaking creations of Babel.

At the end of the medley the King rewarded his loyal supporters with kisses, scarves, and boyish pranks. Then he masterfully mesmerized the noisy zealots into his personal trance with a slow love song. You could feel the magnetism of Elvis' personality, reaching out to touch each individual in a personal way. His performance was a marvel of expertise.

The show came to an end, and without Elvis for distraction, my pain consumed me. Our trip back home was a miserable nightmare. I found it hard to sit comfortably, but Billy, still not realizing the extent of my injury, thought it was funny. He teased and harassed me all the way back to Tampa. I went to see the doctor the day after we got home and he confirmed my suspicions, when he told me in layman terms I'd broken my tail bone.

"How do you fix it?"

"You don't," he said. "It's one of those injuries that has to heal by itself. You're just going to have to baby it for a while"

That's just great, I thought, *with all the work I have ahead of me.* That drive-in restaurant was not going to open by itself.

Billy and I finally came to the conclusion that if we wanted to get married we'd have to go to another county. This was the only way to keep his parole officer from reading about it in the newspaper. We understood the chance we were taking by leaving the county and getting married without permission. But, some rules were made to be broken and this was one of them.

We drove by my Aunt Bethine's house and dropped Jolynn off before heading for Bartow where the marriage took place on April 25, 1972 (Gladys Presley's birthday).

There were no guests, only Billy and me, the marriage license clerk, and a witness provided by the court. I wore blue jeans, my ring was a plain gold band, and it rained. But none of this dampened my happiness. We kept the marriage a secret because Billy had broken parole to do it. But, I knew we were legal now, and that made all the difference in the world as far as my conscience was concerned.

Our wedding night was spent cutting up chickens for the opening of our restaurant the next morning. It was evident from the first day that we had chosen a prime spot. The Sunny South Drive-in, located in Plant City on Highway 39 South, caught the truck drivers traveling the road at night, and we were located near Plant City High School, which brought us teenagers during lunch. Being outside the city limits drew them on the weekends, too, where they figured it was easier to smuggle their bottles of liquor onto our curb.

In the beginning things ran professionally and Billy and I were closer than we'd ever been, working together, and sharing the excitement of being married and starting up a business.

Billy did the cooking, I waited tables on the inside, and we both took care of the curb window. We hired a girl who had just graduated from high school, I'll call Becky (not her real name) to do the curb work.

Billy and I both had family in Plant City, but Bethine patronized our restaurant more than any of the rest. She was the only member of my mother's family who got to know Billy very well, and was the only person who knew we were married. Bethine was divorced with three children and was going with a guy named Preston.

The first time Billy met Preston he told Bethine, "Don't marry him! He will kill you."

"Billy, don't be silly. Preston wouldn't hurt anybody."

"Bethine, believe me. I've lived in the joint long enough to judge a man's character and I'm telling you, that man is fiddlin' without a bow and he'll kill you and he won't even give you a chance. Don't marry him!"

But Bethine, although she seemed to be paying attention to what Billy said, disregarded his warning and eventually married Preston. She was in love.

I was in love too, and really thought everything was going to work out for Billy and me. We had our business now, and nobody knew we were married.

Becky, our new curb girl, started getting eyes for Billy and when I informed her that he was taken she said, "Billy told me you were his business partner and that's all."

She knew we lived together so I can't imagine what words he used to con her about that. But I knew Billy's cheating ways, so unbeknownst to him, I took her aside and told her we were married and even showed her our marriage license. She acted like she was my friend after that. But in the end, I found out she was seeing him behind my back, and I left Billy. My final revenge came when I had the electricity for the drive-in turned off over a holiday weekend and put an end to the restaurant business. I'd be damned if I'd let Becky get everything I'd worked for.

I moved back home with Mama and Pap until I rented a trailer from the lady Mama worked for. She owned a lot of land along the Hillsborough River in Thonotasassa and she had a couple of houses and a few trailers she rented out. Jolynn and I moved into one of the trailers and I bought an old Corvair for fifty dollars. It was an ugly-looking heap, but it ran good. I slowly got on my feet again, then Billy decided he wanted to come back home.

We were living in Thonotasassa in what I called the cow pasture, when I met the best friend I would ever have. One morning Billy stepped outside the trailer and saw this guy with his head under the hood of a car. Billy walked over to see if he could give him a hand, and when the guy lifted his head, Billy couldn't believe it when he discovered Doug, a friend he'd served time with, living next door to us. The hippy girl who'd been our neighbor the day before was now gone, and Doug had moved in during the night.

Billy said, "How in the world I could bump into someone I know, way out here in the boonies, is beyond me."

Doug told Billy his apartment in Orlando had been raided for drugs, and he and his pregnant girlfriend, Darlene, had been arrested and put in jail. Two days after their arrest, Darlene went into labor and was transferred to the hospital where she gave birth to their daughter. Doug escaped from jail, went to the hospital, and stole Darlene and the baby. They fled from Orlando and took sanctuary in this backwoods hideout that a friend had told him about.

I went next door with Billy to meet them and I knew immediately, I'd found a friend for life. Darlene and I were so much alike.

Even our birth dates were only one day apart with ten years between us. I was the oldest.

Being a hairdresser, the first thing I notice about a woman is her hair, and I fell in love with Darlene's long, dark brown tresses the instant I laid eyes on her. That hair, waist length, naturally curly, and thick, thick, thick, was the most beautiful I'd ever seen. She was tiny with boobs like Dolly Parton. And she had a dark mole above her lip.

Doug was not a drug addict, although he did smoke pot. Darlene told me he'd sold drugs to afford a private investigator to search for her oldest daughter, who had been kidnaped by Darlene's ex-husband.

Darlene, Doug, Billy, me, and our kids became like a family. We looked out for each other through good times and bad.

It was now toward the end of 1972, and psychedelic music, flower children, bell bottoms, long hair, and the hippy peace movement were still making a heavy statement. We decorated our trailers with beads, fluorescent posters, lava lamps, and black lights. We entertained ourselves sitting around the floor passing joints and listening to Jimmy Hendrix, Janice Joplin, and, of course, Elvis. We told funny stories, pigged out on pizza, and laughed at absolutely everything.

Darlene loved Elvis and never got tired of hearing my stories. She joined me in sympathy when we heard the latest news reports. According to the press, Priscilla had left Elvis for her karate instructor, Mike Stone. That was hard for me to imagine until I looked at my womanizing husband. Then I shook my head and thought, *But he's not Elvis.*

January of 1973, residents of the cow pasture celebrated New Year's together. I remember this so well, because about a week later everything changed.

Billy had been on his best behavior for three months now and I thought everything was going along fine. Sure, we still had our differences, but nothing serious. He wasn't being unfaithful or fighting with me anymore. And he was working. Then one day, when he was supposed to pick me up from work, he didn't show up. I called his boss and they said he'd quit two days earlier.

Reynaldo's wife, Loida, drove me home where I discovered Billy had packed up and left, taking the new car we had just bought with him. Since I now had no transportation, I had no alternative but to move back home with Mama and Pap.

ABOUT A WEEK AFTER I was with my parents, Mama was frying bacon one morning and the smell sent me rushing to the bathroom. When I came out, she looked at me and said, "Don't tell me. You're pregnant."

I was ecstatic! Even though my circumstances were bad at the time, I was still happy. Jolynn would be six and I would be thirty when this baby was born. I'd wanted lots of children and no amount of people telling me how crazy I was could spoil my happiness. I wanted my children for me. And I worried about my biological clock that was ticking faster with each year that slipped by.

A few days after my pregnancy was confirmed, I saw Elvis in his "Aloha from Hawaii TV" special. I watched him singing and smiling, so pretty, and remembered our special time together. It almost seemed like a dream now and the memories made me want to see him again. But the way my life was going it didn't seem very likely to happen. Oh, I might get to see him in a concert if he came to Tampa. But I missed the more intimate Vegas shows where they didn't announce after the performance, "Elvis has left the building."

I must say, I didn't fret long over the matter. After all, I was going to be a mommy again. And regardless of which road my life took, with or without Billy, I would always have a part of him in this child who was growing beneath my heart. This baby was living proof of our love, the offspring of an elusive love that could never be captured and caged. A physical part of that love that I could hold on to forever.

I worried the entire time I was pregnant that I wouldn't carry to full term. That's how much I wanted this baby. When I called Billy at his mother's house, where I suspected he was, to let him know he was going to be a father, he was elated and wanted us to get back together. I was ready to forgive him again, but unfortunately, I was living at home with my parents and he was staying with his brother and we had no money between us.

One night in February while I was living with my parents, we were all sleeping when the phone rang. I heard Pap get up and go to answer it.

"Hello..."

There was a long pause, then he said, "Oh, no!"

He asked a few questions I couldn't make out since he'd lowered his voice. Then he went and aroused Mama from bed. I heard her say, "What's wrong?" as she went to the phone. The next thing I heard were her screams, "Oh God, no!"

I jumped out of bed and ran into the living room where I saw Mama shaking and crying as she hung up the phone. "Preston shot Bethine in front of Mama's house, then killed himself."

She said Preston tried to kill Bethine's daughters, too, but they ran and, luckily, got away. Bethine's seventeen-year-old son was staying with Mama's baby sister, Geneva, at the time because he didn't like Preston, so he hadn't been around.

The words Billy had said to Bethine came back to haunt me. *Don't marry him. He will kill you.*

Bethine's tragic death devastated our family and was instrumental in opening my eyes somewhat to the danger of my lifestyle. I now realized that bad things could happen to good people.

WHEN I WAS ABOUT FIVE or six months along in my pregnancy, Billy and I moved into an apartment in the new complex Reynaldo had built across the street from his beauty salon. Billy was happy about the baby and I loved him so much, I felt sure he would settle down now and be the husband I longed for.

He went to work for a battery company and started out on the night shift. I could hardly believe the transformation my pregnancy had made in him. He was responsible, devoted, faithful, and so attentive while we waited for the birth of our baby.

Jessica was born on October 8, 1973, and Billy was in total awe of his beautiful baby girl. He proudly boasted his fatherhood, and Jessica took her daily naps on her daddy's chest. Billy sang her lullabies, then watched her sleep as though she would disappear if he took his eyes off her. I thought the baby had finally changed him in a way nothing else had ever been able.

But, by January of '74, he was back to his wandering ways.

WE MOVED TO PLANT CITY and rented a house during the gas shortage. I was the only one working, and having to drive back and forth the distance to Tampa every day, plus waiting in the lines for gasoline, began to wear on my nerves. I think it finally made me step back and see the truth of the situation. And that's when I made up my mind to get out.

I found a house back in Tampa but I didn't tell Billy. Then I started moving my things out of the one in Plant City, a little at a time. Jolynn had two more weeks of school before summer vacation, when I made my final break.

I knew my love for Billy was my weak spot, and I'd always taken him back before, so this time I went on my knees and asked God to show me the way. "Lord, if I can't stop loving him, teach me to learn to live without him."

I was starting to understand Priscilla. No matter how much I loved Elvis, I wasn't his wife. And no matter who a woman's husband might be, it's still no fun sharing him with other women.

SANDRA AND BOB ROSS' WEDDING PHOTO. LAS VEGAS INT'L HOTEL 1973.
(FROM THE COLLECTION OF SANDRA ROSS)

18

A Change Of Habit

1974 - 1975

Sad thing is...you can still love someone and be wrong for them.

— *Elvis Presley*

Sandra and Robert Ross were married August 20, 1973, in a ceremony at the International Hotel in Las Vegas, during one of Elvis' engagements. I was almost eight months pregnant with Jessica and unable to travel. So, I didn't get to make it to the wedding, but Sandra showed me the pictures and told me all about it.

Their wedding was a gift from the Colonel, with Marie Parker standing as Sandra's matron of honor, and Rick Casares, a football player, as Bob's best man. Elvis wasn't in attendance and the Colonel, involved in straightening out some problems with Elvis, had to bow out.

Life is surely stranger than fiction. I remembered when Sandra and I were teens and I told her about my vow to meet Elvis. She'd thought it so far-fetched, she said, "Yeah, and maybe I'll marry his cousin." Well, she hadn't married his cousin, but she had married the Colonel's stepson. Only it hadn't been planned. She just plain-ole fell in love. And I had fulfilled my vow to meet Elvis. Who would have guessed the power of words?

After they were married, Bob and Sandra bought out Bob's partner in the ad agency, then changed the name to Robert Ross Advertising, Inc. Bob had worked as a disk jockey in Tampa for WHBO radio in the early fifties. His background left the door wide open for advertising and Colonel handed him some big accounts.

Bob Ross of Radio Station WHBO, Tampa, Florida, was one of the South's most popular and entertaining radio personalities in the early fifties. His programs, "Sunset Trail" and "Country Jamboree," were high spots every afternoon for his many listeners who gathered around their sets to tap their heels to the lively tunes. Bob's comments and observations made them feel that the world was just a little friendlier place than it had been an hour earlier.

It was no accident that Bob was radio's good neighbor and beloved friend. For nine years he had been a producer following in the footsteps of his stepfather, Col. Parker, who was manager of not only Elvis, but Hank Snow and Eddy Arnold. Bob, too, had lent a hand and managed such great stars as Hank Snow, George Morgan, Slim Whitman, Johnny & Jack, Kitty Wells, and many others. In this way he'd remained in contact with Grand Ole Opry in Nashville. Also, he was talent scout for R.C.A. Victor records. So his wealth of knowledge of country & western music, and his lasting friendships with many top hillbilly artists, made advertising seem like the perfect business to go into.

The "Aloha from Hawaii" satellite special went through Bob and Sandra's agency. They did all the advertising for this major, historical event. Sandra said they had crazy hours because of the huge amount of advertising they handled throughout the world for this show.

I was curious about the Colonel and asked her to describe his home in Palm Springs. She told me her first trip out there was quite interesting. It was before she and Bob were married. As Sandra expressed it:

"I was stuck in the house as a companion to Miz-rie, that's how the Colonel referred to his wife. 'How many shades of blue can there be, Frances? And how many elephants can there be? If it wasn't an elephant, it was a cat. How many cats can there be?'

"The Colonel was getting ready to go to work and the boys

were on tour. Colonel was looking for a companion for Marie, so
Kenneth and I flew out to Los Angeles. One of the Colonel's cronies met us with a private Lear jet, then flew us to Palm Springs.
Before I left home, Bob counseled me on how one behaves with
his mother.

"He said, 'Sandra, now when you play gin with Mama, you
gotta throw the game. You're not good. You're not gonna be
good. You're always going to lose, aren't you?'

"Yahtzee was another game I had to lose. You always had to
throw the game so Marie would win, or else she would tell the
Colonel on you.

"Oh, and the house...there were bars on all the windows, doors,
and the skylights. Marie would hide the keys to the bars. She hid
them over the doors, which were locked up at night. If that place
had caught fire, we would have all burned up. Man, you could not
get out of that house.

"She was stingy with food, too...didn't want to feed you enough.
When she was asleep, Kenneth and I would sneak out to the kitchen
where she'd have the intercom on and say, 'Who's down there?' And
I'd answer, 'We are.' Then she'd say, 'Who is we?' Kenneth was six
years old and the little kid would get hungry.

"Oh, then she would try to feed us bad food with green stuff
growing on it, and the maids would say, 'You don't want that.'
Why in the hell didn't Bob tell me his mother was senile! I
thought. Coffee was very good. It was made with Mountain Valley
water and honey, of course, no sugar. This is what Elvis drank, too.

"Colonel cooked. He had his own big kitchen outside. A monster kitchen, glass enclosed, and air-conditioned so he wouldn't
slop up Marie's kitchen. He liked to cook and he liked to eat. Oh
God yes, did he like to eat! One of his specialties was bouillabaisse,
a fish stew. The way he fixed it was very good.

"I left Palm Springs a little prematurely because I couldn't
stand the heat. Bob hadn't let me take any credit cards or my
check book. He'd given me one hundred dollars and said that was
all I'd need because everything would be taken care of. Then he
left me out there in Hell with no way home. He'd bought a one
way ticket leaving me without a return fare, because Marie, Ken,

and I would be flying together to Vegas to join the men. Then Ken and I would go on home from there with Bob, if I lasted that long, which I didn't.

"I went to the airport and called my girlfriend in San Francisco, then flew out there and called Bob from my friend's house. I told him, 'I'm here. Now figure out a way to get me home.' I had been in Palm Springs for about two weeks. That's all I could hack. I was too frank.

"The Colonel was not a bad man. He loved kids and enjoyed the role of grandpa. Bob had adopted Kenneth after we were married and Ken loved his grandpa. Colonel was good to my baby. Very good to Ken. He would say, 'You like this? Here, honey. Here, have one.' He gave him some little radios and an elephant hide wallet that he still has. It's rather unique, you can't wear out elephant-hide. Colonel gave Ken a watch too, that had been presented to him by Hal Wallis.

"Colonel worked hard for what he got and Colonel was going to keep his money. We didn't see too much of it. He wasn't flamboyant with us. Bob had multiple sclerosis and was in a wheel chair by the time we were married. His doctor bills were so high that Colonel paid for them. He loaned us the money to alter the house for Bob's wheelchair and we made payments on the loan, but had only paid back half when Colonel cancelled the debt. I don't think it was the money that mattered to him. It was just the good faith and the honor of his generation. He did things on a handshake. The Colonel was a moral man.

"Colonel loved power. After money comes power. I think he enjoyed power and being able to manipulate people and their lives. Make them kow-tow. I think that was important to him and he did that real well. So well in fact, the William Morris Agency sent him their new rising stars in the ad game, to serve as gophers for the Colonel. If you can survive that, you can survive any damn thing. You could be bathing the cat or separating the white rocks from the blue rocks in the front yard. Yes, the gravel was part blue and part white. You could be babysitting Miss Marie or cleaning the pool. You were at his beck and call. But what you received from it was the savvy of the man. It made leaders in management and that's why they were sent there, to learn.

"We did advertising for show dates for a lot of personalities: Ricky Nelson, Olivia Newton-John, John Denver, Tom Jones, Engelbert Humperdinck, and of course, Elvis. We did all of his work. There were others that don't come to mind at this time.

"You know, Frances, when Bob and I announced we were getting married, everybody said, Why her? And you know what Bob told them? 'If you don't know Sandra you can't stand her. But once you get to know her you can't help but love her, because she's got soul.' Sandra sighed, That's me...all soul."

Sandra and I didn't see much of each other for the next few years. She was busy with Bob and his illness and I was trying to adjust to life without Billy.

Not long after we'd broken up, Doug was arrested and put in jail, leaving Darlene alone with two children and no job. She'd had another baby and Tina was only a couple of months old. Darlene was afraid that if she went to work, she'd be picked up by the law for the drug charges and escape that were still pending against her. Her biggest fear was losing her children. She did, however, find a way to get family assistance, and was soon receiving a monthly check and food stamps.

The house I rented was a large one and the landlord was in the process of turning it into a duplex. He couldn't lease the adjoining side until it was finished and finances had brought completion to a halt. So he agreed to let Darlene and me share both sides for twenty dollars extra each month.

Living together worked out to be an answer to prayer for both of us. I didn't have to worry with nurseries anymore and Darlene stayed at home and took care of the children, kept house, and cooked. She handed over her check each month to apply to the bills and her food stamps went toward groceries.

Like me, Darlene loved to dance. The one thing she looked forward to at the end of each week was the prospect of going out dancing, and that always depended on whether our budget could afford a baby-sitter.

I remember coming home from work on Fridays and Darlene would have my clothes washed, ironed, and laid out for me. Dinner would be on the table, and she'd be wearing a frolicking gleam in her eyes, while my favorite dance music blared from the radio.

"Can we afford to go out tonight?"

We ribbed each other about how this arrangement appeared, then laughed about it.

Darlene and I had been living together for about six months when her baby came down with a mysterious illness. She was forced to move to Miami where her sister lived, so Tina could be hospitalized.

Tina was diagnosed with leukemia and died about a year later. My heart went out to my friend. I couldn't understand why so many bad things happened to someone as sweet and good as Darlene.

Before she moved, we bought tickets for an Elvis concert at the Curtis Hixon. Unfortunately, she didn't get to make it and told me to let someone else use her ticket to go with me.

My cousin Nancy Leaman, who was visiting from Massachusetts, was thrilled to get to go to the concert. She loved Elvis and had never seen him in person.

My brother Sam and his wife, Nancy, were able to make the concert, too. After the opening acts, there was an intermission before Elvis came on. We walked up to the stage, where Sylvia and some of the others in the group were, and I introduced all three of them to the members of Elvis' group. Then, they invited us to go to Lakeland with them after the concert, for a party at someone's house. I hated to decline but we all had to work the next day. I didn't feel, either, like I could abandon my company. So, when everyone said no, I felt I had to go along with them.

We were heading back to our seats when I ran into my old friend Cliff. I remember thinking, *Wow! Two Elvises in the same building.* Cliff and I talked for a few minutes, but not long because the show was about to start.

The concert revealed Elvis' bad health. He gave us a grand show, but I couldn't help overhearing comments made by people who loved Elvis enough to stand in long lines for his concert tickets. They had laid out the price of admission for this show, which sold out in a day, and I knew they made their diagnoses out of adoring concern. I heard, "Bless his heart, he looks so tired," and I heard, "He must be on drugs, look how fat and puffy he is, but I still love him." Of course my first instinct was to come to his defense by saying, "No one stays a teenager forever."

I was concerned about Elvis' appearance, too. Not because he didn't look handsome, to me he was always princely, but because of his health. I didn't want anything to happen to him. I wanted to talk to Elvis in person again, but I didn't get a chance. The entire entourage took off for Lakeland as soon as they finished the concert.

Not long after, I quit my job at Reynaldo's. Mama and Pap had bought a house for me and built a beauty shop onto the back. Life was less complicated with me working out of my home. I was able to be with my children and escape the nursery nightmare. I put a swing set and a sandbox in the fenced backyard for the children's entertainment and was able to keep my eyes on them while I worked, through the big picture window in the shop.

Doug came down from Orlando to see me not long after I opened my salon. Darlene had told me in her last letter that he was out of prison. But I hadn't heard from him and was surprised by his visit. He said he'd gone by my mother's house and she'd told him where I was living. We talked for a while about his and Darlene's breakup. When our conversation turned to the death of their daughter, I caught some of his sadness from the tremor in his voice.

About a month after Doug's visit, I received a letter from Darlene:

> *Frances, I am so sad over the news I have to tell you. Doug put a gun in his mouth last week and shot himself. I don't know how he could do this to us. You know I still loved him and if he had just given me a little more time, we could have all been together again. Frances, why does everything bad always happen to me?*

I cried when I read her letter. Doug had been a good friend and I couldn't understand his actions any more than Darlene could. I, too, wondered how this was going to affect his family.

I continued working in the shop, putting in long, hard hours the first year, and it paid off. I was soon out of debt and back on my feet better than ever.

The year 1975 had been a busy and prosperous year, and now I needed a vacation and the lure of Las Vegas was pulling me again.

Reports of Elvis' bad health had me concerned and I wanted to see him for myself. I had always felt his life was fragile, and now, I just couldn't shake my feeling of...something.

I started looking for a travel companion among my customers. Naomi was a single lady and, intrigued by my tales of Las Vegas, she agreed to go with me. We made plans for August.

Once again, I fashioned my own wardrobe, and Mama and Nancy kept my children. I'd won a vacation for two in Las Vegas, at a Beeline party, which covered the cost of accommodations at the Stardust Hotel. As much as I wanted to stay at the Hilton where Elvis was, it didn't seem practical to pass up the free lodging. So I booked us at the Stardust.

We arrived in Las Vegas, and just the same as always, the town was plastered from airport to hotel with Elvis' image. But the atmosphere was different than it had been in 1971. Vegas was crowded but it just wasn't the same. I really couldn't put my finger on what was different. It was just a feeling, a premonition of gloom nagging me. I shrugged my intuition, unwilling to let anything darken my mood. I was there to see Elvis, and the sun was sure to shine in the morning.

We checked in at the Stardust, then called over to the Hilton and made reservations for the late show. When we arrived at the hotel that evening, I was hit with the changes in staff. Alex Shoofey was no longer president. In fact, personnel wouldn't even talk about him. They just said, "He's no longer here."

Everything seemed foreign to me. I realized I wouldn't get any special favors from these unfamiliar people. Eula Mae had moved from Las Vegas, therefore, any help I might have received from her was no longer available. The depression of it all stuck to me like Florida humidity and I was unable to shake the ominous feeling.

Our seats were about midway back from the stage. I was shocked when I saw Elvis. He looked tired as he sat on a stool and read to us. I enjoyed the readings and listening to his emotions spill out in comments he could no longer hold back. His costume was elaborate, and his smiles were loving, and from the heart. But his weak health was evident. I questioned some people's lack of compassion and my anger stewed.

I was overwhelmed with protective instincts and wanted to comfort Elvis. I remembered the way he'd soothed me and yearned, so badly, to return that consolation. But I knew this wasn't possible and sensed his need was stronger than his will.

When the show ended, I considered trying to see him, but then I didn't feel the time was right. It was late, and I suspected Elvis would be ready to retire to his bed. Hopefully, those close to him would see to his needs. As we made our way back to the Stardust, the premonition that had been nagging me ever since we got into town was back, with a fury this time.

The next night we made it to both shows. Elvis' condition had not improved any since the night before. Our seats were a little better for the first show, but not close enough for him to see, much less recognize me. And not close enough for me to get a kiss. I was determined though, and I finally reached him at the late performance.

A nice-size tip got us as close as was possible without clout. We were seated in a booth on the same level as Priscilla used to sit. I remember thinking, *These seats may be more comfortable, and have a better panorama, but it sure ain't close enough for my taste.* I wanted to taste Elvis.

When the show got under way, Elvis sometimes interrupted a song and started talking about whatever entered his mind. He was spontaneous about his feelings and seemed a bit spacey. He got a kick out of teasing around with his backup performers. He talked about karate and occasionally, leaned toward spiritual readings. Whatever he chose to talk about, the audience was receptive.

Finally, he kissed a few girls, and I hurried up close to the stage. When he reached me, Elvis leaned over and started to kiss me, then hesitated, really looking at me hard, for just a second. "Do I know you?"

I nodded my head. "I'm Baby Jane."

Recognition lit up his eyes. "You look different."

"So do you, Elvis. But you're still the prettiest man I've ever seen and I love you."

With impatient women pressing for their turn, Elvis kissed me, placed a white silk scarf around my neck, then went on to the next one. But not before our eyes had communicated.

Bittersweet tears silently dampened my face as I made my way back to the booth. Tears, put there by the unspoken message that had transpired between our eyes. Mine had asked, *What's wrong Elvis?* And his had said, *Please don't see the truth.*

I took my seat in the booth and Naomi asked, "What's wrong, Frances? Didn't he remember you?"

Wiping my eyes with the scarf I held in my hand, I sniffed and wept. "Yes, Naomi, he remembered me."

Elvis told a story about a song, then sang "Softly As I Leave You." When he came to the part about dying *long before your arms can pull me back*, I cried harder, sobbing, and sniffing, and thought, *He's sending a message. Trying to tell us something.*

The fans' love went deep for Elvis. We didn't stop caring because he was overweight, and if he chose to sit down and talk, well, we loved listening. We only cared about being in his presence while he sat on stage loving us. We knew we had nothing to prove to Elvis but our love and loyalty. It didn't matter to him who we were or what we looked like. None of that mattered to Elvis. He saw only beauty in love and loyalty. And I thought, *Oh, Dear God, please don't take Elvis from us.*

When the show was over, Naomi and I were walking through the casino and ran into Glen Hardin. We went to the coffee shop together and Glen told us Elvis was in the process of leaving for Memphis as we spoke.

"He's going into the hospital as soon as he gets there. The rest of the engagement has been canceled."

My heart sank. "What's wrong?"

"Well, he wasn't feeling good when we started this gig. But I'm sure he'll be better after a stay in the hospital. Anyway, everybody's packing up and headin' home. There's no show without Elvis."

"Is it bad, Glen? Are you sure he's gonna be alright?"

"Sure...Elvis is gonna be fine. Don't worry." Then changing the subject, he said, "You're looking good. You've lost some weight since the last time you were here."

"Yeah, about fifteen pounds."

"Cut your hair too, I see."

"It's easier to take care of when it's short."

"So, what are you up to?"

"I don't know, now that Elvis is gone. You know me, I come to Vegas just to see his shows."

Glen suggested we get together before he had to leave. But something came up and he had to go sooner than he'd figured. Naomi and I spent the next ten days going to see shows I had previously passed up for Elvis. Although they provided elaborate entertainment, my heart was displaced. It had followed Elvis back to Memphis.

IN 1976, it was announced that Elvis would be back in Tampa for another concert. I paid the son of one of my customers to sit in line overnight and purchase my tickets. I wasn't able to close my shop or I'd have done it myself. The performance sold out the first day, but Darren was at the head of the line, so my seats were close to the front.

This was the last time I saw Elvis. I remember being shocked by his appearance. His eyes said he was tired, and his pride carried his bloated body. I knew in my spirit that we wouldn't have him much longer. I could feel his love, and his precious smile made me cry, because I knew somewhere way down deep inside of me, Elvis was saying good-bye, and we wouldn't have him much longer. I pushed my feelings aside, preferring to believe they were wrong. They just *had* to be wrong.

But something Bitsy Mott (Marie Parker's brother) said confirmed the truth in my heart about Elvis' condition. Sandra and Bob were at this show, seated a couple of rows in front of me. When the concert was over Sandra and I talked.

"He looks so sick, Sandra."

Unshed tears pooled in her eyes. "He is, Frances. Uncle Bitsy went backstage to see Elvis and the boys. When he came back out to sit with us he had tears in his eyes, and he said, 'We're watching a living legend die. Elvis looks just like Gladys did before she passed away.'"

"Don't tell me that, please."

She tried to lighten the mood. "Hey, Frances, some of Elvis' guys came out to our seats to see Bob. One of 'em looked at Kenneth and told Bob, 'God, he looks just like you, Bobby!' and I thought, Hell, there ain't a bit of Bob's blood in that child."

"So what you been up to, Sandra? We ain't seen each other in a long time."

"I know. I'm always busy taking care of Bob."

"Well, tell me something exciting. Have you been to your in-laws lately?"

"We spent Christmas in Palm Springs with the Parkers a couple of years ago. On Christmas day we flew with the Colonel and Marie in a small jet to Los Angeles, to spend the day with Tom Diskin and his young wife. While enroute, Colonel bet the pilot a hundred dollars that he couldn't make it through the pass before another plane. Well, we won! Excitin' enough for you?"

I TALKED WITH SYLVIA after the show but I didn't get to see Elvis. Things were changing and I couldn't help but feel like Elvis' health had everything to do with those changes.

MY HUSBAND EDDIE. 1953.

19

Take My Hand, Precious Lord

1975-1984

Put yourself in a situation that's sinful, then do what Jesus would have done. You'll understand what He was about.

—*Elvis Presley*

I was thirty-two when I took my life-changing step to the altar and received Jesus Christ as my Lord and Savior. Shirley was my customer and an instrument of God. She encouraged me to send my children to Sunday School. The church she attended, Town and Country Church of God, had a bus ministry that would pick them up and bring them home. Mam-ma, Shirley's mother, and also a patron of mine, supervised the kids.

I was convinced in my heart that my children should be raised in the full gospel church. I remember how excited they were when they got home from the service that first Sunday; waving Bible stories they had colored in Sunday school, and both of them talking at the same time.

"Mama, Mama, Mama, please go with us next Sunday," they begged. I looked at the joy on their faces, my two precious children, and my heart melted.

Sunday was my only day to rest and giving it up wasn't easy. I reached for every excusable exemption, but none held up against my love for my children. To be a good mother was my heart's desire and I knew I couldn't do it without the Lord's help.

God was pulling strongly at my heart that Sunday as I fell under conviction to the Holy Spirit, while listening to the sermon. How many times had I rejected this tug at my soul. Was the preacher speaking only to me? Had someone told him I was coming? Did he know my past history and prepare his words just for me?

At the end of the service the congregation was told to bow their heads and close their eyes. The pastor then asked, "Is there anyone here who has never been saved?"

I didn't want to be noticed and couldn't believe it when my hand went up by its own accord. Quickly, I brought it back down to my lap, but not before the pastor had taken note. I sat with my eyes clinched tight, hoping everybody's eyes had been shut and my gesture had gone unnoticed. Suddenly, I felt a hand touch my shoulder. *Oh, no,* I thought, and squeezed my eyes tighter.

A voice whispered, "I saw your hand go up. Do you want to be saved?"

Slowly, I opened my eyes and whispered back, "Yes, I want to be saved, but not today." My mind was praying, *God, if you do answer prayer, please make him go away.*

The voice broke into my thoughts and said, "Today is the day of salvation." Then the pastor slipped his hand in mine, "Come, let's go to the altar."

"Not today, please. I'll do it another time," I pleaded. God knew what it would take to get me down front because it felt like I was being dragged. When we reached the altar and dropped to our knees, Brother Scott began to lead me in the sinner's prayer.

I repeated his words and instantly, they became mine from my heart and I started to cry, anointed tears, that cleansed me and made me into a new creation that very moment. I was on fire from this blessed revelation, receiving an assurance I'd longed for all my life—that I belonged to God. And it had been so simple.

I remember thinking about Elvis and our spiritual conversations and I wished I'd been able to understand the things he tried to explain to me. Then I thought, *This is what it was all about, huh, Elvis?*

I GOT A LETTER FROM DARLENE:

> *Dear Frances, I'm sorry I haven't written you sooner. I've been pretty busy lately. I moved to another place. Can't believe that you and I have birthdays coming up again. They come fast now.*
>
> *Well, Tina would have been two years old May 16th. I went and visited her grave yesterday. It's just hard to believe she's gone. She was my wonderful baby. I just can't get myself to see that she's really gone. She was such a good baby. Even though she suffered a lot, she was still a good baby. I often ask God why he took her away from me, but I don't know! I only know she will always live in my heart.*
>
> *So how is your business going. Making good money? Ha! Why aren't you and Billy making it? I guess 'cause you've been by yourself too long. You're right about me. I've got to have someone that loves me and that I can love back. You only live once, Frances, so make it worthwhile!*
>
> *Well, when you get a chance write me a letter. Give the kids a hug and kiss and take care of yourself. So write soon.*
>
> *Love ya always*
> *Darlene*

Determined to live my life as a Christian, I stopped going out dancing and I chewed pencils in an effort to quit smoking. In other words, I did like so many other misled Christians and worked myself up trying to be righteous, within my own power. I would later learn, all I had to do was give it to the Lord.

Shirley empathized with my struggles, when I confessed how hard it was to live the Christian life. It seemed as though I was giving up everything I'd previously enjoyed. Now, all I did was stay at home and work out of my salon, take care of my children, and go to church on Sundays. I couldn't understand why I continued driving the unnecessary distance to a church where my only affiliation was my customers. There were plenty of denominations around where I lived, but I still made the drive across town, confident that God had my life in His hands.

My struggle to be good continued to be an effort and I murmured my despair to Shirley. I was styling her hair, and she said, "Frances, what you need is a good Christian husband and I'm going to pray for God to send you one. You'll know he's the one, because he'll be a Christian and the desire of your heart. And he'll go to church with you."

I didn't see any way God could answer that prayer. I wasn't even divorced from Billy. And where did I go to meet this Mister Wonderful? Still trying to figure it out for myself, I said, "What are you gonna do Shirley, pray my telephone breaks, then when the Christian phone repair man shows up he'll take one look at me and say, 'Hark! I'm in love'?"

"Have faith, Frances. God will work it out." It seemed I'd heard those words before.

"But I work here in my shop with only women for customers. And I don't go out anymore, where I might be able to meet somebody. Besides, you're forgetting, I'm still married to Billy."

Again, her answer was to have faith. One thing I'd learned was, I had to stop looking for Elvis in the men I married. There was only one Elvis Presley and he belonged to the world. What I really needed was a man who manifested Jesus. I felt this was my only hope of ever having a lasting marriage.

Two days after our conversation a miracle happened. It was after eleven o'clock at night. I had already put the children down to bed, finished cleaning up the shop, and was running the vacuum cleaner over the rest of the house when someone knocked at the door. I was cautious, and wondering who it could be that time of night, I moved the curtain aside and peeked out the window. A policeman was standing on the porch. I thought of Billy. *What's he done now?* But, when I opened the door, I was surprised to see Eddie Keenan.

Eddie was a policeman for the Tampa Police Department and was an old boyfriend of my aunt Colleen. "Eddie Keenan! What are you doing here?"

"Well, I dropped by your mother's house the other day and she told me where you lived. Said you and your children were living here alone. So, since your house was in my patrol district, I told her I'd stop by and check on you periodically."

I invited him in and we talked the usual family catch-up stuff, for about ten or fifteen minutes. When I asked him about his wife and children, a sad look shadowed his face and his beautiful, blue eyes stole my heart.

"I've been divorced since May."

I was shocked. Eddie was a Christian and, in my mind, the perfect husband material. His availability sent my heart to pounding, and after he'd gone, I sat down on the sofa and tried to sort out what his divorce meant to me.

Eddie and Colleen, my mother's sister, had been high school sweethearts when I first met him. I was a child then, about ten years old, and Eddie was twenty-two.

I had a secret crush on Eddie and swiped a picture of him from Aunt Colleen. No one ever suspected my feelings and would only have laughed about it if they had. I kept Eddie's picture throughout the years and had looked at it many times when flipping through my old photo albums. He had joined the navy in 1952 and was sent to Japan. Even though he wasn't there for the entire four years, his duties still kept him in ports far away. He came home to see Colleen every chance he could and they wrote to each other while he was gone. But eventually, she started dating someone else and eloped with Marvin.

When Eddie's tour of duty was over, he came back home and went to see my grandmother. She'd always thought of him like a son. My family was living in the Broadwell house, which he had to pass on his way to Grandaddy's farm, so Eddie dropped by to see us. I can still remember him riding his motorcycle up into our yard, looking so handsome he nearly took my breath away.

I'd just turned thirteen and he was almost twenty-five. If my mama would have known what I was thinking as I stood on the porch watching Daddy and him talk, she would have snatched a knot in my tail, fast. And if I had known then what Eddie revealed to me later, I would have really been in a mess of turnips and bound for the stew pot. He told me, "When I looked at that pretty little blond girl standing on the porch in her blue jeans, I just wanted to toss her onto the back of my motorcycle and ride away with her."

I sat on the sofa, reminiscing, and I remembered when I was married to Lauren the first time, and was working at Harold's

Drive-in restaurant. The place stayed open twenty-four hours and
Eddie patrolled this area of Six Mile Creek. He had a habit of stopping by for coffee and we would talk about our families. I was happily married, but I still couldn't help noticing how handsome
Eddie was in his policeman's uniform.

Funny, Billy and James were both living in Six Mile Creek at
the same time. As large as Tampa was, *how ironic*, I thought, fate
would allow me to recall memories from three husbands, all from
the same time I worked at Harold's, where Eddie patrolled.
Stranger yet, one had lived in prison and one was a cop. I shook my
head and continued to reminisce.

My next encounter with Eddie had been in 1971, when I called
the police to put Lauren out of the house on Dartmouth. I had told
him I wanted a divorce, and asked him to leave, but he'd refused.
When the policeman arrived, I couldn't believe it was Eddie
Keenan at my door. I thought I had it made. Then, Eddie
wouldn't put Lauren out.

"It's his house, too, and since he's made no threats against you,
all I can say is if you don't want to be around him then go somewhere else and stay till it's settled in court."

I took his advice and went to Sandra's for a few nights. Then
Lauren told me I could have the house and he would move out.
But I let him continue to stay in the extra bedroom.

I'd been sitting and pondering old memories for about two
hours when it suddenly hit me! Eddie was the one God had sent to
be my next husband!

The next day was Saturday, my busiest day in the shop. I was
convinced God was preparing a future for me and told my customers I was getting married. Their responses were all the same. Who?
When had all this happened? Wasn't I still married to Billy? When
was the wedding going to take place?

"Oh, he doesn't know about it, yet. But I'm going shopping
for my wedding dress today, just as soon as I'm finished up in
here."

My positive statement brought disbelieving and confused looks to
customers' faces. But as one of them put it, "If anybody can pull
something like this off, Frances, you're the one who can do it."

I bought my dress that day, then waited two weeks for the

phone to ring. When I still hadn't heard from him, I decided it was time to give God a little help in the situation, and I called Eddie. He seemed happy to hear from me and accepted my invitation to dinner for the following evening.

One of the conveniences of working out of my home was being able to put a roast in the oven and check on it while I worked. I prepared an impressive, stick-to-your-ribs, meat and gravy man's kind of meal. Mama used to say the way to a man's heart was through his stomach. Trust me, there's a lot of truth in that statement.

That evening everything was ready on time. The house was clean, dinner was in the oven, salads in the fridge, and the kids were bathed and dressed. I was finishing up my last customer when Eddie knocked on the shop door. I opened it and when I saw him, standing there with flowers in one hand and a bottle of wine in the other, I had to fight to keep from laughing. He was wearing a white, starched, and ironed short-sleeved shirt, with a pair of plaid, high-water pants. He looked like he'd just stepped out of a strawberry patch and cleaned up for courting—like a good-looking redneck farmer.

I hadn't seen Eddie out of uniform but once and that had been when he'd come by the Broadwell house. But he was younger then and wore a black leather jacket and dark pants. Otherwise, he had always been in his navy or police blues when I saw him.

I asked him to come in and he handed me the yellow roses and pineapple wine. While I was getting a vase for the flowers and putting the wine on ice, Eddie took a seat in one of the salon chairs. I returned to my customer and he watched with interest as I finished styling her hair.

I remember, very clearly, sizing Eddie up for a husband while I brushed and combed. *Boy, do I have my work cut out for me,* I thought. *Just as soon as I nail him, I'm going to dress him. He's as handsome as ever, polite, and educated. Wonder why his taste in clothes is so ridiculous? He looks like Clem Kadiddlehopper, for heaven's sake. All he needs is a hat with a feather in it. Oh, well, clothes are easy to change. He sure meets all the other qualifications I want in a husband. He's a good-looking, single, Christian man with a career. A dream come true.*

I finished up in the shop, then Eddie and I went into the living room. I poured him a glass of wine and left him to get acquainted with the girls while I put dinner on the table. If you've never tried to impress a date while having little tell-all kids around, you don't know the embarrassment you're missing.

Jessica was three and Jolynn was nine, and they preceded to tell Eddie that their Mama was looking for a new daddy for them, and she wanted to snag a cop. They got this idea from hearing me say if I ever married again, it would be the complete opposite of Billy—I'd look for a cop next time.

As if this wasn't enough, Jessica decided to crawl up on his lap, stick her tongue in his ear, and tickle him at the same time. "I'm gonna get you! Are you gonna be my new daddy?"

Eddie didn't know how to react, and I was embarrassed and reached over to pull her off his lap, while trying to explain away her babbling, but I just dug myself in deeper.

We ate dinner, then put the kids to bed. Eddie was quiet. I had to carry most of the conversation by myself. We sat in opposite chairs in the living room, talking like we were at a business meeting or something. Not like two people on a date. The evening progressed but the romance of it didn't. I finally concluded that if I didn't initiate the first step, this romance wasn't gonna get started till Eddie's clothes came back in style.

I took him by surprise when suddenly, I jumped up from my chair, walked over to where he was sitting, and plunked myself down in his lap. Then, draping my arms around his neck, I said, "Are you ever going to kiss me or do I have to kiss you?" That's all it took to banish his shyness. Eddie kissed me and we were in love.

He called me a fast mover. I laughed, "Not always. Only when I know what I want."

Eddie was hooked and he knew it. He came over and went to church with me the next day. Our courtship lasted three months and would probably have been shorter but my divorce accounted for the lengthy engagement.

Unable to locate Billy, my lawyer advertised my intent in the newspaper. In the meantime, Eddie and I planned a church wedding, sending out invitations to our families, customers, and friends.

I intended to do this one right. After all, I was a Christian now, marrying a Christian. Jesus would be the cornerstone of our union. We would raise our children and grow old together—a concept I'd never given much thought to in my previous marriages. I was completely committed this time, determined not to end up in the divorce courts ever again.

Eddie was just as devoted and pointed out how it was God who had put us together.

"Like I didn't know that already," I told him. Then it dawned on me, all my boyfriends, and husbands, had had some traits of Elvis about them, and so did Eddie. He had Elvis' spirituality and adventurous heart.

Eddie evaded my efforts to see his house until after we were married. He kept saying it needed a good cleaning because he'd been batching it for six months. This made sense to me, so I let it go and kept busy with my work, the kids, wedding plans, and Christmas shopping. I bought Eddie some new clothes, then, in a hurry to see him out of his Kadiddlehoppers, I told him they were early Christmas presents. He bought my story and proudly wore the stylish outfits.

As the wedding, set for January 29, 1977, drew near, we worried that my divorce might not be final in time. But three days before the big event was scheduled, the papers came through and we breathed a big sigh of relief.

There was something magical about my and Eddie's courtship, and I was so entranced, I failed to get tickets for Elvis' St. Pete performance. Talk about magic, it even snowed. All of Florida, down to Miami, got snow. The cold made red roses for my wedding harder to locate and more expensive when I did find them, but to see Florida looking like a winter wonderland, was worth it.

Our wedding was perfect and the reception a merry success, thanks to the efforts of my girlfriend Debbie and her husband, Hugh, who held the reception for us in their enormous, lovely, sprawling home. Debbie did the flowers and catered the food. She was a busy little angel and her remarkable talents made everything so heavenly.

Mama took the girls straight from the reception to her house so Eddie and I could enjoy a few honeymoon days. We spent our wedding night at Bradenton Beach, then decided the next day to go back to Tampa and hide out at Eddie's house. No one would expect us to be there and it would save money. We had spent so much on the wedding, and neither of us was rich, and I was kind of anxious to see his house, anyway.

I sensed Eddie's hesitation as we got closer to Tampa, and thought to myself, *He hasn't cleaned the house up yet and he's worried about me seeing it. No big deal.* Was I in for a surprise!   It was dark when we pulled up into the yard. Eddie had already told me that the house sat on almost two acres of land. I knew the area. It was a good neighborhood and close to the beaches. To my surprise, it was only a couple of blocks from the church I'd been attending. Now I understood why I'd kept on driving the distance to this particular one. God had it all in hand from the beginning.

The shocking part was the old dilapidated house that appeared to be leaning to one side. And the yard that held an antiquated school bus, a prehistoric motor home that had been rebuilt from an old milk truck, a large broken-down cabin-cruiser boat, and a number of forgotten sheds and buildings that looked as if they were ready to crumble from age and termite destruction.

I stepped out of the car and stood staring, taking it all in while my mouth hung open. This place made Eddie's Kadiddlehopper clothes look like Fred Astaire's in comparison and I thought, *Things always look better in the morning.* Still hoping for the best, I hardly heard his words of explanation as he led me through the front door and switched on a light.

Oh, Lord, God, is this my punishment for all my past sins? I stood staring in uncertainty, at the large kitchen that had no floor.

"I'm sorry about the hole, honey. I was hoping to have it fixed before you saw it." Eddie's explanation was further expressed by the regretful look on his face.

"What happened to the floor?"

"Some of the boards were rotten. So, I took 'em up with plans to replace 'em, but I fell in love and never stayed at home long enough to get the job done."

Bracing myself, I let him lead me around the giant cavity and into the living room where I was met by a pot-bellied wood heater, proudly sitting in the middle of at least three inches of dust and ashes.

Oh, no! I despaired, while trying not to let Eddie see my disappointment. *This has got to be a nightmare. Please, God, let me wake up and find I've been dreaming.* No wonder he hadn't let me see his house before the license was signed.

"I'm sorry about the shape everything is in, honey. But I'll clean it up tomorrow."

Tomorrow, I thought. It would take a bulldozer to plow through this monstrosity, plus at least a year of elbow grease and sweat to clean it up. "Just show me to the bathroom, please, and we'll worry about it tomorrow."

He led me down a hall, then turned on another light, which revealed the smallest bathroom I'd ever seen. The paint was peeling from the walls and the tub was an old-fashioned claw foot. At least it was clean, so I proceeded to run my bath while Eddie went out to the car to bring in our luggage.

I was about to step into the water when I heard a squeeking sound, and looking in the direction of the noise, I stared straight into the evil eyes of a rat the size of a full-grown cat, staring me straight in the face. Eddie heard me screaming and came running with his gun. I was hysterical by the time he reached the bathroom and shot the fearlessly aggressive rodent.

"I figured that's what it was. Darn things keep coming up through the hole in the kitchen floor. I gotta get that fixed tomorrow."

I stood naked and trembling, from fear and the freezing cold house, and let the tears fly.

"Oh, honey," he consoled, "It'll be alright. Tell you what, we'll just stay on at your place till I get this one in shape. That make you feel better?" He held me while I cried, then told me to get in the tub of hot water, and relax while he went to get me a glass of wine.

"Don't leave me, Eddie," I pleaded. "Please don't leave me here alone."

"I'll only be gone a minute, sweetheart." He laid his weapon down on the commode seat. "Nothin's gonna get you, I promise.

But here's the gun if it'll make you feel better." He left the bathroom and I stepped carefully into the steaming water, eased down, closed my eyes, and rested my head against the back of the comfortable old tub. Eddie brought me a glass of pineapple wine then left again to ready our bed.

I sat in the bathtub, sipping the wine, and enjoying the warmth that was beginning to penetrate my shocked system and relax me a bit. *We'll live in my house,* I decided. No way was I gonna move into this atrocity.

Lost in thought and sipping away at the wine, I was parlaying the pluses and minuses of my situation, when a monster house spider decided to come out of hiding and parade himself up the wall beside the tub where my hand was resting.

I flung the wineglass at the huge, creepy-crawly thing, shattering glass into the tub, and screaming and scrambling out of it so fast, it's a wonder I didn't get cut or break my neck.

By the time Eddie reached me the spider had found another hiding place and was nowhere to be seen. I clung to my groom and resolved that the worst had to be over. But I retracted that thought a few minutes later when I crawled between icy sheets, so cold they nearly froze my tears. Eddie quickly hopped into bed beside me and reassured me that he could warm me up. But the sheets were only beginning to thaw when the telephone rang. No one knew where we were. Eddie just figured it must be a wrong number. Whoever it was, they were persistent, so he finally answered it, which turned out to be the worst mistake he could have made that night.

It was the police department. They needed him. They were sorry to bother him, they knew he was on his honeymoon, but they were shorthanded and it was imperative he come to work.

I wasn't about to stay in that house overnight, with only the rats and spiders for company. Eddie was sympathetic and drove me back to my house before reporting in for duty. "What a way to spend our honeymoon, honey, but I'll make it up to you, sweetheart."

ABOUT THREE WEEKS AFTER Eddie and I were wed, I heard from Billy. He was stunned by the news of our divorce and the fact that I'd married a cop. A few weeks later I read in the paper that he was back in jail.

We stayed in my house with the intentions of fixing his up and transferring my beauty shop. But a court battle with his ex-wife forced us to move ahead of schedule.

I was depressed the day we moved. But, instead of wasting my energy crying about the situation, I rolled up my sleeves, put on an Elvis album, and set to work. I dug, and I dug, and the more I dug, the more there was to dig through. It seemed like the work grew rather than lessened. But after about six months, the house finally started to look livable, at least on the inside.

I had redecorated the interior as best I could with sweat, glue, and wallpaper, then dubbed the house "Green Acres," because there wasn't much could be done for the outside. I mean the way that house leaned and all, it was funny looking. But, it kept me entertained.

COL. TOM PARKER INSPECTING SANDRA AND BOB ROSS'S WEDDING CAKE. LAS VEGAS 1973.
(FROM THE COLLECTION OF SANDRA ROSS)

20

Are You Lonesome Tonight

1977-1982

Death is gonna find you regardless of how good you are.
When it's your time, the Lord's gonna take you.

—Elvis Presley

ugust 16, 1977. I was in the bedroom talking with Eddie when the telephone rang. One of the kids answered it and hollered, "Mama, Norma wants to speak to you." Norma was my friend and customer and had stood as my Matron of Honor when Eddie and I had tied the knot.

"Hello, Norma?"

"Frances, have you heard the news?"

"What news?"

"Elvis Presley died."

I stiffened in shock, then quickly reminded myself of how many times untrue rumors had been started about Elvis. But there was a deep, gut-piercing pain in my stomach this time, confirming a truth I didn't want to believe.

"Are you still there?"

"Yes. Yes, I'm here. When did you hear about it?"

"It's all over the news. Go turn your television on."

"Yes. I'll talk to you later."

I hung up the receiver, then, like a sleepwalker trying to out-run the bogeyman, I rushed back to the bedroom and turned on the television. My hopes shattered as I listened to the sad report of Elvis' untimely death. This couldn't be happening. My heart was crushed beneath the pains of truth that my mind rejected. I pinched myself for proof that I wasn't in the middle of a night-mare. I could feel pain. I wasn't crying but I was suffering. Then it hit me, with all the force of a reality one never wants to face.

Elvis was *dead*.

Elvis Presley was, actually, *dead*. The realness of that word, *dead*, kicked me in the belly and stopped my heart.

Strange, I didn't cry. I just stood frozen to the floor, as if time had stopped and everything had come to a sudden standstill. Then I thought, *What's the world gonna be like without Elvis Presley?*

No new songs. No new movies, and no live concerts to look forward to, anticipate, plan for, and dream about. No more reach-ing out to touch Elvis, and no more autographs, scarves, or kisses. I would never have another chance to get my picture taken with him. And Tommy hadn't gotten off his duff and sent his songs to Elvis, so that opportunity was lost forever.

All selfish stuff. But isn't it natural to feel self-centered when you've lost part of yourself? To think about all the what ifs and why didn't I's? Because self has to go on living when love is gone.

I needed to hear his voice so I went to the stereo and put on "Are You Lonesome Tonight," and as I listened to him sing the words "*Do you miss me tonight,*" I thought, in sorrow, of the many people who would be missing him tonight and all the rest of the nights that stretched empty without Elvis. And what about Lisa Marie? She was suffering the greatest loss. She'd lost her daddy, poor baby.

I felt compelled to go to the closet by an urgent longing to be close to Elvis. I pulled out the big old flowered box that held my most precious memories, and I sat down on the floor beside my treasures, and slowly, ran my hands across the top before lifting the lid. I could almost smell the memories escaping.

Closing my eyes, I allowed my mind to drift...to quiet nights spent writing to Elvis. To the sun-kissed days of my youth. And I thought about laughter. My laughter. Elvis' laughter. And music, I thought about music, too. Music that touched the heart of me. Music, birthed from the soul of a poor southern boy. Music that reached out to the oppressed and gave them dreams of better tomorrows. Music that talked to me.

I opened my eyes and looked back to the contents in the box. Lying on top was the blue Summer Festival scarf that Elvis had given me. I picked it up, lovingly caressing the smooth fabric, then buried my face in its softness and inhaled the musty reminder of time. Had it really been six years?

"Oh...Elvis," I sighed, my heart breaking. "I miss you already." But I still didn't cry. "What's wrong with me, Elvis? I love you, why ain't I cryin'?"

Glancing back into the box, this time I saw a clear plastic bag that held inside it a yellow linen napkin. My heart took a sudden leap, and I dropped the scarf onto my lap and grabbed for the package. I held it for a moment, then lifted it up toward the light, studying it. My hands trembled and the open bag slid from my fingers, spilling forth its contents. I reached for my cherished memento and held, tightly to my breast, the napkin Elvis had used to wipe away his sweat. I could see his pretty face in my mind; so close, so beautiful.

The folded cloth was splotched with perspiration stains. I raised it to my nose, closed my eyes, and remembered a handsome man in a white jumpsuit with blue, faraway eyes, and an incredible smile. A man of compassion. A man who believed in making dreams come true. A man whose laugh could light up the darkest corner of my heart. And I remembered the softest lips I'd ever kissed.

I tried to recapture Elvis' essence, the clean-water smell of him, but age had plundered the sweat-stained napkin. Then I closed my eyes and sniffed the air in an effort to remember. Had Elvis been wearing cologne when we kissed?

A person's choice of perfume tells a lot about them. As far as Elvis' preference of fragrance, I read somewhere that he liked Brut. When I had my nose buried in his neck, believe me, I sniffed. And somewhere, far off in my memory, I smelled clean, rich, cool water and a beautiful hint of perfume. Fresh spring water has no taste.

It's invigorating. Refreshing; wet, clean, and crystalline enough to distinguish an individual's personal scent right through the fragrance.

I remember rich, as in the best money can buy. Clean, wet, and rich. If you can smell them, that's how Elvis smelled. But was Elvis wearing Brut? I can't swear that he was. I was too high on my personal cloud to note anything but the raw charisma of my hero.

My eyes went back to the linen napkin I still held in my hand. I couldn't understand why I wasn't crying. I was certainly feeling the pain, but things just didn't seem real. Then the wonderful peace of understanding comforted my heart, and I thought, *He's at rest. Elvis is with his mama and everything is gonna be alright.*

I knew he'd been hurting. No news reports had to tell me Elvis was in pain. I'd seen it on his face and in his eyes and knew we were in danger of losing him. His songs had been telling us for the past two years that the end was near. When I listened closely enough I could hear his messages, sent loud and clear through the words of "I Did It My Way," "The American Trilogy," and "Softly As I Leave You." I think he knew he was dying and struggled, even unto death, to give us what we wanted—a piece of him, because he needed that piece of us, too. Elvis was telling us good-bye in his own unique way.

I was comforted by the part of himself Elvis had given me. He'd been here for me since 1955. Suddenly, it hit me. Elvis was still here for me. He left so much behind; his music, and movies, his lineage through daughter, Lisa Marie, and most of all his spirit.

Thanks for the memories, Elvis. I closed the box and put it away, then went into the kitchen and cooked supper for my family.

REGRETFULLY, I MUST CONFESS to selling a lot of treasures from those memories, a couple of weeks after Elvis' death. I suppose part of it was mourning, and timing was another element. Whatever, it all seems like a fog, now. Anyhow, we needed money to get us through a tight spot. Not realizing their worth, I sold some of my records along with their covers for face value, that I now know were collectors' items. I let menus from Elvis' Vegas performances go for twenty dollars. And scarves? I don't know how many of them I sold. But I did hang onto the Elvis Summer Festival promo and most of the personal stuff.

I felt really bad after selling so much of my collection and I talked to Elvis' old picture about it.

Baby Jane, You did what you had to do. Now quit worryin' about it. Man, when will women ever learn, worryin' don't get you no place. So, why worry?"

E LVIS' WORK on this earth might have been finished but mine wasn't. The first five years of my marriage to Eddie were a menagerie of court wars and adoptions. Eddie adopted my children but lost the battle for custody of his three. I wanted another baby, but Eddie said it was probably just my hormones acting up. I finally agreed with him, and that's when we decided to help children who were already in the world, and needed love. We became foster parents and found our reward in the joy on faces of kids who hadn't smiled in a long time.

Before the foster children came to live with us, we had traveled every summer, allowing our own offspring to select any place within the continental United States that they wanted to go. Then, pulling a camper behind a Volkswagen van, sleeping in tents, and dining on instant oatmeal, cup-a-noodles, and peanut butter and jelly sandwiches, we made all the stops across America. Of course we had the luxury of a porta-potty and a hot plate to heat water.

My choice, naturally, was Graceland. We went there on every vacation. But we never took any trips while we had our precious, foster children. The old van just wouldn't hold all of us, so I never checked on whether it would even have been allowed. But, most important, staying home made the children feel more secure. Some of them had been dragged around the country till travel had no appeal for them.

L ESS THAN A YEAR after Elvis died, Bob Ross passed away. He'd been diagnosed with multiple sclerosis in 1977, after having been confined to a wheelchair since 1973.

On Bob's fifty-second birthday (July 15, 1977), Sandra called me. "Frances, you should see what Elvis sent Bob for his birthday." She was laughing, so hard, I could hardly understand what she was saying. "Elvis has got such a sense of humor, Frances. He sent Bob a very unique card. It says: "Enclosed please find something you've always wanted for your birthday, and inside is a picture of the Colonel on toilet paper, and handwritten by Elvis on the toilet paper is: Happy 52 Birthday, Love, Elvis.'" Then, snickering, she said, "I'll bet a lot of people would like to wipe their behind with the Colonel at some time or another." Now she was howling so hard she was snortin'.

In July of 1978, Bob suffered a fatal heart attack. At the time of his death, Ross Advertising was in the middle of booking and promoting the Tampa Jam and Medicine Show—No. 1.

Colonel Parker sent his regrets and sympathy with Tom Diskin, his right-hand man, who stood in for him at the funeral. Bob's mother, Marie, according to Sandra, had all the symptoms of Alzheimer's, and was so far along in her illness she never knew of her son's death. Sandra tended to the things she had to tend to—dreadful, necessary things—alone, bearing the pain that comes from death and losing the man she loved.

"I walked in a fog", she told me years later. "I was hurled into the middle of that mess of a concert. Didn't know what in the hell I was doing. Try burying your husband one day and facing all that the next."

For the Tampa Jam and Medicine Show—No. 1, they had booked Seals and Croft, Black Oak, Joe Cocker, Wet Willie, Alvin Lee and there were still more to be announced. The concert was held outdoors at Plant Field on August 19, 1978. Although it appeared to be packed, it was a financial bust and investors lost their money.

In the months following the Jam Show, Sandra lived a nightmare. She hired a lawyer and set about closing the agency. "I couldn't run that business," she said, "it was too taxing."

My ex-husband Billy was serving a life sentence plus ninety-nine years for armed robbery and escape, when he and another convict broke out of the close security prison at Raiford, shortly after dark on November 27, 1978. They crawled, cut barbed wire from fences, and skirted electrically charged wiring to gain their freedom.

A guard in the prison tower spotted Billy as he dropped to the ground from the middle fence and shouted for him to halt. Then, he tried to fire his rifle but found the safety catch engaged. Before he could release the safety and fire his weapon, Billy scrambled over the last fence and into the bushes. I'll always believe it was the prayers of his mama that saved his life.

This break was Billy's fifth escape from prison over a fifteen-year period, and the press said, "He's no nickels and dimes man." I worried about him and prayed for his safety while following the news stories.

A couple of weeks after Billy's escape, officials said they were no closer to catching him than the day he made his getaway. He was still at large and they had no idea where he might be. This time it would be three years before he was apprehended. He fled the state of Florida under an alias. I often thought of him. I wondered if my child's father was dead or alive. But deep in my heart, I knew Billy was a survivor, so I continued to send up prayers for his safety.

Over the next three years, we heard occasional news reports saying Billy was still at large. They were filled with speculation and admitted the longer he went undiscovered, the less chance he'd be caught. Eddie and I let Jessica think her father was in the military until she was old enough to seriously wonder and ask questions. But that didn't happen until after Billy was captured and brought back to Florida to serve out the rest of his sentence. And by then, Jessica was eight years old.

Women had always been Billy's weakness, and so it wasn't surprising when I learned the details of his arrest and found out a woman was involved. He wrote me a letter from prison. He said the girl he'd been living with was pregnant with his baby. She had no one to help her and wouldn't be eligible for public assistance until she got her citizenship papers. She'd been born in Germany and had a young son from a previous marriage. Billy knew Eddie and I were Christians, so he asked us, in the name of Jesus, to help her.

A stranger task I have never undertaken. But we agreed to take Alida and her son into our home. We helped her through beauty school, provided her with transportation, and took care of her child while she was in school.

Alida (not her real name) and I had different ways of looking at almost everything. There were times when it was difficult. I know I could not have survived this unconventional arrangement, had it not been for my faith and obedience to God. As the months went by and Alida grew larger with child, our differences magnified and the stress became too much for both of us. Eddie and I found her an apartment and continued to help her until after the birth of her daughter, at which time family assistance finally came through for her.

I know God has a sense of humor, because the night Billy's daughter was born, fate placed me in the labor room with Alida. She had an old Lamaze card from the birth of her previous child, and in the confusion of a busy night at the hospital, she convinced people in charge to let me come in as her coach. During that time we were just two women, sharing in the pain and joy of birth. Although we never became bosom buddies, this experience instilled in us a mutual respect for each other, enough to understand that, though people are different, they are still people underneath the discrepancies.

IN 1982, MY DEAR FRIEND Darlene called me and said she was going to be having surgery at Tampa General Hospital. She had cancer. Her folks wanted to be there for her but couldn't afford a hotel. I told her they were welcome to stay with us. It was the last gesture of love I would be allowed to extend my dearest friend.

It was wonderful to see Darlene again. We had one precious day together at my house before she went into the hospital. I only wished it could have been under different circumstances. The cancer had already begun to drain her strength. After her surgery, there was nothing more that could be done but to wait and pray.

Unfortunately, Darlene spent a year in demoralizing pain before her life ended. During our last telephone conversation, two days before she died at age thirty, Darlene said, "I never got to see

Elvis in person." It made me cry. She'd always been an angel; now Darlene had her wings.

IN 1980, I FELT GOD was calling me to minister the Gospel, so following extensive studies in Christian teaching, I was ordained and licensed a Baptist preacher. Eddie and I were very involved with serving God and our foster children loved going to services with us.

I taught reading at Oldsmar Christian School for a year. This was at the church God had eventually settled our family into after I'd prayed, and prayed, for Him to send me a Holy Ghost filled Baptist preacher. Since I'd been exposed to both the Pentecostal and the Baptist while growing up, my beliefs were a combination of the two denominations.

Brother John Stanton shook up his Oldsmar Baptist Church congregation when, after much study in the Bible, he was shown the need for the Pentecostal experience and received the baptism of the Holy Ghost with the evidence of speaking in tongues.

In 1983, I came home from church one day with Sandra on my mind. So I called her and invited her over for supper. It was good to see her again. We had a nice half-day visit. I asked her how life was treating her and she said, "Working's all I know anymore, Frances."

Sandra had gone back to school after Bob died and eventually became a registered nurse. We talked for a while, then she told me a guy named Dirk Vellenga (Author of *Elvis and the Colonel*) had been writing her and leaving messages on her answering machine. The letters were postmarked from Holland. She said he asked a lot of questions about the Colonel, Marie, and Bob.

"I was not about to give information of such a personal nature to a total stranger. When I called the Colonel about it at the apartment in Beverly Hills, he didn't seem concerned. Frances, that was the first and last time I've had any contact with the Colonel since my husband's death."

Sandra did eventually talk to Vellenga but she didn't have too much to say to him. She knew I'd always wanted to write a book about Elvis, and she told me, "I'm saving the good stuff for you, Frances."

OUR HOUSE CAUGHT ON FIRE while we had our foster children. Eddie was sleeping that day because he was working the night shift at the police department. It was winter and we were still using the old wood heater. I'd gone to the grocery store and had banked up the fire before I left. I wanted the house to stay warm till I got back. I didn't know how much wood to put in the heater, so I just filled 'er on up. I was at the store for about an hour and in good spirits when I headed home.

As I drove up in the yard, I saw people from the real estate office next door, waving at me not to come any closer. I couldn't understand what was going on. They kept yelling, and then I saw flames coming from the roof of our house. And I thought of Eddie.

I jumped out of the van and ran toward the house, then I heard the sirens as fire trucks entered the yard. All I could think was, *Eddie's in there. Oh, God, save my husband!* I ran around to the back bedroom window, ready to toss a brick through, when someone grabbed me by the arms.

"My husband!" I screamed.

I heard a voice shouting, "He's out. He's on the other side of the house trying to put out the fire."

As the words sank into my brain, I fell to the ground and gave in to my emotions, sobbing uncontrollably. "I almost killed him...it's my fault."

And then, those loving arms were holding me. "I'm here, honey, it's okay. It's not your fault." I held onto him like he might disappear in the flames, and I couldn't stop trembling.

The children had been at school. They were safe. My husband was alive and our church helped us to rebuild. God had shown me in His benevolent way that life and love were all that mattered.

Some of my Elvis memorabilia was destroyed in the fire; records warped, and water damage took its toll on other items. I managed to rescue the picture Elvis had autographed to me. And, the contents of my flowered box.

We lived in that house for seven years, and when I was finally contented with where I was, God saw fit to give me a better house. But only after I'd learned He must come first.

I N 1984, we moved into our present home. It didn't take us long to grow used to air conditioning, two bathrooms, and a swimming pool. We took only one more foster child after moving. The possibility of one of them drowning in the pool, added to regulation changes in the system at HRS, were the biggest factors in our decision to quit foster parenting.

J OLYNN GRADUATED from high school in 1985. For her graduation gift, my mother and I took her on a trip to Europe. We toured eight countries and I was amazed at how popular Elvis was over there. Eight years after his death, he was still going strong.

Old memories revived one night while we were in Germany. I'd caught some foreign flu bug that was going around. I was very sick and running a high temperature. I tossed and turned in the bed, delirious from the fever. Then, I slipped into a dreamlike state and Elvis floated in on a cloud of stardust wearing his army dress uniform. I suppose this was because I was in Germany, where he'd spent his army years.

Elvis sat down on the bed beside me, placed his hand on my feverish forehead, and prayed. Then he spoke to me without moving his lips, sort of like mental telepathy. *Baby Jane? Where have you been? I've missed you. You haven't thought of me in a long time.*

"Elvis?...I'm sorry. I've been so busy raising my children and learning about Jesus. But I love you. I'll always love you."

It's okay darlin'. I'll take second place to the Master, any day. I know your heart. He leaned down and kissed me, then sang, "Daddy Bigboots," the lullaby from *GI Blues.*

When I awoke from my dream, the fever was gone. It had seemed so real, the feelings my hallucination provoked were still with me. And I thought, constantly, of Elvis for the rest of that week.

When we got back home from Europe, Jolynn went to work for Taco Bell, then wound up marrying her assistant manager. In 1986, my granddaughter, Tiffany, was born.

I N 1988, Eddie's prayers were finally answered. His only son, Sean, came to live with us. Sean was twenty-seven years old and had served in the marines, then attended the University of California. He'd come for a visit and was with us two weeks when tragedy struck.

Sean had taken his father's kayak out for the day into a swampy area between Tampa and Oldsmar. He said he'd be home before dark. When he didn't show up, long after dark, we started to worry. I knew something was wrong and called the sheriff's department, but I was told we had to wait the usual amount of time for missing adults before they could start a search. By the next afternoon, they became involved and contacted the coast guard.

That first night Sean was missing, I didn't sleep. The second night, I tossed and turned in my bed. When I finally dropped off to sleep, Elvis again visited me in a dream. This time he was wearing a white doctor's coat, like the one he wore in *Change of Habit*. He sat down on the bed next to me and rubbed my hands. *It's okay, sweet baby. Everything is okay. Sean will live. God is teaching him right now, so have faith, little one.*

On the third day, Sean still hadn't been found. It was Valentine's Day. I wanted to stay near the phone so I hadn't gone to church that morning. Mama and Pap were on their way home from the Sunday service, which was in Oldsmar, and as they passed by the area where Sean had gone kayaking, they spotted his car on a downhill embankment where Eddie had missed seeing it in his search. They came straight to the house to tell me about finding the car. I immediately reported it to the sheriff's department, then called Eddie at work. He said he'd meet us at the location.

A helicopter was brought in and flown over the swampy area where sheriffs' deputies finally located Sean's unconscious body. Eddie had taken off on foot into the swamp the moment he saw the car. He found his son when the men in the helicopter signaled his location. When they flew Sean out of the swamp, an ambulance was waiting to carry him to the nearest hospital. I rode with him and prayed as the paramedics administered oxygen and emergency medical treatment. Eddie met us at the hospital.

Sean looked bad. He'd been missing for three days and two of the coldest nights we had experienced that winter. He was suffering from exposure to the elements and his hand and arm were swollen three times their size. His body was dehydrated and he was in a coma. He'd been bitten by a poisonous snake that paralyzed him, and his kidneys had ceased to function. The doctors didn't think they could save his hand and said his kidneys were totally shot.

Sean was hooked up to a dialysis machine, while Eddie prayed by his bedside, and told the doctors that God would heal his son.

"They are not going to remove my son's hand."

Several days later when Sean came out of the coma, he had no memory of what had happened to him. It would be two years later before the memories started to come back. God healed Sean's kidneys in a miraculous way that left no one able to take credit.

Eddie had gone to church one night, not long before Sean was to be released from the hospital. Patti, Eddie's older daughter, had flown to Tampa to see her brother. She and I were at home when Eddie got back from church. He was praising the Lord as he came through the door.

"God healed my son tonight!"

Patti, who believed in God but didn't have the same healing faith as her father, looked concerned.

Eddie told us he'd gone to the altar and stood in for his son's healing. While he was being anointed with oil and prayed for, a lady in the congregation saw a vision over his head, of a water spigot, slowly dripping. Then a hand reached out and opened the faucet to a full flow, and she said within herself, *Lord, I don't understand this, but if you want me to reveal it to Brother Eddie, you will have to cause him to come to me before we leave tonight.*

On the way out of church, Eddie went over to greet the lady and as she told him of her vision, he looked up at the clock and saw it was 9:30 P.M., and knew God had healed his son.

After he recounted this story to us, he went on to bed, while Patti and I stayed up and talked. Patti told me she was worried about her father. She knew kidneys didn't heal themselves and was concerned about her dad not being able to accept the inevitable.

I told her, "Patti, have faith."

The next morning we went to the hospital. The minute we stepped off the elevator, doctors and nurses came rushing toward us. "It's a miracle! There's no other explanation." Sean's kidneys had kicked in and started working at 9:30 P.M. the night before. Patti's face went white just before she threw her arms around her father's neck and hugged him. Sean's kidneys are working today and he still has both hands. Elvis had been right. God had been teaching Sean, and all of the rest of us, a lesson in faith.

EDDIE AND FRANCES ON THEIR WEDDING DAY. 1977.

21

Only The Strong Survive

1988 - 1992

You can't go through life depending on others. That weakens you. You have to depend on yourself.

—*Elvis Presley*

In an effort to supply jobs for his son and son-in-law, Eddie incorporated a security business. A-Interbay Protection was a patrol service that provided drive-by car checks and in-house security for apartments and businesses.

Unfortunately, the business failed to thrive. Eddie had invested all our savings into that company, but due to employee misman-agement of funds, we soon had to take out a loan on our home. Our problems seemed to be insurmountable, and in my misery, I turned to alcohol.

Ava was my closest friend during these trying times. Our friendship went back to 1966, when Ava was in her glory days. Ex-model and owner of several popular nightclubs in Tampa, she was a giving person with a heart of gold. Unfortunately for Ava, there were plenty of takers who fared well from her generosity. By 1990, she was down to her last possessions; her home and its contents. My friend found comfort in the bottle of vodka that was her constant companion.

I don't know how it all started for me. One drink here to forget, another drink there to forget, but I didn't forget. When I was sober, a self-protective mechanism, an inner alarm kept me from dwelling on old memories, memories of times long gone that only brought me pain, the old deep-seated pain I refused to let myself feel. But with the alcohol, it was harder to hold them at bay and the dark childhood memories surfaced, swelling my oppression, washing ashore the debris all around me, and I wanted to fall into an ocean of booze and drown.

I still went to church and read my Bible every day, but there were times when I couldn't hear God. All I could hear was my pain. What a trick alcohol plays on the mind. No wonder it's called spirits.

One evening while I was meditating, and fighting the urge for a drink, depression beat me. I'd been battling my demons all night. The nightmares turned into memories, then the memories faded and came back...faded and came back...like the focus on a camera. They wouldn't stay still long enough for me to apprehend details. Rather, I was left with flashes of nightmarish cruelties that I couldn't think about, let alone make sense of.

The flesh won and I poured myself a drink. I downed it and wanted more. There was only one swig left in the bottle. So, after I'd finished it off, I called Ava. I told her I was coming over for conversation. But in truth, I wanted the bracer I knew would be available to me.

Eddie was at work and Ava lived only a couple of miles from my house. I climbed into the car, backed out of the driveway, and headed down the street. When I came to the end of the road and went to make a right turn, my shoulder-strap pocketbook fell from the seat and somehow got tangled on the accelerator. I reached for it, but found I needed to unhook my safety belt in order to bend the distance. Once I had a grip on the purse I lifted it, then realizing it was caught but not knowing what held it, I yanked on the strap and the car sped forward, out of my control.

I could hear my own voice screaming in my ears and then the shattering of glass and the crunching metal, grinding and cracking. Then everything stopped and the world turned black.

Moments, that seemed an eternity, passed. *Oh, Dear God! What have I done?* Conscious now, I could see I'd hit a parked van and some garbage cans. I panicked, and with no regard for the consequences, started the engine and fled. How I survived the couple of miles to Ava's, only God and his angels know. The hood was smashed up against the front window, and blood threatened to blind my vision further, as it ran down my face and into my eyes. I pulled into the driveway of Ava's house, jumped from the car, and raced to her door. When she answered the bell and saw my condition, the panic I saw in her eyes confirmed my worst fears.

"My face!" I screamed, and reached up to feel glass protruding from everywhere I touched. Fresh sobs escaped my lips as Ava helped me into the house, then, carefully, directed me into a reclining position on the sofa.

"Frances, I'm going to call Eddie. What's his number at work?" I opened my mouth to speak, but the words faded as I slipped back into the safe haven of unconsciousness.

Baby Jane, get a grip.

Elvis? Now I could see him. He was dressed in the same blue casual jumpsuit he'd been wearing when I'd first met him backstage in Vegas.

Baby Jane, you've made a mess of things this time, I'll grant you that. But, you see, honey, you've gotta learn from this experience. Life is too precious to play Russian roulette with it. He kissed me softly then sang "I Was The One."

"Shhh...lie still."

I recognized a voice. "Eddie?"

"Honey, you're in the hospital but you'll be alright. Don't talk."

Fear clutched me in its grip, then Eddie's hand on my arm tightened just a fraction, and I heard him praying. His hand left my arm and I strained my ears to hear him speaking with a sheriff, but I couldn't grasp their conversation. Feeling secure in my husband's abilities, I slipped away to a place where everything was right and problems were nonexistent. And again, Elvis visited me.

Baby Jane, when are you going to learn that you have to be strong? I could see him. He was wearing a white jumpsuit this time. *Honey, listen to me very carefully. You are going to need God's strength in the very near future, even more than you need it now. Stop the drinkin' and read your Bible.* And then he faded away.

I was treated and released to go home. Eddie comforted me, attentively, and without reprimands. But my guilt was still overwhelming. I'd wrecked the car and heaped more trouble onto his already burdened back. Maybe things weren't the way I'd have liked them to be, but alcohol was not the answer. Why had it nearly taken my life to see a truth that should have been apparent to me since childhood? I prayed, asking God to help me. "Lend me Your strength, Lord, for I have none."

Thank God that He is love, and love is having the tenacity to keep the faith, when innocence is gone and the world has turned upside down. I had one more battle with alcohol that again almost took my life before God miraculously intervened.

About a week after my accident, while I was convalescing, Satan attacked me with his ultimate weapon—the memories. Alone at home and feeling sorry for myself, I decided to take a trip to the store and purchase a bottle of cure. After doing that very thing, I poured myself a drink and sat out on the patio, drinking and thinking what a mess my life was.

How could God love me? How could anyone love me? I was a failure and a drunk like my daddy. The spirit of suicide, that spirit that had danced with me all my life, was on me with a vengeance. *Nobody understands me, I thought. Why don't they understand me? Because I'm no good and I don't even know why I'm no good. I want to be good—like Mama. Everybody sees her goodness.*

I remember falling to my knees and praying after making the decision to end my life. *God forgive me if suicide is, in fact, the unforgivable sin. But I just can't stand the nightmares and the horrible memories that forever lurk my mind. What are they about, Lord?* Then, at the last moment, just as I was ready to go for the gun, a hand grabbed my shoulder.

I turned my head and saw what appeared to be an angel. She stood above me with long, flowing, dark hair, clothed in a white gown, and spoke to me. "God sent me to you." Then she prayed a prayer of deliverance and I was set free. Instantly. And I knew it. Free from the memories. Free from suicide. Free from alcohol. Free to serve God and my family with a confidence I'd never before known. Now I knew what Elvis had meant when he'd asked, after praying for me, if I felt free.

I was surprised when I realized my angel was, in fact, a real person. She introduced herself as my new neighbor, Nancy, from across the street. She related to me how she'd been awakened at the midnight hour by her spirit, which was telling her to get to the lady across the street, Now! She questioned herself with *what ifs, and I don't know those people,* then obeyed her spirit.

The next day, she came over to bring me a book. **He Came to Set the Captives Free,** by Rebecca Brown, showed me the root of my problem, then God's word fully delivered me.

I WAS FORTY-SIX when God rescued me from the dark memories. I knew bad things had been done to me when I was a child. Things Mama never knew, or it would have killed her. Sexually abusive things I could never forget, but chose to suppress. I kept them away by burying them under laughter, music, dancing, and pure, undefiled romance. This secret that I bared only to Elvis' picture for years, was the same one I'd actually revealed to him later.

I was feeling better about myself. I'd overcome a lot of difficulties in the past years and was eager to get on with my life. The perfect life, my version of it anyway, seemed within reach. A life of reading, writing, taking some courses at the nearby college, and maybe some travel...a life without catastrophic interruptions.

As I was thinking about all these things and planning my future, the telephone rang. When I answered it, Mama said, "Hello, Sister."

Something in her voice caused me to panic. "What's wrong?" I blurted, without caution.

"Now, don't get upset, but I'm in the hospital. I told Sandy to let me call so you'd know I'm all right."

"What's wrong with you, Mama?"

"They found a large tumor in my ovaries, Sister, but everything's gonna be all right. The doctor's getting me ready for a hysterectomy but I wanted to see you before they take me into surgery."

I felt something in me collapse, and then, just as suddenly, collect itself. "I'll be there as quick as I can get dressed and drive over."

"Sister, I'm at the Centurion Hospital on Dale Mabry, and your grandma is here with us. She's upset. If you could, I'd appreciate it if you'd take her home with you for a few days."

"Of course I will, Mama. Don't you worry about Grandma."

"Drive careful, honey. I love you."

"I love you, too, Mama."

As soon as I hung up, I started to feel the impact of what she had said. The anguish of not being able to unravel hope from denial put me at an impasse. And I cried.

When I reached the hospital, I was met by Pap and the rest of my family. I'd been the last one to be notified. Pap had called everyone else, but for me, Mama told him to bring the phone to her. She knew if I heard the news from anyone else, I'd have killed myself in a panic, trying to get to the hospital.

The doctor came into the waiting room for a consultation with the family at precisely the same time I arrived. He feared it was cancer and said, "But we're hoping to get it all. I can't tell you any more until after the surgery, when we get the lab results."

I knew ovarian cancer was bad and the prognosis was grim. I sank into a nearby chair and let tears I'd been holding back flow. *Not my Mama*, I thought. How could this be happening? Mama did everything right. She didn't smoke or drink. She watched her diet and ate healthy foods. She walked three miles almost every day. She always went for her checkups and followed the doctors' orders to the letter.

No. The doctors were mistaken. They had to be mistaken! Then I remembered Darlene and the bleakness of the situation compounded my misery.

Mama's tumor was malignant, and so began the nightmare that would last for thirteen months. I visited her every day and watched helplessly as she went through the painful ordeal of chemotherapy and radiation. She was a fighter, and I fought the battle with her.

Mama braved the loss of her hair and wore the wig we had bought in preparation. Bible readings and prayer were her greatest comfort, and they united us in a bond that went beyond anything of this earth.

Food became her biggest challenge. For a little woman who had enjoyed eating, the side effects of chemotherapy took away her last pleasure. I was determined to find something that would satisfy her palate and remain in her stomach. At times when I felt helpless, like I wasn't doing enough, Mama reassured me.

"Honey, I just can't eat. When people are nice enough to bring me food, it breaks my heart not to be able to eat it." She started to cry. "I don't want to hurt their feelings. It upsets me. But you...Sister, I can tell you when I can't eat something without getting upset. Then you just smile and keep on trying different things."

Mama reached up, touched my face, and I couldn't hold back my tears any longer. I had to get out of that room for release.

One evening after I got home from the hospital, I suddenly remembered what Elvis had said in the last dream. He had told me that I was going to need God's strength in the near future. How had he known?

I eventually found something Mama could eat—lima beans. Now, every time I look at a lima bean I am reminded of the joy they brought my mother, when at last she could eat something without getting sick.

As time passed it became evident that Mama was fighting a losing battle. But I believed in miracles and refused to accept the inevitable. The day Mama was told there was no more that could be done for her, that it was just a matter of time, she chose to go home and spend the rest of her life in familiar surroundings. Hospice, a nursing organization for the terminally ill, was a blessing, but it never stopped the efforts of my mother's big, loving family. They were all there for her comfort.

Brother John and Sister Peggy Stanton, our pastor and his wife, came almost every day and encouraged Mama to continue fighting. She did fight. Right to the end she fought. Then, on her last day, something happened. She seemed to have reached a decision within herself, and with a courage that showed everyone around her how to die, she smiled and seemed to accept what she couldn't change.

In her final alertness, Mama touched my face and mouthed, "I love you," then slipped into a coma. Assuming she was asleep, I tiptoed out of the room.

As the day wore into evening, everybody knew the end was near. But my spirit had not received the message. At midnight, my family encouraged me to go home and rest. They assured me they would all be near her. Eddie took me by the arm. "Honey, you need to get some rest or you won't be able to go on." I let him lead me to the car with a promise from Aunt Inez that she would call me if there was any change.

We went home and I had barely gone to sleep when I felt Eddie gently touching me. "Honey, Inez just called. Your Mama has gone home to be with Jesus." Eddie enfolded me within his arms and I cried, as much in shock as grief. I'd never known how utterly lonely I would feel. I felt so guilty, too. I should have known it was going to happen. I should have been with her. Was that why I left?

The next couple of days I walked around like a zombie while my family took care of the funeral arrangements. I selected Mama's burial gown in an eggshell color. It was made of a soft thin cotton with lots of lace. One-hundred-percent cotton had been her favorite fabric, and I wanted her to enter heaven in comfort and beauty.

Ava rode with Eddie and me to the funeral. She had lost her mother to cancer a couple of years earlier and could relate to the pain I was experiencing.

Brother John gave my mother's eulogy, which was titled "The Ideal Woman." Afterward, I walked up to her casket and placed a small pink Bible in her hands. She looked beautiful even in death, and so peaceful. I remember thinking, *You're an angel now, Mama... so stay with me or I'll never make it.*

Mama's funeral had the largest attendance of any I'd ever been to. The line of cars seemed to be endless, giving testimony to how well she was thought of, and how so many people loved her.

After the services, out of town friends and family gathered at a nearby restaurant in an effort to console one another. Eddie, at that point, left me in Ava's care. He'd missed so much work in the past week, that after being convinced by Ava that she was capable of taking care of me, he went on to work.

We were sitting in a booth across from each other, talking, when Ava picked up a glass of iced tea. She started to take a sip and suddenly, her hand drew up into a backward knot and she dropped the glass. I quickly looked to her face and saw, with horror, her eyes rolling back into her head. I screamed her name and reached out for her while others rushed to catch her as she slumped over sideways from the booth. Charlie Jo, my cousin who was a paramedic, pulled her gently to the floor and administered CPR while someone else phoned for an ambulance.

My nerves were shattered, but a strength beyond my capacity took hold. I rode in the ambulance with my friend and prayed for God to intervene on her behalf. When we reached the hospital, I was told to stay in the waiting room. A couple of hours went by before I was allowed to see Ava. She was cognizant and wanted to know what had happened. I told her of the event that had landed her in the hospital. Then in her unselfish nature she tried to console me. She apologized for adding to my problems on the day of my mother's funeral.

"Ava, you had no control over what happened, darling. Stop worrying about me and think of yourself for a change."

Ava stayed in the hospital for tests, then was released a few days later with instructions for follow-up treatment. It seemed to the doctors she had experienced a stroke.

ELVIS SIGNING AUTOGRAPHS ON SET OF "FOLLOW THAT DREAM." OCALA 1961.

22

I Believe

Sometimes it's good to get a few words out, no matter if anyone's listening...just to put yourself on your knees.

—*Elvis Presley*

What can be said about Elvis Presley that hasn't already been said? I could say more about the spiritual man. This is a chapter I feel like Elvis would have most wanted me to write. The biggest question in his life was, *Why me, Lord? What is your purpose for Elvis Presley?* I know this because he told me.

Questions have plagued me throughout my life. Questions like, Who am I? Where do I come from? What is my purpose? Why do I do the things I do? Who's really in charge? What happens to me when I die? The Bible tells us to raise up a child in the way he should go and when he is old he will not depart from it.

To understand Elvis Presley we must first understand his spirit, his beliefs. Elvis was raised in the Pentecostal faith as was I. We were taught that God is Love and Forgiveness. God is Omnipotent—He sees all and knows all. He hears and answers prayer. His love knows no boundaries. His forgiveness is eternal. He is selfless and His charity reaches all who are in need. God said He would never forsake us and in our darkest hour He is there. These are the words that were sown into Elvis' heart as a child. And they remained in his heart even when his flesh was weak. Please bear with me as I say it the way my spirit sees it.

Each writer sees through different eyes and writers are as different as their subjects. But as the vision of each author is conveyed to the reader, a clearer picture of the real man emerges.

When people look to the outward, they see only what the physical projects. But spiritual eyes see into a heart and understand.

The Bible tells us that King David prayed in song and praised in dance. It also says he sinned with Bathsheba, then sent her husband to the front line of battle that he would be killed. Yet, God forgave and said of David—*He is a man after my heart.*

Elvis was a man in search of God's heart. His abundance of faith, love, and charity were treasures that exhibited where his heart lay.

That's why it came as no surprise to me that his gospel albums were the only ones to earn him Grammies. I believe they were anointed. Elvis sang gospel music like it was his way of worshiping, praising, and talking to God. And the songs he selected were like prayers and that made me feel like Elvis was particular about what words he sang. He had talked to me a little bit about this when he'd read my brother's music.

When we look closely at the words Elvis sang, we see very clearly inside the man. For instance, when listening to "I Believe," we can see what he hypothesized. Later in his life when he was searching for truth, people accused him of forsaking his Christian roots. But searching for truth only emphasizes a person's love for God. Elvis expressed his true feelings when he sang "There Is No God But God."

I am ever lifted up by the words of "An Evening Prayer," a song that I believe gave solace to the soul of Elvis:

> *If I have wounded a soul today,*
> *If I have caused one's foot to go astray,*
> *If I have walked in my own willful way,*

Dear Lord, forgive.
Forgive the sins I have confessed to Thee,
Forgive my secret sins that I do not see,
Oh, God, watch over and my Keeper be,
Dear Lord, amen.

If there is any question as to who Elvis' God was, he gives the answer in the song "He Is My Everything." Elvis always said there was only one "King" and His name was Jesus.

Elvis' greatest attributes were faith, hope, charity, love, and forgiveness. He forgave in his heart even when he gave no verbal acknowledgement. And I think anybody who knew him realized this.

He had an innocence about him that was best described by Elaine Dundy in her book, *Elvis and Gladys*. She called it, "Elvis innocence, finding no archetype for it. An almost inhuman innocence, and this innocence remained with him all his life."

Elvis read his Bible and prayed. He believed, too, in laying on hands and praying for the sick. Yes, I believe there was more depth to Elvis Presley than human eyes saw.

He'd searched diligently for answers through the sixties, "Trying the spirits." But I think the mid seventies found him more at peace in his heart with the basic truths he'd been raised on. His flesh might have been weak but his spirit *knew truth* and was mighty, and his faith was real. Elvis knew God judged a man by his heart. And I think he found peace in this knowledge.

I SAW THREE of Elvis' Vegas performances in 1975, before he had to cancel due to illness. He appeared to be tired, yet his spirit sang mightily through gospel music and spiritual readings. I saw the life his audience gave to him while his body was dying, and it was apparent to me where his strength came from. It came from his love of God and fellow man.

These performances left a lasting impression on me and it was not long after that I got saved. I believe it might have been something I saw in Elvis as he sang what he felt, that prodded me to take that most meaningful step of my life.

IT WAS 1992, and I had been crazy for Elvis all my life. Even after I got saved, and after Elvis' death, I still loved him. I treasured the picture he autographed to me. I had it professionally framed and hung it on my dining room wall to mark a time in my life I'd never forget.

But after Elvis died in 1977, the same year Eddie and I were married, life got busy for me. I had kids to raise and all that that entails. And it was a time of learning God's ways. Somehow, I'd gotten away from my teen fanaticism and settled into a more mature kind of love for Elvis.

Now, with my children grown and gone, and without Mama around for company, I started to think about finding something to fill the empty hours and days their absence had left. And that's when it occurred to me, now was the time to pursue writing. I hadn't forgotten about telling Elvis I wanted to write a book about him someday.

I signed up for a couple of writing courses at the University of South Florida and finally took pen in hand. I started writing about everything that interested or bothered me. But I was constantly sidetracked by those haunting words, "Write one that'll bring me back to life." But I didn't feel confident enough in my writing, yet, to do Elvis that justice. My notes and handwritten memoirs began to stack up. Finally, one day I gathered up all my writings and sorted them into some semblance of order, and I saw my book! It was right before my eyes. Elvis was my book and by-hound-doggies, Elvis was going to live again!

I remembered, again and again, telling Elvis I wanted to be a writer. I tossed that memory around in my head till I was there.

"Don't write a book about me till I'm dead, then write one that'll bring me back to life." Back to life. Back to life. Over and over, again and again. But, how do I do that? I asked myself.

I started listening more closely to the music that had inspired him. And it was so easy to see—like a musical photograph. Memories played to music in my head, in vivid colors so alive, and feelings I'd never forget cloaked me and I lived them all again.

I SAW A MAN who was loving, emotional, tenderhearted, and generous. A shy man, but observant. A polite man who was sexy and mysterious, with a slight element of danger. A high-strung man, yet a man with an enormous sense of humor who threw himself into everything as though his life depended on it. A man who commanded the focus of attention and would not allow himself to be ignored. A man who was all male and as charming as any romance hero. A man called Elvis, able through his spirit to see into the hearts of people. Then, almost like he could read their minds, compassionately kiss their boo-boos and make them all better. This is what he had made me feel from the beginning. He understood his fans because in a way he was just like them. Elvis knew how it felt to stand on the outside with his face pressed against the window. But more than all this, I saw a spiritual man, and I believe Elvis would want to be remembered as such.

He was an embodiment of contradictions, and by example, a great teacher of right and wrong, showing us how to love and also what traps not to fall into. He expressed himself through music, and if you were listening you knew what was within the man. His moods, his emotions, and his thoughts were declared through the lyrics of his songs. Subsequently, all his mountains, valleys, and trials were recorded for all time on a round, black disc.

WHILE I'M ON THE SUBJECT of what I believe, one question that plagued me was, Why did Elvis come to my room? Which leads to another question. Why did he get the room for me in the first place? I've pondered, and pondered my special gift from Elvis, and the most logical conclusion I've been able to come up with is, *Writing*. I think that word signaled a red flag, then waved it at his curiosity.

You see, during the time I was rooming with Sylvia, my trip up to Elvis' suite, and hanging around backstage and in the dressing rooms, I had ample opportunity to witness a small part of Elvis' personal kingdom. I was the outsider. I remember Elvis' reaction when I told him, "You know I'll probably write a book about all of this someday." His whole demeanor changed and he became like an animal sniffing out a threatening scent.

I believe Elvis recognized something in me that I'd never had faith to see in myself. Something like what only Mama saw in me. Strength and determination—an ability to overcome. So here is my theory:

Elvis was concerned for his privacy. What had this stranger seen or heard that might be damaging to his image? And what was all of her writing talk about? Was she a writer or not? Like a chameleon, Elvis' personality altered to fit the circumstance and to relate to the person, making it a simple matter for him to exhume from me the answer to these two big questions. Who was I, and what was I after?

Elvis' image was very important to him, as was the other side— the personal side. He strived for the *perfect* image. How his fans beheld him was his life's blood. It meant acceptance, and it meant money, and all that he could do with money. He could help people on a personal level, if he had money. Why, he could do anything he wanted and he could enjoy it with people he loved by sharing it with them.

Elvis loved the image. He dressed it, he drove it, he ate it, he lived it, and I think he married it.

I now believe he targeted me for personal investigation the first time I set foot into his private world, up in the penthouse suite. This would explain the interest he showed in me. Then, of course, my mention of writing gave him reason for concern. Is she really a writer? Who is she anyway? And so he set out to find out. But of course, this is just a theory.

KAYE CASON, JESSICA, NANCY MINTON, AND FRANCES. 1996.

23

Words

1992 - 1995

Ambition comes from the brain leadin' the body, instead of the other way around.

—Elvis Presley

The struggle to find my writing identity loomed before me like a great monster ready to gobble me up. But Mama's spirit was with me, planting encouragement within my heart.

You have what it takes, Sister. You just need some reassurance. Go back to school, take a few more courses, then attack it with the same ferocity you've possessed and used throughout your life. And remember, God is on your side.

Could I learn to write and reach the goal I had nourished for thirty-six years? No longer were excuses of caring for my family a way out of facing the real issue. The issue being—did I have it in me to commit, start, and carry through to completion? Was I able to face rejection? *Nothing tried is nothing gained—a good place to start is always at the beginning.*

My typing skills, which were never adequate, had long been forgotten. How could I write a book when I couldn't type? *Pens and pencils have existed long before typewriters were invented. Where there's a will there's a way.* Mama's favorite old cliches were haunting me.

Then one day, while I was trying to write, I placed both hands to my head and shook it as if this exercise would loosen the jargon and force some answers to surface. I picked up the pen, and although words seemed elusive, I started to write. As I wrote I felt a presence. Who was it? I had often felt Mama's spirit but this one held a different aura. It was one of laughter, and music sang within my heart. Who was there? It took me a moment but then I knew. It was Elvis. And for some unknown reason, laughter bubbled up in me like new champagne and I laughed, and I laughed, then laughed some more. I laughed, until a familiar and comforting voice spoke to my heart.

Baby Jane.

The southern voice, thick as molasses, moved like syrup over hot pancakes, right into my heart. "Elvis?" I spoke his name aloud as though his presence was as viable as the pen I held ready to record a message.

Baby, Baby, Baby. The voice came again. *You once told me you wanted to write a book, so what's stoppin' you?*

"Elvis?" I glanced around, almost expecting him to appear physically. "Am I going crazy?" Then I shook my head and tried again to write, but words didn't come.

Then I heard him. *Baby Jane.* I looked up, ever so slightly, from the writing tablet and laid the pen down. I could almost see him now, sitting in the chair across from me. He was laughing, and I remembered the warm feelings I had felt when he used to say, "Baby Jane, you make me laugh." I'd spent my youth pursuing that golden memory.

I know I'm in your heart, but now I'm in your head and I'm here to give you inspiration. Remember when you called me your angel of inspiration? I could see him smiling. It was his famous smile. The one captured and saved on film when at the end of *Love Me Tender,* his ghost appears on the screen.

That's good, Baby Jane. You're beginnin' to visualize. Now pick up the pen and let's write. Bring me back to life. That old magic of Elvis Presley was playing up and down my spine. *You've got back-*

bone, Baby. You always did. That's what I admired about you. You have what it takes and I'm here with you, so let's "rock and roll!"

I picked up the pen and began to write from my heart. It was 1955, and I was eleven years old again, lying across my bed and holding my favorite picture. Elvis' smile reached my heart, and his talking eyes sang to me.

The next day I went to the library and checked out a writer's handbook. Feeling hopeless within the first sentence that told of the competition and how hard it would be to get published, I was encouraged when, in the next paragraph, I read that there were two exceptions: if I were an ex-president, or if I had slept with the ghost of Elvis and could prove it. I hadn't slept with his ghost, but I felt his presence, and heard him when he spoke to my heart.

See, Baby Jane. I've given you the key to unlock all your dreams.

"But Elvis, there are things you told me not to talk about." I spoke these words aloud as if he were right there with me.

And you didn't! Then I heard him again. *I always knew I could trust you. But don't worry, Baby Jane, it's alright to tell it now. Your book will be a success, I promise, because I'll be right here inspirin' you. And your mama, she'll be encouragin' you. We may not be there in the physical, but you know we're real because we live in your heart. Just like when you were a teenager and I was there for you anytime, anyplace. I was real then, wasn't I? Nothing has changed. I'm still around.*

The personalities of Mama and Elvis were reaching out and making contact with my consciousness. I felt them comforting and encouraging me and these manifestations of the spirit allowed me to understand what Jesus meant when he said, "Because I live, ye also shall live."

I called Sandra and told her I was finally going to write that book. She said, "Good, come on over and I'll put on a pot of coffee." I went to her house, we got comfortable, then started reliving the good old days. I asked her if she'd heard from the Colonel.

"Frances, after Bob died, I was just the poor widow who had to go back to school and learn how to support myself. So I figured since I had majored in bedpans and incontinent care during Bob's years of illness, the most logical thing for me to do was become a nurse. So, that's why I'm a registered nurse now. I had difficulty accepting being deserted by my in-laws after seven years of faithful service to Bob. You know, I earned my bachelor's degree in sociology in an effort to understand what was wrong with them. But, I still have not found the answer. The only thing I can rationalize is that I took care of Bob during his long illness, his care wasn't a worry for Colonel and Marie, and after he died my services were no longer required. The worst part of it is, not only did my son, Kenneth, lose his father, but it seems he lost his grandfather, also. It's especially sad since Kenneth idolized the Colonel and emulates much of his savvy. I heard the Colonel's arm was injured in an elevator accident and he lost the use of it."

"Yeah, I think I read the same thing."

"Funny how the spirits move, isn't it? Do you think it was one last karate chop?" Sandra had a teasing, spooky look on her face. "Remember all those stories Papa used to tell us about haints and ghosts? Well, I think maybe there might be something to it." Now she giggled.

"Sandra, may I quote all this you've told me in my book?"

She shrugged her shoulders, took a big draw on her cigarette, and inhaled. "Why not. I guess my name will be mud after this book comes out, but that's alright. Colonel doesn't acknowledge my name anymore, anyhow. Imagine, learning about my mother-in-law's death from you, because you read it in a book!"

"Sandra, are there any last words you'd like to say that would sum up your life?"

"Yes. Since I've been drag racing in a jet with the Colonel, and knocked on my ass by Frances in the casino of the Las Vegas International Hotel, I guess one could say that my life has had its ups and downs."

I SIGNED UP for two more writing courses at the University of South Florida, remembering the last class I'd taken the year before. That first class in "Writing and Getting Published," I had been so green, yet certain I would succeed, I wore my positive attitude, and determination, like a four leaf clover for all to see.

I kept hearing an unfamiliar word passing around the classroom and raised my hand. When the instructor acknowledged me, I asked, "What does critique mean?" All heads turned to look at me.

Their eyes seemed to ask, *What are you doing in this class?* The incident was quite humorous now, considering I'd been sitting in a critiquing group at the time. I wondered how I would embarrass myself this next semester.

This time I found myself in a variety that talked way over my head. They were professional writers in different fields, from editors, to reporters, to teachers, and published writers. That class made me feel like Dolly Parton in a business suit; overwhelmed, uncomfortable, and not sure I fit in. My embarrassment sprang from how dysfunctional, ignorant, and insignificant I felt amidst all their education and professionalism. Would they laugh when they read my work?

Nevertheless, I was the first to raise my hand when Ms. Russo asked, "Who wants to be first?" But the next week, when it was critiqued, (I can sure throw that word around now, can't I?) I was ripped about a lot of things and even though Gianna Russo, the teacher, saw something in my writing—she called it "freshness of truth," and encouraged me, my embarrassment still followed me home. I went to my favorite writing place, then sat down and cried.

Where's your grit, Baby Jane? Believe me, I know what you're feelin'. That's how I felt after I bombed at the Grand Ole Opry. But I didn't let 'em stop me. The Grand Ole Opry just made me more determined. If they laugh at you, honey, there's only one thing to do. Show 'em what you're made of, then take it to the bank!

"That's easy enough for you to say. You're Elvis Presley, the King of Rock and Roll and loved by millions."

And that's what I'm trying to tell you! It wasn't always that way. I remember when my family was so poor we had to practically eat dirt from people like Orville Bean, the owner of the land we lived on. But I showed him. I made him choke on his cotton bolls and I had nothin' more than you have. I had my mama's grit, love, and encouragement, and a talent from God. You have these same gifts. Discover them, honey...hone them and use them. Make your mama proud. And make me proud. Write to the heart of my fans, honey. Put flesh on my bones and make me sing again. Show 'em how much I care. Excite them...make them happy.

I decided in that moment I would face any and all adversity

with a winning determination. I would write and *I would be published*! That ripping I'd taken on my writing was good for me. It showed me where I was strong and it exhibited the areas I needed to work on. Then, that's what I did. I worked.

I completed my courses at the university, then continued to write. Day in and day out, I wrote. Sometimes I was up, at other times I was down, and always I felt the pressure and discouragement that is part of being a writer. But, when I was down, Elvis would come to me. He reminded me of the critics who had called him a flash in the pan. He sympathized with me when I missed my mother.

Baby Jane, when my mama died I wanted to die. I thought I couldn't go on without her love and comfort. The pain of knowin' I would never again see her smile of approval at my accomplishments was almost more than I could bear. After all, what meanin' did they hold for me if Mama wasn't there to enjoy the rewards. It had all been for her! But you see, Baby Jane, your mama's reward is in your achievements.

"Oh, Elvis, you've always understood."

I understand because I've never forgotten. Now pick up that pen and keep writin'. I promise you, when the words seem to be vague and your mind goes blank, I'll come and refresh those memories. Put on a record, or watch a movie. I left a part of myself in each of them. Look for it and write.

"I wish I had a picture of us together, Elvis."

I thought you did. But know this, Baby Jane, sometimes it's necessary for people to see with their hearts what their eyes can't see. God has a reason for all things whether we understand it or not.

Elvis kept his promise and continued to inspire me throughout this book, never once allowing me to see anything but success.

EDDIE AND I went to Las Vegas during the summer of 1992. But Vegas wasn't the same anymore. Elvis no longer occupied the thirtieth floor of the Hilton. Gone was the glamour that had once been the trademark of Vegas, traded for theme parks and family- oriented entertainment.

We were awakened by an earthquake on our first night there, and it set a different atmosphere, and human beings were more aware of their vulnerability and hung close to other people and talked about their fears.

When we returned home it seemed as though things came more from my heart. The earthquake seemed to have shaken the fear of rejection out of me. I didn't panic as easily, and found that in stillness, I received answers that led to what I needed to know, even if I didn't know what that was. The Bible calls it a peace that surpasses all understanding.

The day after we got back home from Vegas, I called Ava and was told she had been hospitalized. I went to see her. The twinkle was still in her eyes when she told me it was all over for her. "I'm dying, Frances, but it's been a great life. Some good, some bad, but I rolled with the punches for a long time." She winked at me and smiled. "I'll tell Elvis hello for you." That was the last time I saw Ava. She died a short time later and it hurt so bad, saying good-bye to another friend. But I was stronger this time.

IN 1993, Eddie and I went back out to Las Vegas. One of the saddest moments was when I watched the sign being pulled down that had so proudly held Elvis' name for years, out in front of the Hilton Hotel, formerly the Las Vegas International. I cried.

Now a new sign stands in its place. I never did like watching the new replace the old. I guess somewhere deep in my heart I'd hoped Lisa Marie would buy the Hilton and change it to the Elvis International Hotel. I felt like it would have given her a stage on which to perform before an audience who would appreciate her. After all, she is part of Elvis and I'm sure he would feel like any other parent—love me, love my child. How could we feel anything but love for Lisa Marie and her children, Danielle and Ben.

I have this image of Lisa Marie doing a music video—her hair is styled like her father's, and she's wearing black, peg-legged pants, a black shirt, a thin white belt, and black and white loafers. She's singing, and she is the spitting image of her daddy. Oh, well...

ICONTINUED TO WRITE, then in January of 1994 I called my sister-in-law Nancy. I told her what I'd been up to since Mama's death, then asked if she felt like doing some typing for me. She was thrilled at the idea, and not only did she type, but also painted two portraits of Elvis. We made plans to go to Graceland for the seventeenth anniversary of Elvis' death. Although I'd been there before, it had been eleven years since my last visit. And I'd never been there during Elvis Week.

Nancy and I drove to Memphis. When we got there I felt like I had come home. The southern hospitality of Memphians just blew me away. And the southern cooking...mmmmm, all my and Elvis' favorites. It made me think of my favorite song, "I Was the One." *You taught them, too, didn't you, Elvis?*

I met so many people and they all had a story. Pauline Bartel, author of **Reel Elvis**, related hers while we waited in line for the candlelight vigil to start. She had discovered Elvis through his movies. Kaye Cason attended Elvis' funeral and has been going to Memphis during Elvis Week since it started. Betty Zogob loves Elvis and relates to his spiritual side.

And the list goes on. But one of my favorite stories came from Yvonne Entjes. She lives in Holland and saves her money to visit Memphis every other year. We came to be friends while at Graceland, then continued to correspond by mail. She wrote me a letter and told me how she became an Elvis fan. I was touched by her message, because it showed me how new generations of Elvis fans get born. Yvonne was kind enough to let me share her story with you:

I want to tell you how I became an Elvis fan and what Elvis means to me. Well, my personal Elvis story began on August 16, 1977. Yes, that's right, on the blackest day ever in the music world. Of course, Elvis was around all my life, but because of my parents. They often told us kids about the things going on in the 1950's and how Elvis became "King." But, you know how kids are at the age of eleven till eighteen. Everything my parents told was old fashion, something to laugh about. Man, that would change!!

In 1975 I saw a music show where they announced that Elvis Presley would become forty years old that week, and because of that special occasion, RCA decided to re-release the song "Jailhouse Rock" for the third time. In about two weeks time, that song became number 1 in the Dutch national Top 100. That same year, they released "My Boy". I liked that song very much, and it's still one of my favorite Elvis songs. It goes without saying that I bought both songs at that time, but I still was not a fan.

On August 16, 1977, I was fourteen years old and had a day off from school. At PM, I went to the store where at that time both my mother and brother worked. As soon as I walked into the store, my brother came up to me and said, "Do you know who died today?" Of course I didn't, and he said, "Elvis Presley!" I just looked at him and said, "Sure!" I didn't believe him, knowing how young Elvis was. But, as soon as I came home that afternoon, I turned the radio on and there it was—he had really died. I spent the whole afternoon listening to Elvis' music. DJs were talking about the man, and fans were in a complete daze, some of them even cried.

That same night on the news I saw the first pictures from what was happening in Memphis, and I saw all those people. You can't imagine how impressive this was to me. As the days went by the impression grew more and more, and it became this urge. I wanted to know more about this man. Why was there more than 80,000 people crying? Why was the whole world completely shaken by the death of this man? Who was he? What did he do to achieve all this? Were my parents right when they told me that he was special?

In the months after Elvis' death I began to read everything about him, and I started to listen to his music and discovered that there was so much more than only

"Jailhouse Rock," "Are You Lonesome Tonight," "It's Now or Never," and "Teddy Bear." I began to understand who Elvis Presley really was...a terrific singer!

In December of 1977, I received "Elvis in Concert" for Christmas and I bought my first book about him. That's when I really fell in love with him. Not long after that, I became a member of the Dutch Elvis Fan Club.

I've met a lot of beautiful people because of Elvis, and they became my friends for life. But, the best thing that happened to me was that after ten years my dream came true. I WAS GOING TO MEMPHIS!!!

I had been saving money for years, and now I was able to go and be close to the man that I loved so much, but didn't really know at all. Well, Memphis in 1987 changed my life. I had a great time, met new friends, but most of all, I saw and learned about Elvis and his fans. And now I'm so proud to say that I'm a member of the wonderful Elvis World.

Taking care of business,
Yvonne Entjes

NANCY AND I HEADED back out to Memphis in August 1995. The weather was hot. Temperatures ranged around a hundred and five with a heat index of a hundred and fifteen. The sweltering heat wave drove fans inside cool, air-conditioned souvenir shops across from Graceland.

Being a writer at heart, I enjoyed the breakfasts at Shoney's, sponsored by Bill Burk, publisher of *Elvis World* magazine, and author of eleven Elvis books. This is where authors give talks. It was at one of these very breakfasts that I'd met Ira Jones, Elvis' army sergeant, the year before. He was back again and sat with Nancy and me. Ira is the sweetest man—like sugar. He kept us spellbound with his Elvis experiences.

As Ira and I exchanged accounts, he told me one on himself, then shyly tried to hide his smile behind his hand. I thought the

story was cute and asked if I could quote him on it. His bashful re-
luctance encouraged me to plead, until he finally said okay. The
sweet shyness of Ira as he told this little story is what made it so
precious to me:

> "Elvis and I were walking along the road together when
> some of his fans spotted him and decided to give chase to
> their idol." Ira kind of hides his mouth behind his hands
> and laughs, "And I was just young and naive enough...to
> think some of them would be coming after me."

I met another army buddy. Bill Taylor, Elvis' lieutenant, gave a
wonderful talk about the kind of soldier Elvis was: "He was a good
team player." Mary Jenkins, Elvis' cook, told us some priceless
Elvis stories during her talk. I liked the ones about when she (May-
wee, as Elvis called her) and Getlow, Elvis' dog, used to get low
and get going when Elvis was on the warpath.

NANCY AND I WENT to the tribute concert. The Sweet Inspirations were on the bill of this show. I had visited with them
backstage at the previous January concert and finally, after twenty-
four years, I returned Sylvia's picture to her that I'd borrowed in
1971. The photo was of the Sweet Inspirations with Tom Jones
and had been Sylvia's favorite snapshot when she'd loaned it to me
so I could have a copy made for myself.

Sylvia was surprised and tickled to get the picture back. We saw
each other again in January, when we were on the "Good Morning
America Show," which took place out in front of Graceland, very
early in the morning on a freezing cold day. But, we didn't get to
talk this summer. Security for Elvis' backup singers was tighter
than I remembered it being for Elvis.

AUGUST 15, 1995. I sat on the bed in my room at the Ramada
Inn, in Memphis. I was writing notes in my journal—*Elvis, tonight your fans will walk up Graceland's driveway, holding candles*

in their hands, and prayers in their hearts. Then I said, aloud, "I wish the weather would cool off a little."

Suddenly, it was almost as though I could feel a breeze right there in my hotel room. And then I heard him. *Baby, have you forgotten what I told you? Nobody gets everything they want.*

How could I have forgotten? "Oh, Elvis, I remember now!"

We had talked about a lot of things. Some I can't recall. I think maybe the dark memories are responsible for shrouding other particulars. However, some had been preserved in gold and all I had to do now was watch a video, or put on a tape, and they embraced me and I lived them all over again—many, many, times.

"Now I remember. We were talking about the Bible, where it says that without a dream a man will perish." Elvis had told me that some of his fondest dreams were beyond his reach. And I said, "But you can have anything you want."

"No, Baby...nobody gets everything they want."

"What do you want that you can't get, Elvis...besides freedom to move around?"

"Don't count that one so lightly. That's a big one itself. But there're others." He talked about the actor George C. Scott. He had loved Scott in *Patton.* "But what I could never understand was when he turned down the Oscar. Man, what I'd give to earn one of those." I remember being impressed by the fact that Elvis had said earn instead of get.

I finished writing in my journal and put the book away. "Thank you, Elvis, for reminding me. I won't forget it again," and I thought, *Nobody gets everything they want, not even Elvis Presley.*

That's right, Baby. But never stop tryin'. I could see him grinning—that alluring, mystical smile.

"Elvis! I know what your special power was!"

Oh, yeah?

"You looked into our hearts, and then you made your home there. Your special power was making yourself live in our hearts. And it doesn't stop there, Elvis. You will always live in the hearts of mankind. You will live for what you gave—for all you left behind. You know something, Elvis? I think you really wanted to be Superman."

I could see him in my mind's eye, smiling.
I almost made 'em believe I was.

I TOOK MY PLACE in line for the candlelight vigil, two red roses in
my hand; one from me, and one for Yvonne Entjes, who was
with Elvis in thought until 1996, when it would be her Graceland
year again. The line had moved fast while Nancy and I talked with
fans. Now, I held my candle out for a piece of light from the eternal flame. Then, silently, I stepped forward and started my ascent
up the hill. This is when Elvis seems to reach out and touch his
fans.

Tranquility, that's what I felt when I passed through the gates,
and all the way up to the Meditation Garden. Horses grazed in the
moonlight and nightbirds sang from the trees. Fresh-mowed grass
and flowers from fans perfumed the night air. Softly, in the background, Elvis was singing. Nobody talked. *So serene and peaceful*, I
thought. *Elvis? You're here, aren't you?* Out of the still night, a
slight breeze fluttered the leaves on a tree to my left.

He walked with me in song in the soft light of a thousand candles, so many they lit up the night. And his sweet voice caressed my
ears, as he sang:
Love letters straight from my heart.

I came to his graveside and laid the roses at his feet. I said a
prayer, then lingered for a moment—just looking. Then, softly, I
whispered, "Elvis, help me here. Where are you?" I could feel him.
"You would be so proud, Elvis. Your fans are the best people. You
taught them how to care."

Then I heard him. *Baby Jane. I am proud. And I'm proud of
you too, honey. I knew you could write that book.*

"You're sure about this, Elvis? I promised you I would never
tell, and the thing about words is, once they're written you can't
take them back."

The air was still. "Elvis, can I ask one more favor of you? Will
you tell my Mama hello? And Darlene and Doug, and Bethine, and
Ava, will you give them all a kiss for me? Tears battled mascara to
streak my face. I was crying! I hadn't cried when Elvis died and

now, I was finally crying! But it wasn't a sad weeping. It was a joyful celebration of life and memories. I thought about that special time Elvis had given me, when our souls had met through the revelation of secrets.

The air thickened with his presence. I felt a warm, uplifting sensation spread through me and cuddle around my heart. I could see his blue, soul-searching eyes, and I heard him say, *You're my special Baby Jane*. And I was. In my heart I would forever be Elvis' Baby Jane.

"Elvis...you're unforgettable."

THE END

Epilogue

I MET BETTY ZOGOB while I was in Memphis: a lovely spiritual lady who loves Elvis. She wrote me a letter after reading an excerpt from *Elvis, You're Unforgettable*, and has allowed me to share it with you:

Dear Frances,

God has blessed and chosen you to be a special friend and connection to Elvis. You have expressed such loving and caring feelings, and thoughts, about Elvis, and I really feel you have been chosen to write these wonderful and positive things. I pray that God will bless you in your endeavor—one that I believe was preordained.

Betty Zogob

Special Thanks

Like Elvis, I give thanks first to my Lord Jesus. Then to my husband, Edward Keenan, for his support, both spiritually and financially, and for always loving me. Without your patience and faith, I don't know how I would have gotten through this book. I also want to thank you for all the meals you cooked, dishes you washed, and clothes you laundered, mended, and ironed. I love you, honey, forever.

To my cousin Sandra Polk Ross. Thanks for abandoning me. Just kiddin' cuz. I love you. Thank you for your interview and the use of the pictures. We had some good times. Thanks for the memories.

To my sister-in-law Nancy Minton for your inspiration, typing skills, and your complete faith in my work. You have been a friend and a wonderful companion on our journeys to Graceland. Thanks, too, for all those trips into town.

Thank you, Eula Mae, for being my friend and showing me the ropes in Las Vegas.

To Sylvia Shemwell for taking me in and being a friend. A special thanks for introducing me to Elvis. To Myrna, Estelle, and Ann, thanks for the memories.

To Gianna Russo, for your editorial expertise. I know you had to literally pull some of the descriptions out of me, but it has been a joy working with you.

To Yvonne Entjes, my Elvis friend from Holland. Thank you for allowing me to include your letter in this book.

Thank you, Pauline Bartel, for looking over a piece of my early work and giving me some invaluable pointers.

To Pap, thanks for being my Dad.

Thank you, brother John and sister Peggy Stanton, for always pointing me to Jesus.

A special thanks to Elvis' fans. Your love keeps him alive.

Thanks to all my kinfolks, and my brothers and sisters at Life Tabernacle. I love you all. And a special thanks to everyone who contributed to this book. I want to especially thank my children for their faith in me: to my two beautiful daughters, Sandy Jolynn Sallee and Billie Jessica Smith, my granddaughter, Tiffany Lauren Sallee, my step-children, Sean Keenan, Patti (Trish) Williams, and my step-grandchildren, Jazlin, Brandon, and Jill Williams, and to all my foster children. I love you and I hope you learn some things from this book that will make your walk through life a whole lot easier. Just hold on to Jesus.

Thank you my brothers: Sam Dalton Minton, thanks for lending me your wife. Tommy Wayne Minton, thank you for all your computer knowledge and the time you spent helping your big sister, and you too, Donna, you've been a supportive sister-in-law.

Thank you, Cliff Denison, for being a good friend. And Lauren and Billy, my ex-husbands and friends, thank you for being such good sports.

I want to thank Bob Baggett, for the superb work you did restoring some of my old photos.

Thank you, Glen Hardin, for being kind.

Thanks to my friend, Todd Rheingold, for offering a writer's shoulder.

Thank you, Betty Zogob, for your spiritual inspirations.

Thank you, Kaye Cason, my Elvis friend.

Thank you, Ira Jones, for your quote and the beautiful pictures of Elvis. I will treasure them always.

Thank you, Bill Burk, for all the insight I received at the breakfasts you sponsored at Shoney's. Keep writing those wonderful books about Elvis that give us facts we can count on for accuracy.

Thank you, Joe Esposito, for your advice on getting published.

A very special thanks to Jane Dystel, for seeing my potential, and also Julie McCarthy for putting my book onto computer disk.

Thanks to my editor, Margie Weber.

And to my publisher, Sally Axelrod, no writer could ask for a better working relationship than I've experienced with you.

Frances Keenan
January 1997
Tampa, Florida

Bibliography

The following books about Elvis, I've used in research, for facts, and memory stimulus.

Bartel, Pauline. *Reel Elvis: The Ultimate Trivia Guide to the King's Movies.* Dallas, Texas: Taylor Publishing Company, 1994.

Burk, Bill E. *Early Elvis: The Tupelo Years.* Memphis, TN: Publisher, Elvis World Magazine, 1994.

Dundy, Elaine. *Elvis and Gladys: The First Revealing Look at How the King's Mother Shaped His Life.* New York, NY: Macmillan Publishing Company, 1985.

Esposito, Joe and Elena Oumano. *Good Rockin' Tonight: Twenty Years On the Road and On the Town With Elvis.* New York, NY: Simon & Schuster, 1994.

Greenwood, Earl and Kathleen Tracy. *The Boy Who Would Be King: An Intimate Portrait Of Elvis Presley by His Cousin.* New York, NY: Dutton Published by the Penguin Group, 1990.

Guralnick, Peter. *Last Train To Memphis: The Rise of Elvis Presley.* Published simultaneously in Canada by Little, Brown & Company (Canada) Limited, 1994.

Jones, Ira as told to Bill E. Burk. *Soldier Boy Elvis.* Memphis, TN. Publisher, Elvis World Magazine, 1992.

Latham, Caroline and Jeannie Sakol. *"E" Is For Elvis: An A-To-Z Illustrated Guide to the King of Rock and Roll.* New York: NAL Books Published by the Penguin Group, 1990.

Pierce, Patricia Jobe. *The Ultimate Elvis: Elvis Presley Day by Day.* New York, NY: Simon & Schuster, 1994.

Presley, Priscilla Beaulieu with Sandra Harmon. *Elvis and Me.* New York, NY: G.P. Putnam's Sons, 1985.

Rovin, Jeff. *The World According To Elvis: Quotes From The King.* New York: HarperPaperbacks—A Division of HarperCollins Publishers, 1992.

Stanley, Billy with George Erikson. *Elvis, My Brother: An Intimate Family Memoir of Life with the King.* New York, NY: St. Martin's Press, 1989.

Vellenga, Dirk with Mick Farren. *Elvis and the Colonel.* New York, NY: Delacorte Press, The Bantam Doubleday Dell Publishing Group, Inc., 1988.

Worth, Fred L. and Steve D. Tamerius. *Elvis: His Life from A to Z.* Chicago Contemporary Books, 1988.

Learn to Listen

Learn to listen like a teddy bear,
With ears open and mouth closed tight.
Learn to forgive like a teddy bear,
With an open heart, not caring who is right.
Learn to love like a teddy bear,
With open arms and imperfect sight.
Do not ask for your life's load lightened,
But for courage to endure.
Do not ask for fulfillment in all your life,
Do not ask for perfection in all you do,
But for the wisdom not to repeat your mistakes.
And finally, do not ask for more,
Before saying, "Thank You,"
For what you have already received.
If you're looking for someone to blame—
Look in the mirror.
There is no challenge that cannot be met,
And dream that cannot be achieved.

Written by one of our
Covenant House kids

(Permission to reprint by Covenant House, America's largest shelter for
homeless and runaway kids)

About the Author

Born on the 4th of August, 1943, in her 80-year-old paternal grandfather's rural farmhouse in Levy County, Florida, Frances Keenan recalls slave stories told by her grandfather, Papa Minton, whose father owned a plantation in Georgia before the Civil War. When Papa Minton married little Granny Minton and moved to Florida, Grandma and Granddaddy Sheffield lived on the Minton land for a while. That's how Frances' mama, Artie Mae, met her daddy.

Firstborn of three children, Frances is descended from two large southern families: nine siblings on her mother's side and eight on her father's side. She is a seventh to ninth generation Floridian. Frequent family reunions have kept Frances closely connected to her roots.

Her first cousin, Sandra Polk Ross, is the daughter-in-law of Col. Parker, Elvis Presley's long-time manager.

Frances attended over seventy of Elvis' concerts—the majority of them in Las Vegas. In 1971, she was befriended by Sylvia Shemwell of the *Sweet Inspirations* (Elvis' back-up singers), and subsequently met Elvis.

Frances worked as a cosmetologist for many years; later was ordained as a Baptist preacher, taught school, and parented foster children. She has two daughters, one granddaughter, three stepchildren, and three step-grandchildren. She and her husband of twenty years, Ed Keenan, reside in Tampa, Florida.

Note from the publisher: Family photograph albums are a Southern tradition. The photographs in this book come from the albums of Frances Keenan, Sandra Ross, and other collectors of Elvis memories—some are family pictures, others are out-of-focus photographs shot by the author, who was overcome with emotion at the thought of seeing Elvis up close. Our intent was to produce a memorable book, with photographs that would help make the book very special. Please let us know if our Elvis book is a welcome addition to your personal library. Your comments are most welcome!